CHARLESTON BUSINESS ON THE EVE OF THE AMERICAN REVOLUTION

Leila Sellers

ARNO·PRESS
&
The New York Times

NEW YORK · 1970

Reprint Edition 1970 by Arno Press Inc.

Reprinted from a copy in The State Historical Society of Wisconsin Library

LC# 72-112571
ISBN 0-405-02474-6

THE RISE OF URBAN AMERICA
ISBN for complete set 0-405-02430-4

Manufactured in the United States of America

CHARLESTON BUSINESS ON THE EVE OF THE AMERICAN REVOLUTION

Charleston Business on the Eve of the American Revolution

BY

LEILA SELLERS, Ph.D.

CHAPEL HILL
THE UNIVERSITY OF NORTH CAROLINA PRESS
1934

PRINTED IN THE UNITED STATES OF AMERICA BY
THE SEEMAN PRESS, DURHAM, NORTH CAROLINA

TO

A. R. S.

PREFACE

Government regulation of business was the central idea of the mercantile system. Regulation was prescribed in order that the state, which was regarded as a mercantile firm, might export more than it imported and so be solvent and even prosperous at the expense of those nations which had an unfavorable balance of trade. The underlying economic principle here was that in trading some nation was bound to get the little end of the bargain and the wise statesman by careful regulation of business provided against this contingency for his state.

This volume is devoted to a detailed description of how business was conducted in an American port before the American Revolution came to deal mercantilism a serious blow. The American business man placed a high value upon his membership in the British Empire whose navy protected his property and whose trade regulation did much to foster his prosperity. But when his economic freedom was too narrowly circumscribed he finally questioned not only the justice of the regulations, but the right of the imperial government to make such regulations for him; and in the name of the rather enigmatic Goddess Liberty he fought a war to establish his point, thus doing his bit unconsciously toward discrediting mercantilism and establishing *laissez-faire,* which being freely translated means let the government keep its hands off business.

In this study an attempt has been made to answer the following questions: First, why did Charleston become in the colonial era the metropolis of the lower South, which thus presented a contrast to the predominantly agricultural and almost townless Chesapeake region? Second, what was the trade territory of Charleston and by what business organization was this territory bound to the city? Third, how was the overseas commerce of the city conducted? Fourth, how did the British government deal with the question of smuggling at Charleston? Fifth, how did British policy in the closing years of the colonial period, including

[vii]

such measures as the Stamp Act and the Townshend Acts, affect
the commercial classes at Charleston? What action did they take
and what results followed?

This study of business life in eighteenth century Charleston
owes much to three South Carolinians who left important records behind them. They are Peter Timothy, editor of the
South Carolina Gazette, Lieutenant Governor Bull, and Henry
Laurens. Timothy's *Gazette* gives important trade statistics for
the period. He belonged to the mechanic class, and, during the
several crises in the decade before the war, his sympathies were
with the small business man and the small planter. These two
classes had few economic ties binding them to England and consequently had developed a strong nativist feeling which sometimes
expressed itself in intolerance of that larger loyalty to the British
Empire which animated the big merchant and planter classes. The
South Carolina Gazette throws an important light on why and
how these classes resisted British regulations of American trade.

William Bull was appointed Lieutenant Governor of South
Carolina on December 6, 1759, and held the office for more than
eighteen years during which time he was called upon at six different periods to act as governor. Bull's abilities were never rewarded with the governorship despite the fact that he was zealously
loyal to the empire and was loved and respected in the province.
During these eighteen years there were several incompetent persons
among those sent out to administer the government. Bull's reports[1] reveal the intimate personal knowledge of one who took
genuine interest and pride in the affairs of the province. They
show a vitality and understanding that are often lacking in the
reports of the titular governors. These only too often appear to
be mere summaries of the reports of subordinates.

If the purpose of the author is realized even in part, it is due
in no small measure to Henry Laurens, Esquire, merchant, planter,
and statesman, whose vibrant personality and many sided interests
lie revealed in that economic history of the Charleston District
prosaically entitled The Letter Books of Henry Laurens, the dates

[1] In the *Public Records of South Carolina*, the South Carolina Historical Commission, Columbia.

of which more than cover the period under consideration.[2] Laurens was a typical big business man of the period, resembling in some respects the modern American big business man but having on the whole broader sympathies than are possible to the modern man in an age of specialization. What strikes one's attention about Laurens is his splendid energy—his natural bent to turn his whole attention to the matter in hand whether it be attending to a wide and varied correspondence including backwoodsmen and English merchant princes, or to the improvement of his estates, or to what he conceives to be for the betterment of his country politically and economically. A man of this type necessarily had the defects of his qualities. Laurens was usually cocksure about the rightness of his contentions, and his egoism was sometimes a little too much in evidence.

This monograph grew out of a study begun several years ago in one of Professor Evarts B. Greene's seminars at Columbia and to him is owed a debt of gratitude for reading and criticising the manuscript and making many helpful suggestions. In fairness to Professor Greene, however, it must be said that he is not responsible for any errors of commission or omission herein contained. Grateful acknowledgment is also here made to Mrs. H. K. Leiding, of Charleston, for the loan of the Kershaw Papers, and to the custodians of libraries in several cities for the many courtesies extended. These include those in the Columbia University Library, in the New York Public Library, in the Library of Congress, in the Charleston Library, and in the Libraries of the South Carolina Historical Commission at Columbia and the South Carolina Historical Society at Charleston.

LEILA SELLERS.

Washington, D. C.
February 27, 1933.

[2] In the library of the South Carolina Historical Society, Charleston.

CONTENTS

CHARLESTON BUSINESS ON THE EVE OF THE AMERICAN REVOLUTION

CHAPTER I

CHARLESTON AND THE CHARLESTON DISTRICT

I

In order to understand the economic history of the British-American colonies, it is necessary to abandon the method of the military and political historian who studies developments in the individual colony or considers the colonies in coördinated groups based principally upon political geography; for business and trade when unhampered by government interference follow the most natural lines of communication and center in those places most convenient for purposes of exchange. Before 1763 there was comparatively free trade within the British Empire and a minimum of government interference in American affairs. Therefore, the colonies of British-America in the eighteenth century fall into certain natural economic groups forming trade districts. In the South there were two such districts: the Chesapeake District including Maryland, Virginia, and certain parts of North Carolina, with a considerable back country which before 1790 included parts of Kentucky, Tennessee and western Pennsylvania; and the Charleston District comprising South Carolina, parts of North Carolina, Georgia, and, after 1763, East and West Florida.

The two principal factors determining the character and scope of colonial business were the nature of the rivers and harbors, and the climate and resources of the country. The influence of waterways is well illustrated in the contrast presented by the Chesapeake and the Charleston districts. Although the exports of Maryland and Virginia to Great Britain were worth nearly as much as those of all the other colonies put together, Norfolk and Baltimore did not become important until after the Revolution. Trade was much diffused throughout these provinces. The numerous navigable streams on which seagoing vessels could penetrate the country permitted the concentration of business in the hands of English and

Scottish factors, the representatives of the British merchants, who established warehouses at convenient locations and dealt with the planter at his wharf. There were no commercial houses to compare with those in Philadelphia, New York, Boston, and Charleston. Tidewater Virginians especially were not concerned in trade except for a few shops here and there. They were predominantly planters.

In the region south of Virginia the waterways were navigable, some of them for more than a hundred miles for small craft, but not for oceangoing vessels, owing to the shoal channels of the inland streams, and this caused the growth of seaports at the available harbors. In North Carolina there was Wilmington; in South Carolina, Charleston, Georgetown, and Beaufort; and in Georgia, Savannah.

Charleston became the commercial capital of the lower southern country despite the fact that the most commodious harbor on the coast, with the greatest depth of water on its bar, was Port Royal, where Beaufort was located. In colonial times ships of more than two hundred tons burden could not cross the harbor bar at Charleston without lightening their cargo. Attracted by a harbor spacious enough, as one writer phrased it, to contain all the royal navy, the English first attempted to make a settlement on Port Royal, but it was abandoned because it was on an island and there was the difficulty of bringing down to the sea the exportable commodities of the interior; besides, there was constant danger in this exposed position of annihilation at the hands of the Spaniards. A move was made to the banks of the Ashley and finally a permanent location was chosen on a neck of land made by the junction of two navigable rivers, the Ashley and the Cooper. These rivers united their waters below the new settlement of Charleston and formed the harbor which opened into the ocean several miles below at Sullivan's Island. Here was not only a good place to land ships, but a place of security easily defended by land and sea. The only approach by land was up "the neck" by a road which was later called "The Path." A wall was erected across "the neck" landward of the city, and guns were stationed on the islands commanding the entrance to the harbor. There was easy communication by means of the Cooper River and the rivers flowing into Winyah Bay, sixty-five miles north of Charleston Harbor, with a hinterland of great resources. Thus Charleston became the point of contact between Carolina and Europe; and the small province of South Carolina, primarily because of its water communications, assumed a position of commanding importance among the British colonies of North America. Rivers furnished highways through the pathless forests to the undeveloped resources of a primeval country; they gave fertility to the soil; they transported the crops to market and brought back into the wilderness those possessions that directly connected the province with the civilization of Europe.

Colonial Charleston was located mostly on the Ashley, but the Cooper was the great highway of trade where most of the wharves were located. Both rivers were navigable, the Ashley for only a short distance; the Cooper for twenty miles above the town for ships and forty for smaller vessels.[1] It was of supreme importance in the early days that overseas vessels could pass up into the freshwater part of the Cooper River and be saved from the dread attack of the worms to which their bottoms were subject in salt water. In fur trading days these rivers facilitated traffic with the Indians; later, sometime before 1700, when the colony entered the second phase of its existence and developed a trade in provisions to Barbadoes, provisions were transported and cattle were driven to market on the rivers and along their banks; in the third stage of the development of the colony, a stage of staple farming on a large scale by the employment of a vast number of African slaves, the waters of the Cooper were alive with traffic. "Notwithstanding we have a few ships of our own," wrote Governor Glen in 1751, "Cooper river appears sometimes a kind of floating market, and we have numbers of Canoes, Boats, and Pettygues that ply incessantly, bringing down the Country Produce to Town and returning with such Necessarys as are wanted by the Planters."[2]

[1] J. F. D. Smyth, *A Tour of the United States*, II, 81; J. D. Schoepf, *Travels in the Confederation*, II, 165. According to Henry Laurens the Cooper was navigable at Mepkin for the largest ships that came to Charleston. Mepkin was twenty-nine miles above Charleston. D. D. Wallace, *Life of Laurens*, 125.

[2] W. A. Schaper, *Sectionalism and Representation in South Carolina*, 269 quoting *P. R. S. C.* MSS, XXIV, 313.

In an age of water transportation Georgetown, on Winyah Bay, sixty-five miles north of Charleston, would have been a magnificent location for a port had the harbor facilities been adequate. Into Winyah Bay pour the waters of the Sampit, the Black, the Black Mingo, the Great Pedee, and the Waccamaw rivers. A little to the south of Georgetown, the Santee River enters the Atlantic. South Carolina contains three great rivers that flow from the mountains to the sea: the Great Pedee (called the Yadkin in North Carolina), the Santee, and the Savannah, which on their journey to the sea are joined by innumerable rivers and smaller tributaries. These rivers are swift streams in the up-country, fit to furnish motive power for mill wheels; on their downward course to the sea they become sluggish yellow rivers of many meanders slanting in a southeasterly direction across the low country. The Savannah, for example, is not more than three hundred miles from its source to its mouth in a direct line, but including meanders it is about five hundred and fifty miles in length. Two of these great rivers find an outlet in or near Winyah Bay, on which Georgetown is located. As early as 1740 the Great Pedee was opened to navigation as far as Cheraw, that is, about one hundred and thirty miles, and great quantities of lumber and naval stores were floated on it to Georgetown. The Santee is formed by two branches in the central part of South Carolina, called the Wateree and the Congaree: the Congaree a few miles northwest of the present city of Columbia subdivides into the Broad and the Saluda; the Wateree above Camden becomes the Catawba. The Congaree in colonial times was navigable as far as the village of Granby, which is in the neighborhood of the present city of Columbia; the Wateree, as far as Camden. Thus nature provided a network of watercourses into the very heart of the province of South Carolina, and emptied the waters of these many rivers into the Atlantic at Georgetown, but gave Georgetown a harbor that would not admit vessels that drew more than ten or twelve feet of water. The result was that Georgetown became a depot where produce was collected to be forwarded to Charleston. In colonial times Georgetown was comparatively of more importance that it is today. It contained two hundred houses in 1784 and was twice as large as Beaufort.[3]

The difficulty of navigating the sea around Bull's Island and down to Charleston caused an interest in inland navigation to spring up. A grand jury in 1770 recommended that a canal be opened between the Santee and Cooper rivers and the Santee canal company was incorporated by the legislature in 1786. When the Santee Canal was opened in 1800, providing a safe inland navigation to Charleston, Georgetown rapidly decreased in importance.

Savannah and Wilmington instead of rivalling the port of Charleston served but to increase the volume of business carried on there. Savannah, on a high sandy bluff on the south side of the Savannah River, was mostly subsidiary to Charleston. It was only after the Revolution that Savannah developed a large independent trade, when the war had revealed the resources of the back country of Georgia and a tide of emigration from Europe and America set in. In 1784 Savannah had one thousand inhabitants. Wilmington, about twice as large as Georgetown, was splendidly located between two branches of the Cape Fear River which commanded considerable inland navigation, but the country about Wilmington was an uninviting sand-barren. A "Lady of Quality" coming directly from the tropical luxuriance of the West Indies, first saw America at Wilmington, and wrote this sentence in her journal: "At last America—a dreary waste of white barren sand and melancholy nodding pines."

At Wilmington was the only good harbor in North Carolina. Ships of three hundred tons burden might enter the port, but the entrance was past dangerous shoals known to seafaring men as the "Rocks of the Cape Fear." Because of these shoals Wilmington employed many small vessels in a coastwise trade to the West Indies, the Northern Colonies, and Charleston.[4]

II

The climate and natural resources of the country account for the character of the Carolina trade. Because of its semi-tropical climate and its potential resources, as well as because it was a No-

[3] Smyth, *Tour*, II, 86.
[4] *Ibid.*, II, 43, 44; David MacPherson, *Annals of Commerce*, IV, 396.

Man's-Land between English Virginia and Spanish Florida, Carolina was competed for by Spain, France, and England. To the English it was the southern extension of Virginia, to the Spaniards it was the northern extension of Florida. Spain claimed it by right of discovery and exploration. France made a settlement in it which was wiped out by the jealous Spaniards; England was the first to make a permanent occupation of it by the establishment of a colony at Charleston in 1670. Thus the founding of Charleston was a by-product of the commercial rivalry of England and Spain, and only another case in which England promoted commerce in a region claimed by Spain.

These nations were not seeking to establish great empires in the New World; they were looking for raw materials abundant only in warm climates. For such materials the sunny region south of Virginia held out great prospects. Here the English were to promote the production of silk and wine to free themselves from dependence on Southern Europe; of hemp and naval stores for their sea power; of provisions to contribute to the prosperity of their West Indian colonies. This southern region was to be eminently successful in the production of two staple crops: rice, which England did not need for her own consumption and whose growth she did not encourage, was destined to create prosperity for the Carolina planter, the Charleston factor, and the British merchant; and indigo, whose story reads like a romance, was to have the distinction of contributing effectively to the promotion of England's industrial supremacy and her dominance of the European market, by freeing her from dependence on the French and Spanish West Indies for the dyes used in her budding textile industry.

The trade of the British-American colonies was confined chiefly to the British Empire; to parts of Europe south of Cape Finisterre, which meant principally Spain, Portugal, and the Mediterranean countries; to certain parts of Africa; and, after 1763, rice was allowed to be carried to the Spanish and French colonies to the southward of Georgia, under certain restrictions. The Northern colonies whose productions were similar to those of the mother country were distinguished by the small volume of their

export trade to Great Britain. They were largely interested in the
fisheries of Labrador and Newfoundland, in ship building, in the
trade to the Mediterranean countries, and in a trade in provisions
to the West Indies, by which indirect means they were able to
make remittances to the mother country for what they required
of European commodities. On the other hand, the southern
colonies, like the West Indies, were distinguished by the great
volume of their direct trade with Great Britain. Their tobacco,
deerskins, rice, indigo, and naval stores were much in demand in
Europe, and the great trade routes of the period ran back and
forth across the Atlantic from Great Britain to the southern and
West Indian colonies. After 1729, when rice was allowed to be
carried outside the empire to the ports south of Cape Finisterre,
another trade route was opened leading from southern Carolina
and Georgia to southern Europe.

In 1769 the number of British ships employed in the trade
between Great Britain and the colonies which later became the
United States of America was as follows:[5]

Colonies	Ships	Seamen
New England	46	552
Rhode Island, Connecticut, and		
New Hampshire	3	36
New York	30	330
Pennsylvania	35	390
Virginia and Maryland	330	3,960
North Carolina	34	408
South Carolina	140	1,680
Georgia	24	240
St. Augustine	2	24
Pensacola	10	120

This table shows that the ships sent out by England to Virginia and Maryland were more than the number employed in the
trade of all the other colonies combined. But the province of
South Carolina, smaller than Maryland, and small enough to be
set in a corner of Virginia, ranked next after these provinces in
the number of ships employed in its export trade. Even a feeble

[5] Adam Anderson, *Origins of Commerce*, IV, 130. These figures refer to British
as distinguished from colonial shipping. New England, New York and Pennsylvania were of course centers of colonial shipbuilding.

colony like North Carolina whose foreign trade was trifling, being mostly in the hands of her neighbors, Virginia and South Carolina, employed more British ships than did New York and nearly as many as Pennsylvania, which contained Philadelphia, the commercial capital of America.

The whole commerce of colonial America to Great Britain was valued at its height at £1,590,000 per annum, and of this sum tobacco, the chief crop of the Chesapeake region, was valued at £700,000 so that the tobacco crop alone was worth nearly as much as the combined exports of all the other American colonies. Ranking next in value after Virginia and Maryland tobacco were the rice and indigo of Carolina, under which name was recorded in the custom house at London all the exports of South Carolina and the exports of North Carolina that were shipped through the port of Charleston. Carolina exports to Great Britain were worth on an average more than the combined exports of all the provinces north of Maryland, and there were two years in the decade from 1763 to 1773 when Carolina exported more to England than did Maryland and Virginia, that is in 1768 and 1769.[6]

During the latter part of the colonial period there was a falling off in the exports of the Chesapeake region to England. The tobacco lands were wearing out and many people were seeking new lands for the growth of this crop in Kentucky and Tennessee.

Year	New England	New York	Pennsylvania	Virginia and Maryland	Carolina
1763	£ 71,253	£ 53,988	£ 38,228	£642,294	£382,366
1764	92,593	53,697	36,258	559,408	341,727
1765	150,690	54,959	25,148	505,671	385,918
1766	146,318	67,020	26,851	460,754	291,519
1767	132,694	61,422	37,641	437,926	395,027
1768	150,898	87,115	59,406	406,048	508,108
1769	133,788	73,466	26,111	361,892	387,114
1770	154,398	69,882	28,109	435,094	278,907
1771	158,218	95,875	31,615	577,848	420,311
1772	132,082	82,707	29,133	528,404	425,923
1773	128,003	76,246	36,652	589,803	456,513

[6] Value of imports into England from America for eleven years as submitted to the Inspection of the British Parliament. From *American Museum*, Oct. 1789, vol. VI., 402. Figures taken from English works and from sources such as parliamentary reports, etc. (although appearing in American publications) are usually sterling. As a rule, figures quoted from American sources and records, with the possible exception of the customs records kept by British officials in this country, are in terms of the local provincial currency.

Those who remained behind converted their tobacco fields into grain fields, developed a greater trade to the West Indies and Scotland, and began to turn to shipbuilding on a small scale. The exports of Virginia and Maryland to Scotland in 1768 were nearly as valuable as those they sent to England, and in 1769 the exports of these provinces to Scotland were more valuable than those to England.[7]

While the Virginia-Maryland exports to England were on a decline, Carolina exports to the mother country were gradually increasing. Carolina was like a well developed plantation just coming into a maximum of production. In 1763 Carolina exports to England were valued at £341,727 and in 1775 at £579,549. This increase was due in great measure to Charleston's control of a large part of the constantly expanding trade of the neighboring provinces of North Carolina and Georgia. Back in the 1730's Charleston was loading annually 220 ships for Europe, and its importance in comparison with commercial centers in the North is shown by the fact that at New York in 1732 only 196 ships arrived and at Philadelphia in 1733 only 173.[8] Before the Revolution the expanding trade of Charleston employed more than 400 ships and the amount of its exports was increasing by leaps and bounds as the following table shows:[9]

SHIPS ENTERING AND CLEARING AT THE PORT OF CHARLESTON

	Entering	Clearing
1755	301	281
1760	245	241
1765	450	444
1770	447	427

On November 30, 1770, Lieutenant Governor Bull wrote to the Earl of Hillsborough that Carolina's commerce kept "equal pace with its agriculture, that its trade extended to all parts of the

[7] Value of the Chesapeake District's Exports. From MacPherson, *Annals,* III, 486, 494-5.

	To England	1768	To Scotland
Maryland	£406,048		£ 97,241
Virginia			273,364
Maryland	£361,892	1769	£ 98,353
Virginia			299,715

[8] J. T. Adams, *Provincial Society,* 1690-1763, 208; S. C. *Gaz.* Dec. 5, 1771.
[9] *Public Records of South Carolina* (British Transcripts), XXXII, p. 401. Cited as *P. R. S. C.*

world consistent with the navigation acts," and that now "near 500 sails of vessels" were employed to carry off superfluous produce and import supplies.

III

Because of its economic value and frontier location the region dominated by Charleston assumed a peculiarly strong military character even for colonial America. Beset by enemies on land and sea, from without and within, it bristled with fortifications. There were Spaniards to the south and west, Frenchmen along the Mississippi, Indians along the border, and domestic enemies in the savage black slaves threatening insurrection.

Forts were built at strategic points in the back country for the triple purpose of giving protection to the frontier inhabitants, of prosecuting the Indian trade, and of resisting the encroachments of the Spanish and French. The Savannah River, the great artery of the Indian trade, was studded with fortifications. At the head of navigation on the Georgia side was Fort Augusta; nearby on the Carolina side was Fort Moore; near the Proclamation Line, beyond which white settlements were not to extend, was Fort Charlotte; and in the heart of the Cherokee country, 300 miles from Charleston, on the Keowee, was Fort Prince George. Four hundred and fifty miles from Charleston was Fort Loudoun, in the Cherokee country, on the Little Tennessee River, in the heart of that region known today to tourists as the "Land of the Sky." Fort Loudoun had been built mostly at the expense of South Carolina, Governor Dinwiddie of Virginia having contributed £1,000 in accordance with the king's commands. It was garrisoned chiefly by troops from Carolina, and here during the French and Indian War 700 soldiers were stationed.[10]

In colonial times Charleston was completely surrounded by a wall and fortifications. Extending along the water front was a general system of fortifications consisting chiefly of batteries on Cooper River; about two miles below the town, on James Island, was Fort Johnson whose guns commanded the channel along which ships must pass to enter and leave the port; on the land side was a wall which changed its location as the town expanded.

[10] *P. R. S. C.*, XXIX, 85-86; *ibid.*, XXXII, 228.

At the time of the Revolution this wall reached to about the section known today as Marion Square, and was a work of tabby, a composition of oyster shell and lime, extending from river to river. Georgetown's bar was considered its best defense. At Beaufort was Fort Lyttleton, built of tabby, mounted with fifteen cannon, and with barracks for one hundred men.[11] Also the powder magazine was mentioned by Lieutenant Governor Bull as one of the defenses of Charleston. The master of every vessel coming into the province was required to pay a duty of half a pound of good serviceable gunpowder for every ton of his vessel. This duty was deposited in the powder magazine.[12]

The king's troops could not garrison all of these fortified places. The colony must do its share. The defense of the province was provided for by militia against foreign foes, and by patrols in the country and night watches in the town against domestic enemies. Every citizen, says Hewatt, joined the military to the civil character. Every man between sixteen and sixty years of age able to bear arms had to enroll in the militia. The duties of militiamen were "to appear completely armed once in every fortnight for muster train and exercise," to do patrol duty, and to be available for a limited time, usually thirty or sixty days, according to the season of the year, when deemed necessary by the Governor or Commander-in-Chief.[13] Merchants and tradesmen found military duty inconvenient because it interrupted business. The planters, however, who were more at leisure on account of the task system of managing their plantations, had plenty of time for military exercise and prided themselves upon their martial spirit.[14]

In 1770 the militia consisted of "about 10,000 men divided into 10 regiments unequal in numbers, but equal in the want of discipline; besides one small nominal regiment of Horse and a voluntary artillery company of 50 men in Charles Town very expert in the use of Cannon." "In the country," wrote Bull,

[11] B. R. Carroll, *Historical Collections of South Carolina*, I, 502-503; *Charleston Yearbook*, 1883, 466; *P. R. S. C.*, XXXII, 389.

[12] Thomas Cooper, ed., *Statutes at Large of South Carolina*, IV, 319-320; see proclamation of Colonel Balfour in the *Royal Gazette*, Sept. 19, 1780.

[13] *S. C. Gaz.*, Nov. 28, 1775; Cooper, *Statutes of S. C.*, IX, 620.

[14] Carroll, *Collections*, I, 208.

"almost every militiaman marches on horseback, of great use for expedition and to avoid Fatigue."[15] The domestic tranquility of the province was provided for by small patrols drawn every two months from each company. Their duty was to ride along the roads and among the Negro houses in small districts in every parish once every week or as occasion required. To preserve good order in Charleston, where there was danger of insurrection because of the great number of slaves from Africa constantly imported, a night watch was established and paid for by money raised from tavern licenses. In 1770 the night watch consisted of 3 commissioned officers, 3 sergeants, 3 corporals, 3 drums, and 96 privates, armed with muskets and cutlasses; one-third mounted guard every night to "prevent disturbances among disorderly negroes and more disorderly soldiers."[16]

It is impossible to determine accurately the population in the colonial period since no official census records were regularly made and kept. For scrappy knowledge the student must sift the information coming from various sources: From the files of old newspapers, from reports of governors to officials in England, from estimates made by the Board of Trade, from the unscientific estimates of the American Congress, from references in old letter books, and from the records of the Society for Propagating the Gospel. The most reliable sources for South Carolina population before the Revolution seem to be the reports made by governors to the Board of Trade from time to time. The figures for the Negro population obtained from such reports are probably as accurate as the count of a census-taker, for in South Carolina taxes were paid on all Negroes and the tax returns indicated plainly the number of Negroes in the province. The white population in these reports was estimated from the militia rolls, one person in every five being considered of military age. From such reports the pre-Revolutionary population of South Carolina may be estimated as follows:

[15] *P. R. S. C.*, XXXII, 383-384.
[16] *Ibid.*, XXXII, 385.

	Whites	Blacks	Total
1748	25,000	39,000	64,000[17]
1760	31,000	52,000	83,000[18]
1769	45,000	80,000	125,000[19]
1773	65,000	110,000	175,000[20]

The census of 1790 gave the white population of South Carolina as 140,178 and the black as 108,895—total 249,073. The decrease in the Negro population was due no doubt to the fact that the British had either destroyed or carried away numbers of slaves during the war, and the increase in the white population to the tide of emigration from Europe that set in after the war.[21]

Georgia had a population of about 9,000 in 1760, 26,000 in 1770 and 55,000, in 1780; while North Carolina's population in 1760 was about 115,000, in 1770 about 230,000, and in 1780 about 300,000.[22]

In the summer of 1770 the number of dwelling houses in Charleston was counted and found to be 1,292, from which Lieutenant Governor Bull estimated the population to be 5,030 whites and 5,831 black, "employed chiefly as domestic servants and mechanics."[23] On January 22, 1775, Henry Laurens wrote to his son John, who was in school in England, that he had been in Charleston seven weeks during which time bells had not tolled four times. He considered this a very extraordinary circumstance in a town containing about 14,000 persons. This is very good testimony both as to the population of Charleston and mortality in the colonial period.

The *Gazette of the State of South Carolina* published on September 14, 1786 an account of the number of houses taken from actual count of certain American towns as follows:

[17] Glenn to B. T. (?), Carroll, *Collections*, II, 218.
[18] Bull to the B. T., *P. R. S. C.* XXVIII, 352.
[19] *Ibid.*, XXXII, 122-124.
[20] Wm. S. Rossiter, ed., *A Century of Population and Growth*, 1790-1900, p. 7. E. B. Greene and V. D. Harrington, *American Population before the Federal Census of 1790.*
[21] *Ibid.*, and John Drayton, *A View of South Carolina as respects her Natural and civil Concerns*, 103.
[22] Rossiter, *A Century of Population and Growth*, 4.
[23] *P. R. S. C.*, XXXII, 388.

Philadelphia	4,600	Alexandria	300
New York	3,500	Richmond	280
Boston	2,100	Petersburg	290
Baltimore	1,900	Williamsburg	230
Charleston	1,500		

Boston, the account says, "by accurate calculation lately made has been found to contain 14,640 inhabitants, exclusive of strangers," which gives about seven persons to a house; so counting there were estimated to be in Philadelphia 32,200 inhabitants; in New York 24,500; in Baltimore 13,300; and in Charleston 10,780. This way of figuring gives Charleston considerably less population than she had a decade earlier by Mr. Laurens's off-hand esimate. Perhaps this way of estimating population did not give Charleston full credit for her colored population, for there were families that kept as many as fourteen slaves on their household premises. The parishes of St. Philip's and St. Michael's in which Charleston is located had by the census of 1790, 8,089 white and 8,831 black population, giving a total of 16,920 inhabitants; while Baltimore had by the census of 1790, 13,503 inhabitants.

Thus Charleston, in 1770, with a population of about 11,000, half of whom were Negroes, was the fourth city of British-America and the commercial capital of the South. However insignificant this population may appear to modern eyes, it compares very favorably with that of the old cities of Great Britain with whom Charleston traded chiefly. In fact, London is the only one of them that would be classified today according to population as a city of the first rank. Bristol, next largest to London, had a population of 95,000 in 1761; Birmingham about 50,000; Manchester 50,000 to 60,000; Glasgow 26,000 to 27,000.[24]

IV

Charleston had assumed in colonial times the general appearance that it has today. Hewatt tells us that most of the houses were built of brick, although travelers reported that only the most "considerable buildings" were of brick, the others being of cypress and yellow pine; many of the houses were three stories high,

[24] Anderson, *Origins of Com.*, III, 624-625.

"some elegant and all neat habitations, within genteely furnished and exposed as much as possible to the refreshing breezes from the sea"; and many "were encumbered with balconies and piazzas found convenient and even necessary during the hot season as retreats to enjoy fresh air." Pumps were installed at regular intervals throughout the town. Only footways were paved and brick pavements were used only on the principal streets. The inhabitants suffered much from dust in dry, and from mud in wet weather. The public buildings were the Exchange, the State House, an Armory, two churches for the Episcopalians, one for the Presbyterians, two for the French and two for the German Protestants, besides meeting houses for the Congregationalists and the Jews. The most conspicuous building in the town was St. Michael's Church whose tower 190 feet high served as a landmark for incoming ships.[25]

Some idea of the appearance and character of the city can be gained by viewing it first through the provincial eyes of Josiah Quincy, of Massachusetts, who visited Charleston in 1775 and viewed his voyage in the light of a journey to a foreign country; and then through the more sophisticated eyes of a European visitor, the Marquis de Chastellux, who was in Charleston in 1784. "This town," wrote Quincy, "makes a most beautiful appearance as you come up to it, and in many respects a magnificent one. I can only say in general, that in grandeur, splendour of buildings, decorations, equipages, numbers, shippings, and indeed in almost everything, it far surpasses all I ever saw, or ever expected to see, in America. Of their manners, literature, understanding, spirit of true liberty, policy and government, I can form no adequate judgment. All seems at present to be trade, riches, magnificence, and great state in everything; much gayety and dissipation."[26]

The Marquis de Chastellux said Charleston was a commercial town in which strangers abounded, as at Marseilles and Amsterdam; that manners were consequently polished and easy; that the inhabitants loved pleasure, the arts, society; and that the country

[25] Carroll, *Collections*, I, 603; Newton D. Mereness, ed., *Travels in the American Colonies*, 398.
[26] *Journal of Josiah Quincy*, 72-73.

was more European in its manners than any other in America.[27] The marquis was writing at a time when all American ports had been thrown open to European trade by the successful issue of the Revolutionary War; and of the numerous vessels from many quarters of the globe that crowded Charleston harbor there was scarcely one in five that bore the stars and stripes. As one writer phrased it "flags of Hamburg, Bremen, Altona, and Lubeck, and an occasional Spanish and Portuguese flag made up the variety."

The amount and character of public business conducted by the city was noteworthy. The city officials, elected by the freeholders of St. Philip's and St. Michael's parishes, consisted of vestrymen, churchwardens, firemasters, commissioners of the market, wood and coal measurers, and packers of beef and pork. The vestrymen and churchwardens were the most important of the city fathers because of their double character as civil officers and custodians of the public morals. The churchwardens levied taxes on slaves, real estate, and money at interest, for the support of the king's government; they also held elections, for the church was still in matters of government the partner of the state. Sometimes they conducted lotteries for the purpose of defraying extraordinary expenses. For example, there was a lottery proposed by the city council in the *City Gazette* of January 13, 1790, the purpose of which was the repairing the Exchange, which was in a "ruinous condition," and completing certain streets.

The lottery was a popular scheme for raising money for benevolent purposes. In 1773 the Delaware Lottery was being advertised throughout America. Its purpose was to raise the sum of five thousand six hundred and twenty-five pounds (or 15,000 dollars) for the use of the College of New Jersey, now Princeton University.[28] Public lotteries were common, but private lotteries were under the ban of the law. Under the law of South Carolina, enacted September 13, 1762, persons who "presumed to set up lotteries under the denomination of sales of houses, lands, plate, jewels, goods, wares, merchandizes and other things by chance," were subject to a fine of £1,000 proclamation money

[27] *Travels in North America*, II, 187-188; E. S. Thomas, *Reminiscences of the Last Sixty Years*, I, 31.
[28] *S. C. Gaz.*, July 5, 1773.

and 12 months jail sentence "without bail or mainprize," because lotteries were highly prejudicial to the public, and to the trade of the province and tended to defraud his Majesty's subjects.[29]

Moreover, church officials saw that the sabbath was duly observed. Charleston was a cavalier city. Its people went to the theatre to see shows given by traveling companies of actors; they attended concerts; they belonged to many exclusive societies; they liked to dance, and the Church of England minister, upon one occasion at least, thought it a part of his duty to advance a sufficient sum to secure for his people a dancing master, which in New England would have been enough to disgrace any minister. But Charleston also had its blue laws in conformity with Puritan ideals. The traveler Schoepf tells us that on Sunday all shops were closed and no sort of game or music was permitted. During the church service watchmen went about to lay hold upon idlers in the streets and upon all who were not upon urgent business or visiting the sick, and compel them to turn aside into some church or pay a fine of 2s. 4d. The grand jury of Charleston could present as a grievance in 1770 "The want of public stocks to make example of sabbath breakers, profane swearers, drunkards, and other disorderly persons."[30]

Fire prevention was difficult in a city full of careless Negroes and wooden houses, and Charleston had many disastrous fires. Fires sometimes originated from boiling pitch, tar, and turpentine within the city and from fires made by Negroes who watched rice upon the wharves at night, a practice that exposed the houses near the quays to danger. To prevent fire a certain section of the water front was set aside for the boiling of pitch, tar, and turpentine and persons who prepared their naval stores elsewhere in the city were subject to a fine. Also neglect to have one's chimney swept was punishable by fine. The law provided that if any chimney within the city took fire and blazed at the top, the tenant or owner was subject to a fine of £5.[31] Previous to 1783 fires were extinguished by citizens who obtained water from pumps or wells to convey directly to the fire. In June, 1784, a company

[29] Cooper, *Statutes of S. C.*, IV, 180.
[30] *Travels*, II, 222; *S. C. Gaz.*, Jan. 25, 1770.
[31] *Gaz. of the State of S. C.*, Aug. 28, 1786.

called the Hand-in-Hand Fire Company was organized, the members of which were required not only to pass buckets from one to another to extinguish the fire, but also to rescue the private property of the individual members of the company.

The establishment of public lamps "for usefulness in time of fire and to prevent Robbery" was recommended by a grand jury about the time there was much excitement in America over the parliamentary tax on tea, glass, paper, etc. The light situation is set forth in the following paragraph from the *South Carolina Gazette* of March 29, 1770:

"At the beginning of last Winter, a few public-spirited Gentlemen in this Town, set the Example to light the Streets, by putting up Lamps at their Doors; many others would have done so, at the same time but were restrained by the Consideration that they would thereby give Encouragement to the sale of an Article of British Manufacture for which we are unconstitutionally taxed. However, the great Utility of them having been observed, in time of Fire, and upon other Occasions, the Number is now increased to near 100; and the Legislature hath ordered some to be put up at all the Public Buildings and at the Houses where the Fire Engines are Lodged. But for the duty on glass, 'tis thought there would, by this time, have been between 4 and 500 Globe Lamps imported, and distributed through this Town; and it seems to be the earnest wish of the Inhabitants that an Act may be passed the present Session, for completely lighting all the Streets, with such Lamps as we can have made. In Philadelphia they have them of their own glass."

The lamps being installed, the problem arose of inflicting suitable punishment on those "mischievous and ill-disposed" persons who should break them. A city ordinance of 1784 decreed that the breaker of a lamp should forfeit on conviction the sum of £20 currency if the offender were a white person, and if a slave, he was to be whipped through the streets not exceeding 39 lashes unless the owner should pay his forfeit. One half of the fine went to the informer and the other half to the public treasurer, if it were a public lamp, otherwise it was to go to the owner of the broken lamp.[32]

There were three markets in Charleston: two for vegetables, meat, etc., and one for fish. The markets opened each morning at the rising of the sun, with the ringing of the market bells. Persons offering anything for sale before the ringing of the market bells were subject to fine and imprisonment: if free, the offender was fined 40 shillings; if slave, he was given corporal punishment of 39 lashes and was confined in the stocks not exceeding 6 hours. The sanitary conditions in and around these markets can be realized from the frequent references made in books of travel to the numerous buzzards to be seen in the city, which were unharmed because they lived only on carrion. Wrote Schoepf: "They eat up what sloth has not removed out of the way, and so have a great part in maintaining cleanliness and keeping off unwholesome vapors from dead beasts and filth."[33]

A law enacted on April 7, 1770, authorized the erection of a fish market "on the low water lot belonging to the public situated to the Eastward of the Bay of Charlestown, directly opposite to Queen Street." Hitherto fish had been offered for sale on stands and benches on the bay of Charleston and in the public streets "to the great nuisance of the inhabitants." At the new fish market it was lawful for all persons to buy and sell fish every day in the year, Sunday excepted, "from daylight to eight of the clock in the evening." Since Negroes, mulattoes, mestizoes, the principal persons who carried on the business of fishing, were apt to be disorderly, any two commissioners were authorized to confine, riotous, disorderly and drunken Negroes in the stocks for not more than two hours, and if the offense were repeated, a majority of the commissioners or two justices of the peace might order such offenders publicly whipped. Probably because of the frequency of disorders in the Fish Market, the public stocks were located there. The surplus fund after the expenses of the maintenance of the market were paid, was turned over to the churchwardens and vestry of St. Philips, in which parish the market was located, to

[32] *Digests of the Ordinances of Charleston*, 1784-1844, Sec. XVI, 409.
[33] *Columbian Herald*, October 16, 1786; Schoepf, *Travels*, II, 195.

be used for the poor of the parishes of St. Philip's and St. Michael's.[34]

Cornering or monopolizing the market was strictly contrary to the law. Medieval regulations concerning the forestaller, the regrater and the engrosser were still in force in eighteenth century Charleston. Forestalling was "buying or contracting for any merchandise, victuals, or anything whatsoever, on the way coming by land or water to any fair or market, or coming from beyond sea to any port, &c. to be sold, or causing the same to be bought; or dissuading people by word, letter, message or otherwise, from bringing such things to market, or persuading them to enhance the price after they are brought hither." Regrating was "buying or obtaining in any fair or market any grain, wine, fish, butter, cheese, candles, tallow, sheep, lambs, calves, swine, pigs, geese, capons, chickens, pidgeons, conies, or other dead victuals whatsoever, brought to a fair or market to be sold there, and setting up the same again in the same fair, market, or places, or some other fair or market within four miles." "Engrossing was getting into possession by buying, contracting or through promise butter, cheese, fish, or other dead victuals whatever, of like necessary or common use, with intent to sell them again." Any person guilty of either forestalling, regrating, or engrossing, upon conviction by two witnesses, was condemned to the loss of the goods bought and imprisonment for two months for the first offense; to the loss of double the value of the goods and six months imprisonment for the second offense; and for the third offense to the loss of all his goods, to be set upon the pillory, and to be imprisoned at the court's pleasure.[35]

The commissioners of the market once duly elected must accept the office, which was without salary, or pay a fine of £10 sterling; but no person was obliged to serve more than one year in any term of seven years. The commissioners fixed the standard of weights and measure, the rental price of stalls (a certain number of stalls being set apart for the use of the planters to expose their commodities for sale), the price for stalling, killing, cutting

[34] *Digests of the Ordinances of Charleston*, 1783 to 1844, 406-407.
[35] *The Columbian Herald*, Sept. 25, 1786.

up, and selling cattle, hogs, etc. In the *South Carolina Gazette* of October 31, 1774, we may see the commissioners of the market in action. They, with two magistrates, spent the week-end on a tour of inspection: they fined the butchers "for killing on Sunday contrary to the law"; they visited the wharves where they tried and adjusted "weights Beams & Scales"; and concluded by trying the bakers bread, which was found deficient in weight and 900 half crown loaves were seized and distributed to the poor. "Some of the Brown Bread used chiefly by the poor wanted no less than 17 ounces, white in general 4 to 7 ounces of the proper weight." After 1783, when Charleston was incorporated, the Intendant and Wardens became the official inspectors of bread and the city council determined in the assize of bread such matters as the size, weight, content, and price of a loaf of bread. The council also prescribed penalties for such misdemeanors as underweight, failure to mark bread with the baker's initials, and fraudulent mixture. The following is an example of the assize of bread:

Superfine flour being at 8 dollars per barrel, of 196 net, second at 7 dollars, and country flour at 5 dollars, the loaves must weigh as follows:

		lb.	oz.
White bread	8d. loaf	2	14
	4d. "	1	7
Wheaten bread	8d. loaf	3	3
	4d. "	1	9
Household bread	8d. loaf	3	14
	4d. "	1	15

Bakers notwithstanding the watchful care exercised over their business by the government were capable of going on a strike. The readers of the *Charleston Morning Post* and *Daily Advertiser* for November 14, 1786, read this notice from the bakers of Charleston:

"To the Public: This is to give notice that we the Bakers of this city unanimously shall stop baking after this day the 13th inst. at which time the late ordinance of the City Council is to take place; as we find that we cannot in justice to the support of our trade or families comply therewith. Since the City Council have had the regulation of the assize of bread, instead of granting us a redress of grievances complained of in our former petition, they have repealed all former acts, and to bake up to the present assize is not in our power, for they require a greater quantity of baked bread out of a hundred of flour than it will really make, without allowing anything for the support of ourselves and families."

CHAPTER II
THE TRADE TERRITORY OF CHARLESTON

I

Charleston was the metropolis of the immense southern Indian country several hundred miles to the west and southwest of the city, where traffic with the Indians was carried on under the direction of a superintendent sent out by the British government. In addition to this, it was the trade center for the prosperous tidewater section of South Carolina; it plied a considerable back country trade with the frontier settlers of western North and South Carolina; a coastal trade with the tidewater section of North Carolina, especially with the Cape Fear country; a trade by land and sea with Georgia; and, after 1763, a coastal trade with East and West Florida. Charleston was thus the commercial capital of an immense region and became a sort of city-state, drawing to itself all the wealth of the surrounding country, which gave it a prestige the memory of which has never faded. Uninformed people even to this day have an idea that South Carolina consists of the picturesque old city of Charleston and a vague hinterland of sand and pines.

Geographically, South Carolina is divided like all Gaul into three parts: a low and level coastal plain extending from 100 to 200 miles from the sea; a middle country, known as the Piedmont, more elevated and rising a hundred miles or more from the fall line to the mountains; and beyond this, the mountains. Socially and economically, in colonial times, South Carolina was divided into two sections—the low country and the up-country.

The low country along the sea coast consists of an almost dead level of sand, pine barrens, and swamps. The arable land before the introduction of commercial fertilizers was confined mostly to the river valleys; here rice and indigo were cultivated by means of slave labor on great plantations ranging in size from 3,000 to 40,000 acres, and exported directly to Europe. The waste of sand and pines between the immediate seaboard area and the western portion of the coastal plain was used as a range for cattle or left unoccupied and served in the early days as a barrier between the low country and the up-country.

The typical plantation consisted of swamp land for growing rice, relatively high land for growing provisions and indigo, and pine barrens. A small part of the land was cleared, a still smaller part cultivated, and the greater part pine barrens.

In the low country a plantation might consist of as much as 300 acres of cleared land. Away from the rice coast, where only occasional patches of rice were grown and the planter's money crop was indigo, a hundred or two acres of cleared land was called a plantation. The number of Negroes employed depended upon the quantity of swamp land in the plantation; for the swamp land required a vast amount of human toil in unwholesome surroundings before it was fit for the cultivation of rice. The heavy forest growth of the swamp had to be cleared away, ditches dug, embankments constructed and reserves of water prepared for irrigating the crop. Twenty-five or thirty Negroes seem to have been the number employed on the average plantation. Ralph Izard, whom the census of 1790 reported to be next to the largest planter in the state of South Carolina, owned 594 Negroes distributed on eight plantations, in three parishes, and he had besides ten other slaves in Charleston. Izard's home plantation, "The Elms," contained 1,400 acres, of which 300 were in cultivation. Dr. Pringle, however, who was considered only a small planter because he owned only 1,900 acres, employed 70 or 80 Negroes on 240 acres of cleared land, but this was probably because 200 acres of his land was swamp.[1]

The small amount of land in cultivation was due largely to the crude sort of farming everywhere practised. Husbandry tools were of the kind that had been in use for centuries. The land was not ploughed or harrowed but hoed, the hoe being the principal implement used before the Revolution in the cultivation of rice, indigo, corn, and other crops. Harvesting was done with the

[1] La Rochefoucauld-Liancourt, *Travels through the United States of North America*, I, 586; *ibid.*, II, 599.

sickle and scythe. The flail had replaced the trampling out of grain by oxen, and rice was "manufactured" at infinite cost of human labor with mortar and pestle, although a few progressive planters had introduced rice mills operated by horse power. Timothy Ford wrote in his diary in 1784: "The number of slaves supply the almost total want of instruments of husbandry; & the dint of muscular force the want of invention and improvement."[2]

Farming was still to a certain extent a migratory occupation. The man who wished to establish a plantation obtained a tract of land, whose quality he judged by the kind of trees growing upon it. Good swamp contained white oak and cypress, good high land oak and hickory. When the land was cleared, he surrounded it with a fence to exclude the cattle, sheep, and hogs, and here he planted year after year rice and indigo until the land was exhausted. Then he forsook his clearing, abandoning it to grass, weeds, bushes and forest, and took up fresh land. A principal cause for land exhaustion was ignorance of the use of fertilizers. Although there were vast numbers of cattle in the country and oxen were probably used more as draught animals than horses, manuring and the rotation of crops to renew the fertility of the soil were not practised. Small wonder then that an acre of land produced only from 2 to 4 barrels of rice weighing 625 pounds; or 15 to 20 bushels of corn, 25 bushels per acre being considered a great crop; or a hundred bushels of potatoes. As late as 1784 a traveler could write of South Carolina farming: "Here they never use any manure." Then, overseers were commonly paid as wages a percentage of the crop, which spurred them on to produce great crops each year without regard to preserving the fertility of the soil.

Soil exhaustion, with the consequent need of constantly opening up new lands, the existence of impenetrable swamps, and land speculation account for the large estates in the tidewater section of South Carolina. Then the manifold activities of plantation life required a large field for their scope. The planter was not only a farmer, but frequently a lumberman and cattle raiser. A variety of employment was necessary to keep the Negro, a costly

[2] Published in the *S. C. Hist. & Gen. Mag.*, XIII, 143-183.

investment, busy; for allowing him to be idle was like having money out without bringing in any interest. No idleness was permitted on a well regulated plantation and there were few holidays, Christmas being one of them. From spring until September slaves were kept busy cultivating rice, indigo, and provision land. In the autumn some of them beat out rice in crude hand mills, a task that was not completed when spring ploughing began; others cleared land, sawed boards and scantling, split rails, made staves and shingles, coopered barrels and casks, cobbled shoes, made negro clothing, did carpenter work. The plantation was economically almost self-sufficing, and in a crisis, such as that brought about by the Revolution, could be made absolutely so. The planter lived at home. He raised cattle, hogs, sheep, potatoes, corn, and other provisions, sufficient for himself and his slaves. Only the wealthy planter owned the boat that transported his crops to market, and freight charges were so high that the ordinary planter could not afford to pay for the transportation of provisions. Indian corn was important in the list of provisions grown on the plantation. "Our growth of corn," wrote Henry Laurens, "is esteemed superior to all the Northward produce at every market and is generally dearer than any other." Southern corn sometimes brought five shillings more per bushel than that from the northern colonies. The southerners' fondness for corn dishes was being established. Travelers commented upon their predilection for hominy "big and little" and meal and hominy formed an essential part of the diet of slaves both in the southern colonies and in the West Indies. Besides corn, the planter exported some cattle and hogs to the West Indies, but a good number of these were needed at home for the support of slaves. From the point of view of the Charleston business man the plantation was important mostly as a source of rice and indigo and as a market for African slaves and European manufactures of various kinds to supply the master and his slaves. Since the plantation in its relation to the business world at Charleston is dealt with more at length in later chapters, this brief account will suffice at this point and we shall now consider more in detail the economic evolution of the up-country and its relation to Charleston.[3a]

II

For more than sixty years after the founding of Charleston the up-country was occupied only by the Indians and the fur traders. It was only in the decade of the 1750's that the Carolina back country above the middle course of the rivers began to fill up with white people, mostly Scotch-Irish and Germans from Pennsylvania, and English from Maryland and Virginia. Braddock's defeat in 1755 exposed the frontiers of Pennsylvania and Virginia to the warriors of the Six Nations, and hastened the occupation of the up-country. The successful termination of England's war with France in 1763 gave security to the frontier and immensely stimulated the peopling of the up-country.

Hewatt writes that within the space of a year after 1763 more than a thousand families came to Carolina driving their cattle, hogs, and horses before them; that incredible numbers of people attended the sittings of the governor and his council, which occurred once a month, in order to obtain lands granted in small tracts of from 50 to 300 acres. A Charleston item in the *Georgia Gazette* for April 21, 1763, states that "near 1,000 families" had arrived at Long Cane's (now Abbeville County, South Carolina) within the last 12 months, that improvements in that settlement were almost incredible and that "near 4,000 families" were expected. From the neighborhood of Ninety-Six, in South Carolina, it was reported that "upwards of 300 families" had passed that town in about three months time in order to settle the lands thereabouts, and that the Cherokee Indians were behaving in the most friendly manner.[3] The Indians, along with the herds of buffalo and deer, began to disappear, and Charleston's export trade in skins and furs, which had been an important source of wealth, began to decline. By 1777 Henry Laurens could write to a correspondent that South Carolina was already "well covered by inhabitants"

[3a] For South Carolina agriculture see, Carroll, *Collections*, II, 196 *et seq.*; Weston, *Documents Connected with the History of South Carolina*, 65; *American Husbandry*, I, 387-397.
[3] Alexander Hewatt, *An Historical Account of the Rise and Progress of the Colonies of South Carolina and Georgia*, II, 274; *Ga. Gaz.*, July 7, 1763.

and "comfortably settled" from 250 to 300 miles to the west by people from England, Scotland, Ireland, and "thousands from France," that the Indians had been pushed back 300 miles from the sea.

The productions of the back country were similar to those of the mother country and the colonies of the North; and here the emigrants from the North established a society like that to which they had been accustomed at home. It became a land of small shops, small farms, household manufactures, big families, plenty of food, but not much contact with the outside world. The women wove, the men farmed. Patches of flax, hemp, and cotton were cultivated; almost everybody kept a few sheep. There was a spinning wheel and loom in almost every house, where were manufactured cloth of flax, wool and cotton. Wheat, oats, barley, rye, Indian corn, indigo, tobacco, and madder were cultivated. There were good pastures for horses, black cattle, sheep, and hogs; and fowls of all sorts were abundant. Men made their husbandry tools, tanned leather, distilled drinks from peaches, apples, barley, and other grains, substituting honey for sugar.[4]

Thus in the Carolina backwoods grew up a society antagonistic to that of the low country: a land of Dissenters, instead of Church of England men; a land of small farms and shops, instead of large plantations and large mercantile establishments; a land of household manufactures, saw mills, flour mills, stocking mills, instead of a region dependent on England for all of its supplies; a land of small buyers, instead of purchasers who must supply the needs of large plantations; a land of democracy where men had to earn their livings in the sweat of their brows, instead of an aristocracy where one lost caste by performing manual labor.

A potent factor in the development of the back country was England's policy of permitting manufactures where they did not interfere with her own and encouraging agricultural expansion by various expedients, such as the exemption of certain exports from duties for limited periods, giving bounties on certain commodities, and granting lands to settlers upon easy terms.

[4] Laurens to Christo Zahn, Aug. 13, 1777; P. R. S. C., XXXII, 31; Marquis de Chastellaux, Travels in North America in the Years 1780, 1781 and 1782, II, 36-40.

Parliament granted bounties to encourage the manufactures of Great Britain or to promote her naval supremacy, such as those upon indigo, flax, hemp, tobacco, silk, wine, lumber, and naval stores. The legislature of South Carolina also gave bounties for raising silk, wine, oil, barley, wheat, hemp, flax, cotton, indigo, and ginger.[5] And it was the provincial bounty which produced, in many cases, the desired result, for much of Carolina back country produce was not considered worthy of the parliamentary bounty. In 1769 the Carolina hemp growers collected a bounty of £20,000 sterling.[6] Perhaps most of this hemp went to Philadelphia, Boston, and Rhode Island to be used in the shipbuilding industry. The assembly of South Carolina was offering in 1771 a bounty of ten shillings current money upon every one hundred pounds of flour "equal in weight and goodness to the best flour imported from the northern colonies," and at the same time was laying a duty of five shillings current money upon every one hundred pounds of flour imported from the other colonies.[7] The purpose of this legislation was doubtless to encourage the further expansion of the flour milling industry. By 1770 the back country was supplying the home market and was exporting 4,000 barrels of flour a year.[8] By 1796 there were warehouses of inspection for flour not only in the ports of Charleston, Georgetown, and Beaufort, but in back country villages like Camden, Columbia, Granby, and Vienna, in the far-west of Abbeville County.[9]

Raising cattle and hogs was an important occupation of the back countrymen. Even in the plantation district men sometimes owned as many as a thousand cattle and it was said to be a common thing to own two or three hundred. In the wilds of Georgia the conditions were particularly favorable for cattle-raising and sometimes herds of as many as five or six thousand head were advertised.[10] William Bartram, the naturalist, while traveling in South Carolina and Georgia in 1773 was entertained on a cattle

[5] P. R. S. C. XXXII, 31.
[6] Ibid., XXX, 500.
[7] S. C. Gaz., March 28, 1771.
[8] P. R. S. C., XXXII, 395-396.
[9] S. C. Gaz., October 15, 1772; Cooper, Statutes of S. C., IV, 291-294.
[10] For advertisements of cattle see Gaz. of the State of Ga., April 2, 1783 and S. C. Gaz., March 29, 1773.

ranch, about fifty miles up the Savannah River from the town of Savannah. The whole stock of cattle was about fifteen hundred although the owner had recently acquired his herd. Great quantities of beef were disposed of at Charleston, but all the milk products, such as butter and cheese, were consumed in the cattleman's household in support of his slaves, who were employed in squaring pine and cypress lumber for the West Indian market.[11]

Stock raising conditions in the later colonial period are well described by William Gerard de Brahm, who was appointed Surveyor General for the Southern District in 1764. De Brahm wrote that cattle had multiplied so greatly in South Carolina that to make room for the immense yearly increase, great herds were driven into the neighboring province of Georgia, and there kept between the Savannah and Ogechee rivers, by cowpen-keepers who moved about from pasture to pasture "like ancient Patriarchs or modern Bedewins"; that the cowpen-keepers determined the number of their flocks by the number of calves which they marked every spring and fall; thus "if 300 calves a year were marked, the cattleman reckoned his stock at 400 heifers, 500 cows, and 300 steers—in all 1,500 head, besides horses"; that the purchaser of 300 head of cattle was allowed 124 cows, 80 steers, including bulls, 90 heifers and 6 horses, for which he paid £300 sterling, and the cattle were delivered gratis on the other side of one, two, or three streams according as the cowpen-keeper was in want of selling.[12] After reading such a description, one feels it was not accidental that two of the battles fought in Carolina during the Revolution were called respectively "Cowpens" and "Blackstock."

There were expert horsemen, much like the modern western cowboys, who rode the range, and who once a year assembled the cattle for the young to be counted and to pick out those intended for market. Sometimes the cattle were fattened on corn fodder and rice straw, but most often they were killed just as they came out of the woods. The cattle and hogs of each farm were dis-

[11] Wm. Bartram, *Travels Through North and South Carolina, Georgia, East and West Florida, 1773-1778*, 310-313.
[12] P. C. Weston, ed., *Documents connected with the history of South Carolina*, 200.

tinguished by special earmarks and the horses were branded. A registry of each owner's brand was kept at Charleston and falsification or extinguishment of the mark was a felony.

Newspaper advertising reflects the prevailing interest in stock-raising and the qualities that recommended stock to purchasers. The word "tame" was much in evidence. Such phrases as these stand out in the advertisements: "A stock of tame cattle"; "tame plantation cattle"; "a stock of fine, tame, well governed cattle"; or as a special recommendation, "a young cow bred up to the town." There were advertisements in the Charleston papers of herds of cattle ranging in number from about 200 to 2,000, of which the following is a specimen:

"To be sold.
On Thurs., the 26 Day of Apr. next, at the Vendue House in Charles Town precisely at 12 O'clock at Noon.
A Stock of about Two thousand Head, more or less, of fine Black Cattle, with Stock of Horses and Provisions; Together, with 100 Acres of Land, whereupon the Cowpen is settled. This stock is well known to be as fine a Stock as any in the Province; It formerly belonged to Capt. James Mac-Pherson, who disposed of it to Benj. Waring and Ralph Izard, Esq; etc.
William Davis."

The inspectors of beef and pork were important city officials at Charleston where cattle were butchered and prepared for the market. Cattle were also shipped alive to the West Indies or Philadelphia. It was contrary to the law to kill cattle until they had been in town twelve hours and in 1783, when Charleston was incorporated, it was forbidden to kill cattle within the limits of the town. North Carolina was a great hog-raising province, and thousands of these animals from North Carolina found a market in Virginia and South Carolina. Cattle were selling in 1784 at from three to six Spanish dollars per head, and hogs as low as from three to three and a half Spanish dollars per hundred.[13]

The great problem of the landlocked up-country was transportation. The swift streams were excellent for turning mill wheels but of no use in transporting crops to market. Trade with

[13] For account of cattle see Smyth, *Tour*, II, 78-79; Schoepf, *Travels*, II, 108-110; La Rochefoucauld-Liancourt, *Travels*, 601; *American Museum*, "Notes on the United States," July 1790.

Charleston on any large scale had to be deferred until wagon roads could be built. These had to pass over a forbidding pine barren before the market in the low country could be reached. The back countryman, therefore, turned his eyes to the northward whence he came, and found it easier to drive his cattle to the markets of Philadelphia and New York along the existing trails through the mountains rather than blaze a trail across the country to Charleston. Nevertheless communication with the low country must have been established at an early date for by 1763 the province had become almost economically self-sufficing. The low country was exporting quantities of rice and indigo to Europe; with the development of the up-country, Charleston's import trade in provisions from the North began to fall off, and at the same time the former trade in provisions to the West Indies was reëstablished and became flourishing. Trade with the Indians was declining, but was still considerable and deerskins yet formed one of the most important exports from Charleston.

Most of the back country trade was by wagon. Before the Santee Canal was cut in the 1790's, connecting the Santee and Cooper rivers, the produce of North and South Carolina, collected along the Broad, the Saluda, the Wateree, and the Catawba, the waters of which join in their course to form the Santee, was often shipped on the Santee in small boats to Georgetown, where it frequently had to be reshipped in coastwise vessels to Charleston. The difficulty of navigating the sea down to Charleston and of working up the rapid stream on the return trip caused many people of upper Carolina, even along the rivers, to resort to wagon traffic; and for the greatest part of the back country the wagon was the only means of conveying crops to market.

There was a phenomenal development of the back country trade before the Revolution. Early in the 1760's that race of backwoodsmen described by travelers as of a yellowish hue and sallow cadaverous complexions, contrasting unfavorably with the opulent and well-bred planters, was hauling produce to market and bringing out necessary supplies in covered wagons drawn by four or six horses, two abreast, often traversing distances of three hundred miles or more. Before the Revolution as many as three

thousand wagons per year from the back country passed over the
ferries coming into Charleston, and the merchants of the city
found it worth their while to build large wagon yards in the rear
of their stores for the accommodation of wagoners. Some merchants built stores outside of the city gates to cater especially to
the back country trade.[14]   The *South Carolina Gazette* for December 5, 1771, contained this observation: "Last Monday a
gentleman counted no less than 113 waggons on the Road to
Town, most of them loaded with 2 Hogsheads of Tobacco, besides
Indico, Hemp, Butter, Tallow, Beef, Wax, and many other
articles; who carry on their return Rum, Sugar, Salt, and European goods. The most ever observed on the Road before, in one
Day, was 30, and that was reckoned extraordinary."
    Wagoning became a profitable business. The trip to Charles-
ton from the back country might take two or three weeks, for the
rate of travel was twenty or twenty-five miles a day; but the wag-
oner lived at almost as little expense on the road as he did at
home, except for an occasional glass of rum at an inn or ordinary.
He brought along his meal, bacon, and cheese and prepared his
meals as he camped in the woods, while his horses grazed nearby.
On the way down, business sometimes fell in his way when the
crossroads' storekeeper hired him to haul out his goods or sold him
produce. The roads were the great handicap to business. They
were so bad in places that several wagoners had to club together
to get over bad places; but the assembly was remedying this condition by appropriating money to widen narrow roads and improve
roads generally, because of "the great & increasing inland Trade"
carried on by means of wagons.[15]
    Charleston developed a trade with the back parts of North
Carolina both by water and land. Some of the rivers of North
Carolina, like the Broad, the Catawba, and the Pedee (Yadkin)
become navigable after they pass into South Carolina, where they
find an outlet to the sea. By means of such rivers the fur traders
from Charleston had penetrated western North Carolina before

[14] *P. R. S. C.*, XXXII, 282.
[15] For accounts of back country trade see Smyth, *Tour*, I, 205; Mereness,
Travels; Journal of Lord Adam Gordon, 1764-1765, 399; La Rochefoucauld-
Liancourt, *Travels*, I, 630; S. C. Locals, No. 4, H. P. Archer, 8.

the immigrants arrived. The boundary line between the Carolinas was not finally adjusted until the eve of the Revolution, and the government at Charleston was accustomed to regard the upper courses of these rivers as a part of South Carolina. In 1770 when the matter of the boundary line was under consideration, the agent of South Carolina represented to the Board of Trade that the South Carolina government had been accustomed to make grants of land to European immigrants upon the branches of the Broad River; that settlers along the Broad and Catawba had collected bounties offered by the South Carolina legislature on hemp and naval stores; and that it would be an injustice to these people to annex them to North Carolina for that would mean that they must abandon cheap water transportation to Charleston for expensive land transportation to the markets of North Carolina by means of wagon and cattle.[16]

The western settlers of North Carolina and Georgia found a readier sale for their produce in the brisker market at Charleston than in the nearer towns of Wilmington and Savannah. When Charleston was being besieged by the British in 1779, the governors of South Carolina, North Carolina, and Georgia presented a memorandum to Lord George Germain in which they expressed their belief that the back settlers of North Carolina would be compelled to submit on the fall of Charleston, because they were dependent for necessary supplies upon that market to which they had been sending for many years past "upwards of 2,000 wagons annually to vend their produce and secure necessities for their families."[17]

III

The physical geography of North Carolina ordained that in an age of water transportation it should develop little independent trade. The bulk of its exports reached the outside world through the merchants of Virginia and South Carolina or by means of the New England traders. North Carolina had no proud tidewater aristocracy. It was predominantly a land of few slaves and free labor, of crude plenty and little culture. With a population nearly

[16] P. R. S. C., XXXII, 225-230.
[17] P. R. S. C., XXXVI, 80-81.

twice as large as that of South Carolina, it possessed not a single important seaport. There were navigable rivers in abundance, but shoal water, sand banks, and low islands and bars rendered the passage into them dangerous. Edenton, New Berne, and Wilmington were on navigable rivers, but at some distance from the sea. Edenton, in the northeastern part of the province, on Albemarle Sound, at the mouth of Roanoke River, was 35 or 40 miles from the sea in a direct line, but the circuitous channels leading to it were 180 miles long. New Berne, on the Neuse, in the central section of the coast, was a hundred miles from the sea. The entrance to the harbor at Wilmington, on the southeastern coast, as we have seen, was considered dangerous on account of shifting shoals. Thus it happened that North Carolinians carried their produce in small vessels to the markets in Virginia or to Charleston and brought from thence their supply of European goods.[18]

There was little communication between the northern and southern coasts of North Carolina, because of the difficulties of navigation. The settlements on the Albemarle and Pamlico sounds and the Neuse traded principally with Virginia and the New England traders. The Albemarle section, isolated and lonely, with its small population and feeble government, was still a sort of sub-province of Virginia. Its chief crop, tobacco, was transported by land carriage to Petersburg, in Virginia, until after the Revolution, when the construction of the Dismal Swamp canal, connecting Albemarle Sound with the Elizabeth River, transferred its trade to Norfolk. The settlements on Pamlico Sound and the Neuse trafficked mostly with the New Englanders. These "Dutchmen of America" plied a brisk trade with the small towns along the coast of North Carolina, South Carolina, and Georgia. They usually came to the southern ports in the fall, bringing in their schooners and shallops such commodities as cider, cheese, apples, gingerbread, hides, potatoes, European goods, and rum, which they bartered for pelts, pitch, tar, and tobacco, and returned

[18] Adams, *Provincial Society*, 207-208; *Collections of the Georgia Hist. Society*, III, 165.

North in the spring. Virginia regarded them as poachers upon her tobacco trade and watched their activities with jealous eyes.

All kinds of imported merchandise were exceedingly dear in North Carolina because of the bad navigation and lack of trade competition. "The New England farmers," says James T. Adams, in quoting Hugh Meredith's *Account of the Cape Fear Country,* "were hard milkers." In the 1730's the cheapest goods in the Cape Fear country were fifty per cent dearer than at Philadelphia and most things one hundred per cent. Prices were probably unavoidably high in North Carolina and were due more to geography than to any hard milking on the part of the New England traders. It is not uncommon even at the present for shopkeepers in isolated country sections to ask forty or fifty per cent more for certain articles than one has to pay in the city. That is the reason why the mail-order houses and the chain stores have come into being. The New Englanders could make only one trip in the course of the year and bring only a small quantity of goods at each trip in their small craft, while the large merchantmen made at least two trips to Europe in a year. The New Englanders were obliged to spend the winter in one or several places along the coast, not only to peddle their goods, but also because navigation in North Carolina waters in winter was dangerous. Large ships did not like to make the trip even in summer. Also the New Englanders had to pay high prices for money, the object of their quest, in order to make remittances to England for part of their stock in trade. It was the universal complaint of the small-town people that they could keep no money among them because the northerners gave a price for "Guineas, Moidores Johannes's Pistols & Dollars far above their real and intrinsic value."[18a]

The most prosperous section of North Carolina was the Cape Fear region. Brunswick, formerly the capital of the province, was yielding precedence in the later colonial era to Wilmington, whose special advantage was its location at the meeting of the two navigable branches of the Cape Fear River, extending far back into the interior. The northeast branch on which Wilmington is located contained the longest river navigation in the province.

[18a] Collections of Ga. Hist. Soc., III, 165.

It was navigable for vessels of eighteen or twenty tons for a hundred miles to Cross Creek, rechristened Fayetteville, in honor of Lafayette, after the Revolution. Here numerous thrifty Scotch Highlanders, adherents of the old and the young Pretenders, had taken refuge. As late as 1770 the South Carolina newspapers were announcing the arrival of 1,200 Highlanders in the Cape Fear River to settle North Carolina.

Cross Creek forwarded naval stores, lumber, pork, and furs to Wilmington, which had a little direct trade with London, Bristol, and Glasgow; some trade in lumber and provisions with the West Indies; a small coastwise trade with the northern provinces; and a flourishing trade in rice, indigo, lumber and naval stores with Charleston.[19] In 1788 when Wilmington had not yet recovered from the economic effects of the Revolution, her exports for the year were: 2,902,606 feet of lumber, 4,934,670 shingles, 225,999 hogshead staves, 334,258 barrel staves, 1,406 hogsheads of tobacco, 26,587 barrels of tar, 356 barrels of pitch, 6,540 barrels of turpentine, 99 barrels of pork, 522 tierces of rice.[20]

As the above exports show, the chief industry of the Cape Fear country was the production of lumber and naval stores. The yellow pines of North Carolina were making themselves famous. Before the Revolution 130,000 barrels of naval stores went annually from North Carolina to England. As early as 1767 there were fifty saw mills on the Cape Fear and its tributaries cutting seven and a half million feet of lumber annually. There were official inspectors of turpentine, rosin, pitch, boards, shingles, casks, and staves.[21] The Journal of a Lady of Quality gives us an insight into the colonial lumbering business. This Scotch lady, Janet Schaw, visited, in 1775, her brother, John Rutherford, on his plantation Bowland, at Rocky Point off the Cape Fear, and wrote as follows in her journal:

"[John Rutherford] makes a great deal of tar and turpentine, but his grand work is a saw-mill, the finest I ever met with. It cuts three thousand lumbers (which are our own dales [deals]) a

[19] Elkanah Watson, *Men and Times of the Revolution*, 49; James Sprunt, *Cape Fear Chronicles*, 49-50; La Rochefoucauld-Liancourt, *Travels*, I, 635.
[20] *State Gaz. of North Carolina*, May 14, 1789.
[21] MacPherson, *Annals of Com.*, III, 569.

day, and can double the number when necessity demands it. The woods round him are immense, and he has a vast piece of water, which by a creek communicates with the river, by which he sends down all the lumber, tar and pitch, as it rises every tide sufficiently high to bear any weight. This is done on what is called rafts, built upon a flat with dales, and the barrels depending from the sides. In this manner they will float you down fifty thousand deals at once, and 100 or 200 barrels, and they leave room in the centre for the people to stay on, who have nothing to do but prevent its running on shore, as it is floated down by the tides, and they must lay to, between tide and tide, it having no power to move but by the force of the stream." The raft system may be illustrated from the county records of Brunswick from which the following extract is taken: "Large rafts of lumber are frequently brought down the river and by stress of weather are broke and lyable to be lost. Persons picking up the scattered lumber, boats, or goods are to advertise the same in public places."[22]

Yellow pines were bringing some culture into North Carolina. The "Lady of Quality" wrote of an old gentleman who lived on a plantation called Hunt Hill which furnished lumber, staves, hoops, and ends for barrels, and casks for the West Indian trade. He had numerous slaves which had been "bred" to be coopers and carpenters and was able to load a raft once in a fortnight. Although he lived in a house little better than a Negro hut, his income was from twelve to fifteen hundred pounds sterling per year, and he possessed such treasures as a library "with fine globes and Mathematical instruments of all kinds, also a set of noble telescopes."[23]

A letter of Governor Tryon to the Board of Trade on March 7, 1768, indicates that much of the naval stores of North Carolina went to the credit of South Carolina. Tryon wrote that he had been told that all vessels entering and clearing at the port of London from either of the Carolinas were entered on the custom books as trading to and from Carolina generally without distinction of North and South Carolina; that when the agents of South Carolina and Georgia solicited from Parliament legisla-

[22] *Journal of a Lady of Quality*, 184-185 and note p. 81.
[23] *Ibid.*, p. 185.

tion permitting the exportation of rice to certain foreign markets, the exports from the two Carolinas were extracted from the custom books and placed to the credit of South Carolina and served to swell the importance of that government, while a great majority of the naval stores were actually shipped from North Carolina. Tryon requested that North Carolina might have the credit of its own exports and produce. This request was never granted, probably because of the difficulty of keeping separate accounts.[24] The comparative volume of the foreign trade of North and South Carolina to places other than Great Britain may be surmised from the following account of the value in sterling money of the exports of the two provinces in 1769:[25]

	To Great Britain	To Southern Europe	To W. I.	To Africa
N. C.		£ 3,238-3-7	£ 27,944-7-9	£ 71-15-4
	£405,014-13-1			
S. C.		£72,881-9-3	£59,814-11-6	£619-16-9

IV

In Georgia the Carolina merchants and planters found the excellent navigation which excited their enthusiasm at home. Here were lands fully as good as those on the seacoast of South Carolina, and that too at a time when inland swamp land was becoming scarce and therefore dear; for it was not until about the time of the Revolution that the tide flow system of irrigation was introduced which opened large new areas along the coast to the cultivation of rice.[26]

The successful termination of the war with France, which gave security to the frontier, immensely stimulated the demand in South Carolina for Georgia lands and excited great hopes of riches in the bosoms of the planters. In 1767 Henry Laurens, a Charleston merchant who had invested largely in plantations in South Carolina and Georgia, was requesting Governor Wright, of Georgia, to have some person appointed to enter and clear vessels at Frederica or Darien; to have beacons and other landmarks put

[24] Colonial Records of North Carolina, VII, 695-696.
[25] MacPherson, Annals of Com., III, 572.
[26] J. G. W. de Brahm, History of Georgia, 21.

down at St. Simon's or Jekyl's Island, and, to procure a pilot for one or the other of these places.[27] Laurens had "settled" at least three Georgia plantations at this time. He prophesied that within the space of twenty years the region about the Altamaha and Turtle rivers, the Saltilla and the Great and Little St. Marys would load "300 sails of vessels" per annum with rice, pitch, tar, turpentine, hemp, indigo, masts, pine and cypress lumber, Indian corn and peas, and live stock. He believed there was a prospect of producing silk and madder and that shipbuilding would prosper on account of the quantities of oak, pine, and cedar to be found. The prosperity of the plantations promoted the growth of ports, such as, Frederica, Darien and Sunbury.

The boundary between South Carolina and Georgia had not been fixed and much Georgia land was granted by the Carolina government to its citizens. After the Revolution the Georgia government called in question the validity of the titles to some of these lands, and this was the occasion of much bitter feeling on the part of the South Carolina investors and of some sharp financial losses. The region south of the River Altamaha at first was regarded as Carolina territory; a fort had been erected at Frederica which had been garrisoned for many years by detachments of troops from South Carolina. After the war thousands of acres in this region were petitioned for by soldiers, merchants, and planters. *The South Carolina Gazette* of April 2-9, 1763, says: "We hear, that upwards of 400,000 acres of land, to the Southward of the river Altamaha were petitioned for last Tuesday and warrants issued for about 300,000." Thousands of acres were granted to great merchants like Henry Laurens, Aaron Loocock, Joseph Kershaw; to great planters like Stephen Bull and Thomas Shubrick; and to politicians like Sir Egerton Leigh and William Bull. One of the most modest petitions for Altamaha lands was that of Francis Marion, which called for only 500 acres, while Rawlins Lowndes and many others were asking for as much as 7,500 acres. But the grants of Georgia lands made by South Carolina were insignificant compared to the grants of East Florida lands, ranging in quantity from ten to twenty thousand acres,

[27] To Jonathan Bryan, Sept. 4, 1767.

which were being made by Great Britain at this time to influential noblemen, merchants and politicians.[28]

The development of Georgia was probably more rapid than that of any other of the British-American colonies. Some of the best Georgia lands could be bought in 1760 for prices ranging from 3 shillings to 10 shillings Georgia currency per acre; in 1784, however, the best Georgia lands were selling for £3 to £12 sterling per acre, and this at a time when much land in the South was thrown on the market on account of the debtor-creditor situation just after the war and land prices as a consequence were greatly reduced.[29]   In the decade ending 1773 Georgia exports exceeded her imports for six years.   In 1764 her exports to the mother country were valued at £31,325.   By 1774 they had tripled in value and brought £103,477.[30]

The big money commodities in Georgia were the same as those of South Carolina.   In 1760 Georgia shipped 3,283 barrels of rice to Great Britain; in 1770—22,129 barrels.   In 1760 her exports of indigo were 11,746 pounds; in 1770—22,136 pounds. The Georgia skin trade during the later colonial period was increasing at the expense of that of South Carolina.   In 1760 she exported 65,765 pounds of deerskins; in 1770—284,840 pounds.[31]

Georgia had a large trade to the West Indies, where lumber, cattle, and provisions were exchanged for rum, sugar, and Negroes; a large coastwise trade with Charleston, where rice, indigo, and provisions were exchanged for Negroes, European goods and West Indian products; a small direct trade with Great Britain from which she received European goods and African Negroes; and a small trade with the northern provinces from whom she bought flour, biscuit, and other provisions.[32]   In 1762 Georgia trade employed 22 square rigged vessels and 35 sloops making 2,784 tons; ten years later Georgia was employing 84 square rigged vessels and 135 sloops making 11,246 tons.[33]

[28] *Council Journal,* 1763, pp. 43, 76.
[29] Smyth, *Tour,* II, 50; Laurens to Habersham, November 16, 1768.
[30] MacPherson, *Annals of Com.,* III, 409-585.
[31] *Ibid.*
[32] *Col. of Ga. Hist. Soc.,* III, 165.
[33] *American Museum,* IV, Sept., 1788, p. 278.

V

By the acquisition of Florida in 1763 a new trade territory was added to the Charleston District and a new field of investment was opened to the merchants and planters. There was little prospect of eastern Florida developing for some time an independent trade. The only approach was by sea, and the bar before St. Augustine which shifted its position from time to time rendered the navigation dangerous for large ships. The British for administrative purposes divided the immense territory of Florida: East Florida, with its capital at St. Augustine, consisted of the present state of Florida with the exception of a small section west of the Apalachicola River; and West Florida, with its capital at Pensacola, embraced the coasts of the present states of Alabama, Mississippi, and that part of Louisiana east of the Mississippi River. In this vast territory, in the widely separated settlements at St. Augustine, Pensacola, and Mobile, at the time of the evacuation of the Spanish there were, at the most, not more than 7,000 Europeans.

At the end of the Seven Years War when the English exchanged Havana, the center of the Spanish-American Empire, which they had captured in 1762, for the sandy waste of Florida, almost destitute of population, it seemed an unequal bargain. There were, however, economic and military reasons for the transfer. From West Florida lumber of the finest kind—live oak, cedar, pine—could be shipped to the West Indies and the northern colonies; then Pensacola, on Pensacola Bay, was excellently located to carry on trade with Mexico, Vera Cruz, Campeachy, and New Orleans; and finally, the acquisition of West Florida would enable the English to reap the full fruits of the expulsion of the French from the Mississippi, and establish a vast fur trade with the Indians along its banks as far north as the Illinois River. And this too at a time when the Carolina skin trade was on the decline on account of the occupation of the frontier by white settlers and because of the great distances from which skins had to be transported to Charleston.[34]

East Florida was valued because St. Augustine was well sit-

[34] *Ga. Gaz.*, Jan. 10, 1765, Gov. George Johnson's Description of East Florida.

uated to surprise the Spanish ships in time of war; for the vessels from Carthegena, Porto Bello, and Vera Cruz on their way to Havana and Old Spain must pass out of the Gulf of Mexico, double the capes of Florida, and then be carried forcibly northward along the gulf stream by the trade winds toward St. Augustine, where a few English war ships could take every loaded vessel before it could pass out to sea. Also the acquisition of East Florida rounded out the English continental possessions and gave security to the other colonies, particularly to South Carolina and Georgia, whose slaves would no longer have a motive for disappearing across the Spanish border. And lastly, the English were securing, in a region where Spain's only business had been trade with the Indians, a new field for pursuing their favorite program of agricultural expansion, so successfully carried out in the colonies from Massachusetts to Georgia.[35]

The first Florida real estate boom was initiated shortly after 1763. Advertisements began to appear in the provincial and the English newspapers and in governors' proclamations setting forth in extravagant terms the advantages to be obtained in East Florida. It was said that in Florida there was sufficient pasturage for cattle the year round, and that cattle and deer were already there in abundance; that two crops of Indian corn could be made in a year and indigo cut four times a year; that there was fertile soil along the rivers for rice plantations, and that sugar plantations like those in the West Indies could be established. Lands were granted on the same easy terms as in South Carolina except that a quit rent of four shillings proclamation money on every 100 acres was required in South Carolina, while in Florida a quit rent of only one-half penny per acre was due after five years. In South Carolina three acres in each 100 had to be cleared per year, while in Florida, it was sufficient to clear three out of every fifty acres of plantable land within three years.[36]

Many thousand acres in East Florida were granted to members of Parliament and merchants of England and to wealthy

[35] *Gentleman's Magazine*, Oct., 1766, XXXVI, 486.
[36] See Governor Grant's Proclamation, Dec. 3, 1764 and *S. C. Gaz.*, Apr. 2-9, 1764.

merchants and planters in Carolina. The *South Carolina Gazette* of February 9-16, 1767, reported that "Last week the king in council passed 42 grants of land in East Florida, most of them to gentlemen of considerable fortune" and that "10 noblemen and 15 members of Parliament had already obtained grants for the purpose of establishing plantations there." Two types of settlements were made in East Florida: Plantations like those in the West Indies and Carolina where attempts were made to produce rice, indigo, sugar, and cotton by means of slave labor; and small farms like those in Georgia and the back parts of the Carolinas where poor European immigrants centered their labors chiefly on the introduction of the wine and silk culture.

Carolinians were especially interested in the plantation settlements. Men like Sir William Campbell, who had married a Carolinian and resided at Wasana, S. C., and Francis Kinloch, of Winyah, S. C., obtained grants of 20,000 acres in East Florida. Other Carolinians of exalted position at St. Augustine were William Drayton, the Chief Justice, a member of a prominent Carolina family, and John Moultrie (a brother of General William Moultrie who was distinguished in the defense of Charleston in 1776) who became Lieutenant Governor of East Florida. Probably the most extensive plantation establishment in East Florida was the sugar plantation on Halifax River of Richard Oswald, Esq., an English slave merchant, who was one of the negotiators of the peace of Paris in 1783.[37]

There were two remarkable attempts to colonize Florida by means of the poor white immigrant. Denys Rolle, a wealthy country gentleman of Devonshire founded a settlement in 1765-1769 at Charlotia, now called Rollestown, on the St. Johns River, which consisted of a motley group of about 300 indentured servants, mostly women, from the gutters of London. In 1767-1768, Dr. Andrew Turnbull, a wealthy Scotchman, made a settlement about sixty miles below St. Augustine, on Mosquito (now Ponce de Leon) Inlet, and called it New Smyrna in honor of the birthplace of his wife in Asia Minor. The settlers consisted of more than

[37] *Acts of the Privy Council*, Col. Ser., VI, 439; *ibid.*, IV, 813-815; Carita Doggett, *Dr. Andrew Turnbull and the New Smyrna Colony of Florida*, 23, 86.

1,400 people from Greece, Italy, and the Island of Minorca, by means of whom Turnbull attempted to establish the silk and wine culture. Both of these attempts ended in failure, Rolle's because of his visionary and impractical character, Turnbull's principally on account of religious dissensions among the settlers and his own personal and political quarrels with the colonial authorities.[38]

The Florida boom began to collapse about the time of the founding of Turnbull's colony. On May 28, 1768, Henry Laurens was writing to Richard Oswald that the "damp upon East Florida credit was not unknown to the people of Charles Town." It did not take long to discover that East Florida was not sufficiently supplied with fresh water streams to make rice profitable; that sugar works could not be successful because of the sudden freezes to which Florida is subject. But indigo of an excellent quality was grown; some of it sold in 1771 for 8s. 9d. sterling a pound at Garraway's Coffee House in London, a much higher price than Carolina indigo was bringing.[39]

On account of the lack of a good harbor the channel of commerce of East Florida was through Charleston and for this reason double freight and insurance were charged on East Florida products. The Charleston merchant profited by these ventures in East Florida. He was often the agent for the absentee British investor and received fees for visiting Florida and making a report of its lands. Many, if not all, of the settlements were financed through Charleston, and the merchant's rum, Negroes, rice, corn, and other provisions found a ready sale in the new settlements. For example, it was through Henry Laurens that Governor Grant of East Florida provided for the Greeks of Turnbull's colony, and Turnbull himself after his colony was established sent large orders to Charleston for supplies. Also Denys Rolle's indentured servants were forwarded to the St. Johns River through the agency of the Charleston merchant.[40]

Charleston's relations with West Florida were not so intimate. The Pensacola Packet and other vessels plied regularly between

[38] Doggett, *Dr. Andrew Turnbull*, 23, 86.
[39] MacPherson, *Annals of Com.*, III, 514.
[40] Laurens to Turnbull, Aug. 17, 1768.

Charleston and Pensacola; the king's packet boat could make the trip in eighteen days. A road was established in 1767 between St. Augustine and Pensacola by way of St. Marks Apalachee. The Spaniards, who took charge of French Louisiana in 1767, were good neighbors because, said Lieutenant Governor Bull, they were "not actuated by such a restless spirit of extending their territories as the French." Their occupation of Louisiana meant that more of that desirable commodity, Spanish money, would find its way to Charleston. But all of the advantages that came to Charleston by way of West Florida trade were probably overbalanced by the fact that the furs and skins of the Southwest Indians were now finding outlets at Mobile and Pensacola. In 1769 ten ships and 120 seamen were employed in the direct trade between Pensacola and Great Britain.[41]

[41] *S. C. Gaz.*, July 5, 1770 and Sept. 15, 1767; *P. R. S. C.*, XXXII, 103-104; Anderson, *Origins of Com.*, III, 130.

CHAPTER III

THE CHARLESTON FACTOR

I

Since Carolina was a new country of colonial status, overseas business was carried on almost exclusively by means of credit and was directed by factors or commission merchants who acted as agents of British firms. Those representatives of the British merchants who dominated the external trade of the Charleston District seem to have been generally called Charleston factors and it is the name which will be applied to them in this work. The internal trade of the district was in the hands of retailers who acted principally as agents of the Charleston factors, but also as independent traders. The most important group of retailers were called country factors. We shall hear more of them in the following chapter.

The Charleston factor was not only a merchant but a banker and broker as well. In his character as merchant, he sold merchandise sent out to him by the British firms and bought rice, indigo, deerskins, naval stores, and other produce for his British correspondents; in his character as financier, he managed the fiscal system and controlled the financial life of the country. The Charleston factor derived his importance from his connection with the British merchants, who gave him a year's credit for merchandise, paid him a commission (usually five per cent) for selling merchandise and buying rice and indigo, and furnished him in the bill of exchange a medium by which he could purchase cargoes in any part of the world with which he was allowed to trade.

As a merchant proper the Charleston factor was interested in selling goods in wholesale quantities to the retailers; in monopolizing and supervising the shipping business; in selling slaves, chiefly Negroes, sent to him directly from Africa; in participating in the immigrant and indentured servant business; and in directing the skin trade. As a financial representative of the British merchants he was chiefly concerned in operating the credit system of the country, in recommending and making investments for his customers in Great Britain and America; in manipulating means of exchange to the advantage of the British merchants and incidentally to his own advantage.

The wholesale trade, then, of the Charleston District was largely in the hands of the Charleston factor, whose chief stock in trade was naturally derived from England and Scotland or from the East Indies and Europe through the channel of England. In addition to being a factor, he was often an independent trader, importing and exporting on his own account, with correspondents not only in Great Britain, but in the West Indies, the Wine Islands, Portugal, Spain, and the cities of Flanders, Holland, and Germany. Henry Laurens, who was one of the greatest of the Charleston factors, had correspondents in the following places: Liverpool, London, Oxford, Bristol, Cowes, Poole, Glasgow, Jamaica, Barbadoes, New Providence, Tortola, St. Christopher, St. Kitts, Antigua, St. Augustine, Oporto, Lisbon, Madrid, Havana, Guadeloupe, Boston, New York, Philadelphia, Rotterdam, and after 1775, Rochelle, Nantes, Bordeaux.*

The wholesale dealers were the great advertisers of the time. They advertised their merchandise in terms of the current exchange. Since £700 currency was equal to £100 sterling selling goods at 7 for 1, was selling at prime cost. Goods were advertised to be sold for cash or ready money, for produce, for short or long credit. Short credit seems to have been for one-three-six months; long credit anything beyond six months, usually a year. The following is an example of the terms advertised by wholesale dealers:

> "Selling off at
> Prime cost.
> Whole at 7 for 1 with 9 months credit without
> interest, and Payments will be made easy.
> To any person taking three thousand Pounds,
> 8 for one with six months credit.
> To anyone taking Five Hundred Pounds, 8
> for one with 3 months credit.
> 250 Pounds 8½ for one 3 months credit.
> For sums under, 8 & Half for one cash.   Isaac Motte."

---

* Wallace's *Life of Henry Laurens* has been helpfully suggestive in this chapter and the one on the Foreign Slave Trade. Professor Wallace has also made numerous corrections and suggestions, many of which have been incorporated in this book.

The chief requisites for holding the much envied and profitable position of factor to the big British firms were capital and successful experience as a clerk extending over a series of years, with some merchant firm, preferably in England or Carolina. Capital was required for the numerous cargoes of slaves, which were the most valuable merchandise handled by the English and Carolina firms; to provide for the housing and marketing of the great quantity of goods sent out for the Indian trade, the plantation trade, the back country trade, the coastal trade; to buy partnerships in vessels, for the English merchant secured the interest and fidelity of his Charleston factor by allowing him partnerships in overseas ships, and the entire or partial ownership of inland and coastwise vessels was absolutely essential to the prosperity of the business of the Charleston factor.

Successful experience as a merchant's clerk was required of the young man aspiring to be a factor for British firms. The merchant's clerk was often an articled apprentice, although sons of men of high social rank commonly assisted the Charleston factors in loading ships, making invoices, and marking rice barrels. Governor Wright, of Georgia, was glad to get such employment for his son with Henry Laurens; and James Habersham, who acted as governor in Governor Wright's absence, was disappointed when his son Joseph failed to get such employment in Charleston because most of the houses in town were under engagement to take the sons, nephews, or other relatives of their principal customers.[1]

The prospective Charleston factor who had served a regular clerkship in a counting house was at an advantage when he began his career. It gave him opportunities for a visit to the frontier of the province and voyages to the West Indies, Portugal, and Great Britain "to establish a correspondence with the merchants trading to Carolina & obtain a share of their commissions"; with perhaps also a trip to Amsterdam, Rotterdam, and Hamburg. Such an itinerary was actually followed by John Hopton after he ended a five-year clerkship with Henry Laurens. First of all, he made a tour of five hundred miles into the frontier country to get a first hand impression of the business situation there; after which

[1] Laurens to Wright and to Habersham, Jan. 25, 1768.

he was ready for his foreign travels. His former employer furnished him with letters of credit to the merchants at the places he visited, assuring them of the "safety" of any bills he might draw. They were informed that he would begin "commercial life upon as good footing as any man he had known in Carolina"; for his father not only was paying his expenses so that he could travel genteelly in the character of a young merchant, but he was setting him up in business with the very large capital of £2,000 sterling. Laurens and Gabriel Manigault, two well established and rich merchants, also assisted Hopton in getting a start in business by taking each a one-fourth "concern" in the cargo of rice by which he was accompanied, "to give him an introduction into trade and assist him in making West Indian correspondents." Finally, Laurens and another merchant, probably William Head, were sureties for Hopton so that he could obtain the sale of African cargoes. Their recommendatory letter reads as follows:[2]

John Hopton   8 Apr. 1771
    In order more effectually to Enable you to make offers & accept the Sale of African cargoes—We hereby bind ourselves, to be your sureties in the Sum of £10,000 Pounds Stg.—for due Performance of any contract which you may make for the Sale of such Cargoes,—assuring our Friends generally & particularly Richard Oswald Esq—Oswald Grant & Co. Proprietors of Bance Island & Messrs Ross & Mill in London that we think you in all Respects capable of rendering as good account of Sales for negroes as any Gentleman in Charles Town of your age and Experience— to which you and these Friends who shall be pleased to entrust you, may depend upon the additional aid of
                                          W.H.
Signed by   & H.L.

The sequel to this story is as interesting as its beginning. Hopton made his grand tour, secured correspondents, obtained commissions, and became in the period before the Revolution one of the greatest of the Charleston merchants.[3]

    We shall hear more of the business of the Charleston factor as a commodity merchant in the chapter on the retailers, and of

[2] The above recommendatory letter, contrary to Laurens' usual custom, is copied carelessly in his letter book.
[3] Laurens to Mayne & Co., Aug. I, 1770; to Cowles & Co., Feb. 18, 1771; to R. Grubb, March 6, 1771; to Bright & Co., Jan. 12, 1770.

his activity as a slave merchant and a dealer in immigrants and indentured servants, in the chapters dealing with those subjects. In fact, there is hardly a chapter in the rest of the book that does not deal directly or indirectly with some phase of the manifold business activity of the Charleston factor. The rest of this chapter will treat of the Charleston factor as a dispenser of credit, and as the chief operator and controller of shipping in the country.

II

The most lucrative branch of the plantation business was furnishing slaves on credit to the planters. This phase of the Charleston factor's business attained an unprecedented development in the latter part of the seventeenth and early eighteenth centuries, when the British program of agricultural expansion pursued so successfully in the American colonies began to promise a special development in South Carolina, owing to the mild climate, fertile soil, and abundant water courses on which crops could be transported to market and manufactures carried to the interior. Important also was the emergence of two staple crops, rice and indigo, much in demand in Europe, which required for their cultivation the importation of vast numbers of African slaves. Thus agriculture in South Carolina promoted the prosperity of the ship owners, the merchants, and the manufacturers of Great Britain, three important classes influential in the councils of the empire. For these reasons South Carolina received much more attention from the British government than did most of the other colonies.

In 1704 rice was "enumerated," which meant that the market for it was limited to Great Britain or the British colonies, and also that the planter must take for his rice what the British middleman chose to give him. Also a prohibitive duty was placed on the rice consumed in England in order to protect the English farmer's grain; but a drawback of duties was allowed on rice reexported to its natural market in northern Europe where three-fourths of it was consumed. The first governmental concession came to Carolina rice in 1730, when the rule that the colonies must find a market for their "enumerated" produce within the empire was relaxed by allowing rice from South Carolina to be shipped to any part of Europe south of Cape Finisterre in ships built in Great Britain and navigated according to law. Two reasons for this concession were that rice is a perishable commodity and had sometimes been damaged by being shipped first to England and reshipped there to Spain, Portugal, and the Mediterranean countries; besides, the English merchants wished Carolina rice to compete in the southern European markets with the rice of Italy and the Levant. The privilege of exporting rice to southern Europe was given to North Carolina, Georgia, and the two Floridas as the plantation system spread to those provinces.

In 1764 the market was further enlarged by a second concession by Parliament which allowed rice from South Carolina and Georgia to be carried to any part of America south of Georgia on the payment of duties equivalent to what the rice would have paid if it had been exported to England and reshipped on a drawback, that is one half British duty on rice. This privilege was granted to North Carolina in 1765. The purpose of this legislation was to allow these provinces to retain markets entered when Great Britain had been in possession of certain of the West Indies during the war with France. While this was an important concession, it did not mean as much as the concession of 1730, for Charleston's trade with the French and Spanish West Indies was not large. It did mean, however, that the Charleston exporter's business with the West Indies was placed on the same footing as the British merchant's, and it did give greater opportunities to the ship carriers of the northern colonies.[4]

The indigo industry, which produced a crop of wealthy planters, could not have existed without a subsidy from the British government. In order to promote the manufactures of Great Britain, indigo was put on the list of "enumerated" goods in 1748 and was granted a bounty of 6 pence per pound.[4a] Also a duty was

[4] For rice legislation see 3rd and 4th Anne C. V, §12; 3rd Geo. II, C. XXVIII; 4th Geo. III, C. XXVII; Carroll, *Collections*, II, 266; MacPherson, *Annals of Com.*, III, 401. The Northern continental colonies, however, protested against this concession because it allowed rice to compete with other foodstuffs in the French and Spanish colonial markets. Beer, *British Colonial Policy*, 1754-1765, 225.

[4a] The assembly of South Carolina, because of the distress in the state occasioned by French and Spanish interference with English shipping, had given a bounty of 9 pence per pound on indigo in 1744. This had been repealed in 1746.

placed on foreign indigo imported into the British Empire. The result of this favoring legislation was that South Carolina and, in a lesser degree, North Carolina, Georgia, and East Florida, were able to supply the principal part of the dye used in the English textile manufactures. And the price received for Carolina indigo was not greatly inferior to that given in England for Spanish and French, which was a superior dye.

Trade in most of British-America was subordinated to agriculture. It was especially so in the South where "big business" was concerned in the production of staple crops for the European market. The plantation became a great business enterprise organized upon a capitalistic basis, which resulted in a sort of agricultural industrialism. The plantation business was run mostly on credit. The credit system had been extended to South Carolina when it was found that rice could be grown with profit on the inland swamps of that province. The plantation system had been introduced from the West Indies and the British merchants had discovered that it was "good business" to furnish slaves on credit for the rice fields. They had to pay 5% interest for capital in England. They received 8% interest on their investment in South Carolina (in the early days 10 and 12 per cent), and were able in addition to sell through their factors at Charleston plantation equipment and European manufactures to the planters at greatly enhanced prices. Capital invested in land and slaves was so profitable that the planters could pay interest annually and discharge the principal of their debt in a few years. The merchants made fortunes in the Carolina trade and some of the planters became so prosperous that by 1730 they were sending their sons to England to be educated.

The planters lived chiefly on the produce of their estates and went into debt mostly for slaves and plantation supplies. In Timothy Ford's diary, written in 1785, we have this account of the credit situation:

It had been the custom of the merchants to sell the goods negroes &c to the planters at one years credit, and so universally did it obtain that the planters scarcely pretended to deal on any other terms. It was convenient for both—for the planter because when he got his crop to market in the fall he

could command money—for the merchant because that was the time of
making remittance; so that the planter had nothing to do but to draw on
his factor for his arrears in rice or indigo; & the merchant recd. and
shipped it off. But this habit of giving & obtaining long and extensive
credit implied or begot a great deal of honour & punctuality in dealing—
'twas the merchants to cultivate it because he recd. a proportional profit on
his goods—it was the planters interest to support it because he got goods
at his pleasure & paid at his leisure. . . . At the commencement of the war
. . . the denomination of debtor & creditor must have included all the men
in the State. [Planters and merchants—] one charged with debts across
the water the other indebted to the merchants.[5]

Jefferson's statement that in Virginia "debts had become
hereditary from father to son for many generations, so that the
planters were a species of property annexed to certain mercantile
houses in London" has been frequently quoted to create the impression that the southern planters as a class were eternally in debt
and eternally at enmity with their creditors whom they regarded
as extortionate plunderers.[6] If it be true that the planting class
was in economic bondage to the British merchants, the servitude
in South Carolina was probably of a less galling nature than in
Virginia, where the British factors monopolized the plantation
trade, and where, during Jefferson's day, agriculture was in a
painful state of transition from the cultivation of tobacco to grain.

In South Carolina agriculture was in a healthy expanding
condition, and capital was constantly being invested in land and
slaves. The successful termination of the war with France made
new areas safe for plantations in Georgia and East Florida; the
British merchants extended credit to the planters almost without
limit and they reaped a harvest through the steadily increasing
exports reaching England through the port of Charleston and
through the steadily widening market for merchandise and
Negro slaves. South Carolina planters were in debt because they
lived in a new country into which great quantities of capital were
being poured in order that a future harvest might be reaped. Their
indebtedness was a temporary condition and the planters as a class
were eager to ship their produce to England as soon as possible in

[5] *S. C. Hist. & Gen. Mag.*, XIII, 201-202.
[6] Jefferson's *Writings*, Ford ed., IV, 155.

order to sustain their credit. There was, it is true, a constant drain of capital to England to pay for slaves, but when indebtedness threatened to become chronic, the sovereign remedy was applied of cutting off for a season the importation of slaves. When this form of capital was excluded from the province, even the poor planters were able to clear themselves of debt.

Colonial agriculture in South Carolina compares favorably in hopefulness of outlook with modern farming in the state, whether it was pursued in the back parts of the province by a farmer who tilled his own soil and collected bounties from the government on his wheat and hemp, or on a large plantation where many slaves were employed. Capital could be borrowed for 8 per cent in colonial times, even as it is today; a charge account then as now was run with a merchant, who if he were honest, charged no more than 9½ or 10 for one for goods that in Charleston were selling for 8 or 8½ for one in cash. The land and slaves of the planter were sold for debt, even as are the farms of the South Carolina farmers today, but with a difference of degree. Any county newspaper in the state today (1929) contains more advertisements of lands to be sold for taxes or under mortgage than did any issue of the *South Carolina Gazette* (whose circulation extended into North Carolina, Georgia and Florida) notices of lands and slaves to be sold for debt. The Charleston factor found it worth while "to carry" his debtor and secure himself by taking a mortgage on his land and slaves and a lien on his crop, if necessary; for in good crop years the wealthy planters laid by money, and the "poor and middling" planters got out of debt, and perhaps had a surplus to invest in slaves. If not, the latter were ready to strain their resources in order to enlarge their plantation operations and get in the big planter class; and for this reason they were excellent customers for slaves. And there must have been many good crop years in the prosperous period just before the Revolution; for South Carolina's exports exceeded her imports to Great Britain for ten of the twelve years preceding the war.[7]

[7] Hewatt, *Hist. of S. C. and Ga.*, 186; Laurens to Lloyd & Barton, Dec. 24, 1764; MacPherson, *Annals of Com.*, III, 384-599. Slaves are not included in the imports from Great Britain.

Plantations were of course the great investments of the period. The mechanic, the money lender, the minister, the merchant put their money in lands and slaves. The extent to which a minister, who was a poorly paid official, might engage in planting is reflected in the following advertisement from the *South Carolina Gazette* of February 2-9, 1767:

At Public Vendue,
at Mr. Thomas Nightingales' on Charles Town Neck.
One hundred and twenty valuable slaves, (belonging to the Rev. Mr. Robert Smith); among whom are good sawyers, squarers, carpenters, wheelwrights, blacksmiths, taylors, shoemakers, cooks, washers, seamstresses, and several handy boys and girls. Conditions 12 mos. credit, paying interest and giving good security.
Jan. 12, 1767.   Sam. Prioleau, Jun. & Comp.

The person here referred to was the rector of St. Philip's, described in Peletiah Webster's Journal as "an English Gent., educated at the University of Cambridge; a very social & polite clergyman."

The Charleston factor invested in lands and slaves and operated plantations to such an extent that it was often difficult to determine whether his dominant interest was planting or merchandising. He frequently resided like a country gentleman on a plantation along the banks of the Ashley or Cooper, where the seats of the oldest and wealthiest families lay, in a colonial mansion appropriately set amidst acres of cultivated parks and gardens. It was through the Charleston factor that the British investors received the information and obtained the means to make investments in the Charleston District. These investments often assumed the form of a partnership between the British investor and the local merchant. For example, William Knox, the agent of Georgia, owned 198 slaves and several plantations which were operated through a copartnership with James Habersham of Savannah.[7a]

The terms of such a copartnership proposed in 1768 between Richard Oswald, merchant of London, Henry Laurens, merchant of Charleston, and John Louis Gervais, who through successful

[7a] *Ga. Col. Recs.*, VI, 25.

plantation ventures was able later to set up as a merchant in Charleston, emphasizes very forcibly the fact that it was human chattels that gave value to land. Gervais and Laurens had received through their family rights a grant of 13,000 acres of land at Long Canes, in Ninety-Six District of South Carolina, for which they had probably been at no expense except for the fees demanded at the land office. They proposed a partnership with Oswald on the following terms. Each was to furnish 20 working hands and £150 sterling (equal to £1,050 currency) for building houses and purchasing cattle, wagons, and plantation tools. Gervais was to have the superintendence of the farms. Oswald was asked to send out a good carpenter and wheelwright to serve for three years; the former to superintend the putting up of buildings, the latter to make wagons. He was to pay their passage and a share of their wages. The following was to be Oswald's "concern" in the business as outlined by Laurens:

Dr.   Cr.

One third part of 13,000 Acres of Land at Long Canes in South Carolina held in company with John Lewis Gervais & Henry Laurens.

Dr.	Cr.
To Amount of cost and Clothing with Tools & first provisions of 20 Negroes at £350 each which being high will admit of two or three Little ones included £7,000	By 1/3 of 13,000 Acres 4,333 1/3 Acres at a very low estimation when cleared & including Houses & Stock of Cattle, Waggons &c. only at 20/ £4,335
Expence of Houses Cattle Waggons &c £1,050	Balance capital reduced to ..£3,716
£8,050	£8,050

For which Balance there will remain the original value of the Negroes— £7,000.[8]

At the time the proposition was made to him Oswald had lost heavily by setting up a sugar plantation in East Florida and was not looking upon plantation ventures with unprejudiced eyes. He therefore declined the proposition of Laurens and Gervais.

William Gerard de Brahm made an estimate of the first cost

[8] Laurens to Oswald, April 27, 1768. Laurens' estimate of costs is expressed in provincial currency rather than in English sterling.

and necessary expenses for the first year on a rice plantation as follows:

Supposing the Land to be purchased @ 10/ acre V:G: 200 acres	100-0-0
To build Barn and Pounding Machine purchasing boards & Timber	220-0-0
To purchase 40 working hands @ £45	1800-0-0
To purchase working Oxen and Horses	60-0-0
To two Carts and Collars	10-0-0
To Hoes, Axes, Spades, and other Plantation Tools	30-0-0
To amount Expences for Tax & Quit Rent £5 .. & first years Provisions £50	55-0-0
To Overseer's Wages	50-0-0
To Negro Shoes £6-10-0 Do clothing £20-0-0 & Blankets annum £5-6	31-16-0
To Box of Medicines & Doctors fees £20—for Deaths of Negroes per an. £100	120-0-0

£2476-16-0

The forty Negroes, de Brahm calculated, would cultivate 130 acres of rice and 70 acres of provision land; the rice at 40s. would bring £700, which would be more than 28 per cent interest on the investment and the planter would be at no expense the following year for provisions.

This estimate presents some interesting contrasts in the relative cheapness of land and dearness of labor in a new country. Could there be a more forceful illustration of the preciousness of human labor than the fact that the Georgia planter was required to spend only £100 for land while the hands to make the land productive cost £1,800? The planter paid for the plantable part of his plantation, that is, the part cleared and in a condition to produce crops, or that part capable of being cleared and cultivated. In some instances, it seems, the high land adjoining the swamps was thrown in gratis to conclude the bargain. Even the necessary outbuildings and such equipment as a pounding machine made on the plantation cost more than twice the amount spent for land due to the human labor expended in their production. The overseer's wages for a year came to half the cost of the land, and an amount equal to the cost of the land had to be counted as part of the necessary expense on account of the losses to be sustained from the death of the laborers.[9]

The income from plantations probably ranged all the way from four or five hundred pounds to eight or ten thousand pounds sterling. The cost of laborers and plantation equipment being so great, it did not pay to attempt to cultivate less than a hundred acres. Drayton wrote that plantations existed whose annual value was $80,000, others $10,000 to $20,000, the majority probably from $3,000 to $6,000. Henry Laurens made about £500 sterling annually on Mepkin, his home plantation, thirty miles from Charleston, on the Cooper River, and considered it an excellent income. On Mepkin Laurens worked forty or fifty Negroes and grew Indian corn, wheat, and "all the produce of the best high lands (very little rice)." Besides Mepkin Laurens owned in South Carolina plantations called Mt. Tacitus and Ninety-Six; and the following plantations in Georgia: Broughton Island, on the Altamaha River; New Hope, on the opposite side of the river; Wright's Savannah, on the Savannah River nearly opposite the town of Savannah; and Turtle River. The four Georgia plantations, which were a hundred miles or more from Mepkin, were more valuable than the plantations in South Carolina because they had been more recently established and were in an extremely fertile country. These plantations were at their best about the time the Revolution came and Laurens said he expected to have reaped from the Georgia states alone 10,000 guineas annually if the war had not come just when it did.[10]

III

The great importing merchant found it as profitable to own the boats that transported rice and indigo to market as the railroad baron finds it to his interest to own the railroad operating in the coal district, but in his efforts to monopolize the shipping business he encountered rivals in the great planters who owned plantations scattered through Carolina, Georgia, and even as far south as

[9] De Brahm, *Hist. of Georgia*, 51. For other estimates see *American Husbandry*, 407-408, 415-426.

[10] Drayton, *View of So. Ca.*, 110; Laurens to Oswald, April 27, 1768; Wallace, *Laurens*, 21.

East Florida, and were therefore interested in boat ownership; as well as in the country factors and country merchants whose business could not go on without boats.[11] Besides, there was a considerable class, including shipmasters and seamen, shipbuilders and repairers, the keepers of ropewalks and fishermen, who earned their livelihoods because of the several hundred ships that entered and cleared at Charleston each year, and on account of the numerous vessels employed in the inland and coastwise trade of the province.

Despite the fact that only a small percentage of the vessels employed in the foreign trade was built in the province, shipbuilding was an important industry in colonial Carolina. One at least of the large fortunes in South Carolina belonged to a shipwright. Henry Laurens wrote in 1771 to a correspondent of "Mr. John Rose our great shipwright who came in recommended to me with a Broad Ax on his shoulder in the year 1749 and who has since acquired a fortune of perhaps £30,000 stg. or more by his honest industry."[12] A fortune of £30,000 sterling was as much as many of the greatest of the merchants acquired by means of trade.

Ramsay says that shipbuilding began to engage the attention of South Carolinians about the year 1740, that five shipyards were erected between 1740 and 1773, and that twenty-four square-rigged vessels were built, besides sloops and schooners. The gazettes corroborate in part Ramsay's statement. They mention ships under construction or being launched at Hobcaw and Hilton Head. Up the Path at Mrs. Frost's (on Cooper River), was Captain Cochrane's shipyard—possibly Captain Robert Cochrane who took an important part in the attempt to open direct trade between Charleston and the French ports during the Revolution. At Beaufort, Port Royal, some of the largest ships in the Carolina trade were built, for example, the "Rose Island," capacity 1,800 barrels of rice, built for Mr. Shubrick of London by Emre at Beaufort, in 1766.[13] Bloody Point, on the Savannah, below Beaufort and not far from Cockspur, was a popular place for building ships because it was in the center of a great plantation district and

[11] See the chapter on the Retailers and on Rice for a further illustration of this rivalry.
[12] To Wm. Cowles, June 4, 1771.
[13] S. C. Gaz., June 2-9, 1766.

vessels constructed and launched there were sure of obtaining an early freight of rice. Bloody Point was probably on the Georgia side of the Savannah, but Charleston merchants frequently had their vessels built there. Laurens, for example, had the "Friendship" built at Bloody Point on what he considered favorable terms, the vessel costing £1,300 sterling at £5 per ton. The disadvantages for shipbuilding in Carolina just about counterbalanced the advantages. The great drawback was the high price of skilled labor, but there were excellent timbers for shipbuilding and excellent cargoes for ships once they were built.

When the business outlook was very gloomy because the British Parliament had passed the Townshend Acts, and South Carolina, along with the other American colonies, had entered into non-importation agreements to bring about the repeal of the obnoxious legislation, the *South Carolina Gazette* made the following statement:

"It has been computed, that there are (built and owned in this province) upward of 130 Boats and Schooners, three-fourths of them deck'd carrying from 10 to 50 tons at 4 barrels of rice to the ton, employed in bringing the Country Produce to this market, of which near 100 will soon be out of employ: And their burthen together is reckoned 3,500 tons."[14] Probably 130 more vessels, some of a capacity of 70 tons (280 barrels of rice), were employed in the coastal trade to Georgia, East Florida and the West Indies.

There were three classes of vessels employed in the Charleston trade: Inland boats of a few tons burden carried on the interior trade of the province because of the danger of large vessels being grounded on the shoals in the rivers. The largest vessel of this type had trunk masts that had to be folded when they passed under a bridge. In the maritime parts of the province where most of the great plantations lay, rice and indigo were conveyed to market in vessels with standing masts, decked to protect the produce from the weather. These "decked periaugers" drew too much water to pass far up the channels of the inland waterways. They were essentially coasters, some of them of fifty tons burden,

[14] *Gazette* of June 27, 1768.

which collected produce from the landings of the plantations and from the depots of the port towns. Vessels of the same type, some of them, however, of seventy tons burden, carried on the coastal trade.[14a]

The inland boats and the "decked periaugers" were probably owned principally by Charleston business men. Some of the West Indian coasters were owned by Charleston merchants and some in partnership by Charleston and West Indian merchants, The ships employed in the European trade ranged from 200 to 500 tons burden, although a 500 ton vessel was considered a very large ship. The great majority of the vessels carried from 1,000 to 1,200 barrels of rice, that is, they were from 250 to 300 tons in capacity. The *South Carolina Gazette* of April 10, 1775, reported the arrival of a new ship the "Maria Wilhelmina," burden 800 tons, the largest ship that had ever been built in New York and that had ever entered Charleston harbor. Most of the overseas ships were owned by British merchants who allowed their Charleston factors a sufficient partnership in vessels to make it to their interest to be faithful and efficient partners. Laurens wrote during the Revolution that before the war about 400 "sail of vessels" were usually employed in the trade of South Carolina, one-tenth of which were owned in the state.[15]

Carolina merchants of course did not confine their ownership to Carolina-built vessels or even give such vessels a preference. The majority of the great merchants were probably Englishmen or Scotchmen, many of whom regarded Carolina as an excellent place for making a fortune to be spent in England. Both of the men who were Laurens' partners for a number of years retired to Shropshire to spend the comfortable fortunes they had made merchandising in Carolina. Such business men, as the Revolution approached, were taunted with the epithet "birds of passage" by the radical patriot leaders, and they were regarded with suspicion because they had no great stake in the future of the province and could not be trusted to resist with the proper spirit "the tyranny"

[14a] P. R. S. C., VI, 320.

[15] Frank Moore, ed., *Materials for History*, 186. Sometimes the captain owned his own vessel which he manned with his slaves and did a profitable business in the coastal trade.

of the mother country. On the other hand, many of the great merchants identified their fortunes with the patriot cause and did valiant service for the liberty of America.

Intercolonial business was burdened with provincial duties on rum, sugar, molasses from the West Indies, and also on rum, biscuit of several sorts, and flour from the northern provinces, but the export trade of Carolina was promoted by a provincial law which allowed a drawback of three-fourths of duties on all goods re-exported within six months.[16] The agent of the Charleston factor in the intercolonial business was the captain of the merchant vessel, who in an age of barter became a merchant himself and had to bear heavy responsibility.

The character of the coastal business carried on for the Charleston factor by the captain of his vessels may be illustrated from the correspondence of Henry Laurens. In December, 1767, Laurens' schooner *Wambaw*, bound for St. Augustine, was loaded partly on his account with rum, corn, and sugar, which were consigned to Captain Peacock for sale. On arrival at St. Augustine Captain Peacock applied at the custom house for a certificate to cancel his bond for non-enumerated goods, he adjusted and collected freight money agreeable to the bills of lading for the rest of the cargo, and the sums due from the passengers. He had been instructed by Laurens not to stay in St. Augustine longer than six or seven days, during which time he was to dispose of Laurens' part of the cargo to such persons as were recommended to him "as safe and punctual dealers," for cash or a credit of three months. He applied to Governor Grant to exchange the collected money for a bill of exchange and that part of the cargo that remained unsold he turned over to one of Laurens' East Florida correspondents. After ballasting his vessel with stones and shells he cleared out for Georgia and touched at Darien, where he received a permit to load with rough rice and shingles. He then proceeded to Laurens' plantation on Broughton Island, in the Altamaha River, where he threw out his ballast and took on a cargo of rice, boards, planks and shingles, which ballasted his vessel for the return trip. Laurens' final admonition to Captain Peacock was characteristic,

[16] Cooper, *Statutes of S. C.*, IV, 150.

it was: "Be careful in all your steps to comply with the acts of trade."[17]

The function performed by the captain of a West Indian vessel differed only in scope from that of the captain of a more modest continental coaster. These vessels trafficked along the Carolina-Georgia-Florida coast and finally landed in the West Indies. Laurens' schooner *Brother's Endeavor*, in February, 1770, was loaded with rum, gunpowder, Dutch brick, and other goods. Captain Magnus Watson was instructed to go first to Sunbury in Georgia and barter the rum for corn at the rate of "1½ bushels for I gal. or thereabouts"; the gunpowder for Georgia money, for Indian corn, for cash, or for "any substantial man's note payable in one month." In this way 150 bushels of corn were to be obtained to carry to the plantation at the Altamaha. The Dutch brick were to be bartered to Lachlan McIntosh, a planter, for shingles, and the unsalable goods were to be left with the overseer at Broughton Island plantation, from which it may be inferred that Laurens might have had a community store under the oversight of his overseer. At the plantation after loading with shingles and rough rice, Captain Watson proceeded to Kingston, Jamaica, where his cargo was disposed of for cash or barter and a return cargo of "neat full proof of Rum, the very finest & dryest Muscavado Sugar, Melasses and 1,500 to 3,000 weight of best coffee" was obtained. Captain Watson was instructed to call on Mr. Meyler, a delinquent correspondent of Laurens' and endeavor to prevail on him to give a promise of remittance.[18]

Money itself was considered not only a means of exchange, but an article of barter or merchandise. For example, Laurens instructed the captain of a West Indian vessel to dispose of his cargo to the best advantage for ready money and to invest the proceeds in "good Rum of a fine Color & full proof, or in negroes, or in dollars." If the rum was selling higher than a certain price then the captain was to lay out the money "in fine healthy young Negro Lads & Men," if they could be had within certain limits; if neither rum nor negroes were to be obtained within the limits

[17] Laurens to Peacock, Dec. 14, 1767.
[18] To Capt. Watson, Feb. 15, 1770.

fixed by Laurens, then the captain was to bring home the money in silver.[19]

The schooner *Brother's Endeavor* commanded by Captain Magnus Watson, was a typical coaster. It was a little more than a fifty ton vessel and carried a little more than two hundred barrels of rice. It cost Laurens £500 sterling, and was manned by Captain Watson and his mate and two foremast men, besides two negro seamen valued at £150 sterling. Captain Watson received £5 sterling per month "commencing the day he went over the bar" at Charleston, which was more than the customary wages of the captain of·a West Indian coasting vessel. Out of these wages he was to "agree on the men's wages & the Mate's upon the best terms he could." "The negroes," wrote Laurens, "are entitled to no wages being my property as slaves, except clothing & provisions from me & good usage from you." In addition, Watson received five per cent commission on all goods he sold on Laurens' account.[20]

IV

Perhaps the greatest part of the trade of the Charleston District was conducted by first or second-hand barter, and for this reason an indispensable part of the merchant's equipment for business, in addition to his store of goods, consisted of storehouses to contain produce brought in by the farmer or planter, which the merchant paid for partly or wholly in merchandise. In fact, in the early colonial period it had been necessary for the treasurers, like Pharaoh of Egypt three thousand years before Christ, to keep granaries and cattle pens, in which to receive taxes and from which to make payment of public debts; and in the troubled period following the war, Virginia was obliged to pass acts declaring tobacco, flour, grain, and skins acceptable in payment of taxes, and to construct warehouses for the reception of such commodities. It was the custom in Carolina for merchants in advertising their goods to specify what commodities were acceptable in exchange and the prevalence of barter sometimes caused a merchant to publish a long advertisement in which he gave a list of all he had for sale

[19] To Capt. Richard Todd, Sept. 23, 1767.
[20] To Capt. Magnus Watson, Feb. 15, 1770.

and all that he wished to exchange, of which the following is an example:

To be sold by the Subscriber.
Forty large Hogsheads and 30 Tierces of New Rum—
Ten Hogsheads of Jamaica Rum—Six half and one Whole
Chests of Bohea Tea—Twenty Dozen of Women's Black
Callimance Shoes, made at Lynn near Boston in New
England—Twenty half quintals of very Best Isle
of Shoals Table Fish—with a quantity of Wooden
bowls, Racks, and Mast Hoops, Also, a few
Barrels of Train Oil and Blubber.

Josiah Smith, Jun.

Wanted immediately, By said Smith
And for which he will Barter any of above-mentioned articles:
Twenty Thousand weight of the best Water-rotted Hemp, clean & bright.
Fifteen hundred weight of very best Copper and Purple Indico, in large and dry Squares.
Sixty Barrels of Rice, to be very clean, bright, and whole grains.
Two Hundred Sides of thoroughly tann'd, well cur'd Soals.
Twenty Barrels of thick and large Corn-fed Pork, well cur'd, in tight strong Casks.
Twenty Kegs of white, & clean saved Hogs' Lard, to weigh from 60 to 100 lb. each.
One Hundred Barrels of Good Tar,—in tight strong Casks, to be full hoop'd, and free from Water.
Twenty Chaldrons of Smith Coals.

Other means of exchange were furnished by hard money, paper money, and bills of exchange. Hard money consisted mostly of foreign coin brought in by trade with Southern Europe, the West Indies and South America, especially Spanish and Portuguese coins. This specie was hard to retain. Some of the silver left the country for the payment of the king's duties, especially under the operation of the Townshend Acts. Then Carolina tourists who liked to summer in Rhode Island, Philadelphia, New York, or Boston found it convenient to use hard money on their travels, particularly half johannes and dollars. Also traders from the northern colonies carried out much foreign coin, for the chief object of their quest was not Carolina produce but hard money with which to make remittances to the mother country. And finally, all the trading people at Charleston found hard money a very satisfactory remittance to Great Britain in that it was present cash. Not only was there no discount on it but there was often a premium, although freight on it was an item to be considered.

The traders in Charleston, as elsewhere in the colonies, tried to remedy the chronic scarcity of hard money by placing a high value upon it. Thus, in 1771, the money lenders and merchants entered into an agreement to receive foreign gold and silver at advanced rates. The agreement was not confined to milled money alone, but extended to unmilled of sufficient weight, with certain exceptions. Foreign coin was to pass according to the following table.[21]

SPECIES	Standard weight		Weight now received at		Former value in currency			Now valued at in currency		
	Dwt.	Gr.	Dwt.	Gr.	£	S.	D.	£	S.	D.
Johannes............	18	11	18	0	25	4	0	26	0	0
Halves.............	9	5½	9	0	12	12	0	13	0	0
Quarters...........	4	14½	4	12	6	6	0	6	10	0
Half Quarters.......	2	7	2	6	3	3	0	3	5	0
Moidores...........	6	21	6	20	9	9	0	9	15	0
Halves...........	3	10½	3	10	4	14	6	4	17	6
Quarters.........	1	17½	1	17	2	7	3	2	8	9
Half Quarters.......	0	18½	0	18½	1	3	7½	1	4	4½
Doubloons..........	17	8	17	0	23	0	0	24	0	0
Double Pistoles......	8	16	8	12	11	10	0	12	0	0
Pistoles............	4	8	4	6	5	15	0	6	0	0
Halves............	2	4	2	3	2	17	6	3	0	0
Dollars............	17	12	17	8	1	11	6	1	12	6
Halves............	8	18	8	16	0	15	0	0	16	3
Quarters...........	4	9	4	8	0	7	0	0	8	1½
Half Quarters......	2	4½	2	4	0	3	9	0	4	0¼
Pistarines..........	0	0	0	0	0	6	0	0	6	3

The presence of unmilled money gave great opportunities to the counterfeiters and there were frequent accounts in the newspapers of villains passing off base, cut and clipped coins on the unwary.

There was little English money in the colonies and the hard money of the different European nations, particularly of France, Spain, and Portugal passed at par with sterling as the value of the metal warranted. While foreign money was of the same value

[21] *S. C. Gaz.*, Feb. 28 and March 7, 1771; *ibid.*, Oct. 29-Nov. 5, 1763.

as sterling in all the colonies, it was rated differently in the different colonies. For example, the commonly used silver coin known as the Seville piece of eight passed at 4s. 8d. in South Carolina and Georgia; at 6s. in New England; and at 8s. in New York and North Carolina. In English sterling, however, the same coin was equivalent to 4s. 6d. Queen Anne attempted to bring order out of the confusion resulting from the existence of colonial currencies of different values by issuing a proclamation in 1704, which was enacted into parliamentary statute in 1707, creating what was known as proclamation money. By this law a person was forbidden to accept foreign money as worth more than a third the value of his colonial money, that is the ratio of proclamation was fixed at 4 to 3, in other words, £100 sterling was equal to £133 proclamation. This legislation failed, however, of its purpose, which was, as the statute recites, to prevent foreign money "being drawn from one plantation to another to the great prejudice of trade." Hard money was in such demand that it was impossible to prevent business men of the different colonies from entering into agreements to receive it at advanced rates, as we have already seen.[22]

V

Paper money in South Carolina represented the debt which the colony had incurred in the various frontier wars. Bills of credit were first issued in 1703 to pay for the Carolina phase of Queen Anne's War, which involved the colony in the fruitless and expensive siege of St. Augustine. This issue was for £6,000, which was afterwards increased to £10,000, and was loaned to the planters at 12 per cent interest.

After Queen Anne's War the British were busy exploring the possibilities of that valuable trade concession which they had gained in the Treaty of Utrecht, called the Asiento. By this they were allowed to furnish Spanish America with Negro slaves at the rate of four thousand a year for fifty years, but they were forbidden to sell other commodities to the Spanish colonies, except that once a year a British ship of five hundred tons burden

[22] Cooper, *Statutes of S. C.*, I, 428; 6th Anne Cap. XXX; Channing, *History of the U. S.*, II, 495-499.

might visit Porto Bello on the Isthmus of Panama for purposes of general trade. There was peace in Europe from 1713 to 1739; but an active commercial war was in progress in America, particularly in the southern colonies which were being used by English vessels as a base from which to carry on an illegal trade with the Spanish dependencies. Spain retaliated by establishing coast guards to keep watch on the English, by laying oppressive restrictions on English bottoms trading in the Spanish colonies, and by seizing and condemning English vessels. By 1739 the smouldering flames burst into open warfare between Spain and England in the so-called War of Jenkins' Ear.

But long before this time South Carolina had been put to great expense for equipping a land expedition against Spanish Florida in 1728 and for fitting out a vessel against the *Guarda Costas,* which, with various other expenses, such as those incurred for the expedition against the Tuscarora Indians in North Carolina, for the Yemassee War, and for suppression of the pirates, left the province with a debt of about £106,500. The new royal government, therefore, allowed the assembly to issue paper money to the amount of its debts on condition that it provide for strengthening the military defence of the province by voting a bounty on the importation of foreign Protestants. The bills of credit for £106,500 issued by the assembly on August 20, 1731, were the only paper money the province had until the Revolution, although in the period after 1763 trade was constantly expanding. Periodically when the bills became obliterated and worn they were called in and reissued. Thus bills were exchanged in 1748, 1767, 1769 and 1771. No sinking fund was provided, but the paper money of South Carolina passed so readily in Georgia and North Carolina that premiums were given for it. In 1710 the rate of exchange with sterling was 1½ for 1; by 1730, however, the exchange was at 7 for 1, because in addition to the war debt, heavy importations of Negroes had taken place which kept the province always in debt.[23]

The planter whose crops commanded sterling values was in

[23] Carroll *Collections*, II, 256-257; P. R. S. C., XXXIII, 26-27, 33-106; *ibid.*, XXXI., 278-279.

favor of increasing the amount of paper currency, while the merchant whose capital was tied up in outstanding notes and bonds was for calling it in and sinking it so that his debtors would not be able to pay him in depreciated currency. The British government, being at this time largely dominated by the commercial classes, came to the rescue of the colonial merchant by passing the Restraining Act of 1764 which prohibited paper bills of credit issued thereafter in the colonies from being made a legal tender in payment of debts.[24]   Thereupon petitions from the colonies and from the merchants of London trading to North America began to pour in on the Board of Trade, Parliament, and the King. These set forth the distress to which the petitioners were reduced by want of a medium of commerce and the impossibility of debtors making remittances to their creditors on account of the scarcity of gold and silver coin, and prayed for issues of paper currency.

A petition of the assembly of South Carolina to the king on November 28, 1766, stated that many of the South Carolina bills had been long worn out and destroyed and that not more than £70,000 was in circulation, an amount less than that which the province contributed to the support of the king's government annually.[25] Henry Laurens wrote that the whole currency of South Carolina, including gold and silver, was not equal to more than one-fifth of the value of the rice and indigo crop of 1769.[26]

The assembly became the agency through which the planters conducted their campaign for paper money, while the council was the organ of the king's government, and to some extent of the colonial merchants.   As the quarrel became more bitter, the assembly used its prerogative of originating and framing money bills to embarrass the government by presenting tax bills which it knew the council would have to reject, and consequently no tax bills were passed in South Carolina from 1769-1774, and the king's officials of course went unpaid.

In 1774, when the chronic scarcity of hard money was unusually acute, the assembly in order that it might avoid the neces-

[24] 4th George III, Cap. XXXIV.
[25] P. R. S. C., XXXI, 278-279.
[26] To Reynolds Getly & Co., Sept. 20, 1770.

sity of passing tax acts and at the same time pay for the public services, took advantage of the parliamentary act which provided that paper issued by the government of the colonies as security to their public creditors should be receivable by the public treasurers as legal tender for payment of duties, taxes, etc., and assumed the power, without the consent of the council and governor, to order their clerk to issue certificates of indebtedness to the public creditors certifying that such sums were due and would be provided for in the first tax bill that should pass. To guard against counterfeiting, five of the members as well as the clerk signed these promises to pay. This act seemed to the uninitiated a praiseworthy effort on the part of the legislative body to provide for the payment of public obligations, but it was really a subterfuge for issuing some £200,000 currency as a circulating medium despite the prohibition of Parliament. The members of the assembly, the merchants and the planters agreed to receive these certificates as money. The Charleston Chamber of Commerce, which had been organized in the latter part of 1773, accepted the certificates, and they passed into general circulation. Thus the business men of the city were placing the stamp of their approval upon a measure of the assembly which in effect created and issued money without the consent of the Crown.

Lieutenant Governor Bull described the reception of this extra-legal money in a letter to the Earl of Dartmouth: "The people shift it about from hand to hand with an eager impatience, almost like a hot iron, not only to discharge pressing engagements, but many fear it will prove a loss in the possession of the last holder." Nevertheless, the king's servants had been starved into submission and only one official refused to receive the certificates in lieu of legal money for his service. Bull, however, who, like the others, had received no salary since 1769 and to whom a large amount was due, refused the certificates because he regarded it as inconsistent with his duty as governor "to countenance such an unwarranted Emission calculated as much to elude royal Instructions as to relieve Public Creditors." And he had the courage to repeat his refusal when the assembly issued other certificates of indebtedness in 1775.[27]

Since the paper money issued by the legislature was inadequate for purposes of trade, commercial instruments, such as notes and bonds, and certificates of various kinds passed in business transactions. The bonds of planters of reputation, particularly those given as security for the payment of Negroes, passed like money: Negroes, houses, stores, and other property were advertised to be sold for them. Also certificates of proclamation money issued by the commissioners of the Indian trade in payment for merchandise and services were receivable for duties and taxes and were a form of money used in intra-provincial dealings. At the warehouses of inspection, sellers of produce were not paid until the ship came to take away the commodities, which might not be for months, and in lieu of payment, certificates were issued stating usually the warehouse number, brand, quality and value of the produce. These passed in business transactions and were, to all intents and purposes, a kind of money. Any person counterfeiting a flour certificate was subject to a fine of £500 current money and to stand in the pillory two hours; but in the period after the Revolution when the tobacco industry was being developed, the death penalty was prescribed for counterfeiting a tobacco certificate.[28]

In the following story of bills of exchange the reader will be impressed at every turn with the fact that the merchants of England and of the colonies in the eighteenth century were performing many of the important functions now exercised by bankers. Throughout the colonies a merchant's bill of exchange, which ranged in amount from twenty shillings to many thousand pounds, drawn upon some well known firm, especially of London, had a currency similar to that of bankers' bills today. Not only was it common for the great English merchants to conduct a private banking business; but the same kind of business was being done in a lesser degree by a colonial merchant like Henry Laurens in Charleston, who was the "merchant" or banker of Mr. Samuel

[27] For the story of certificates of indebtedness see MacPherson, *Annals of Com.*, III, 538; *P. R. S. C.*, XXXIV, 36; *ibid.*, XXXV, 24; *S. C. Gaz.*, Aug. 23, 1773.
[28] *S. C. Gaz.*, March 28, 1771; Cooper, *Statutes of S. C.*, IV, 330.

Johnston, of Edenton, North Carolina, or of Mr. James Habersham, of Savannah, or of some humble Indian trader out in the backwoods. The merchants of the crossroads and villages made deposits with him when they wished to send their remittances to England, or he furnished credit to the young merchant starting out in business, or he drew bills for planters who needed to go on a journey or meet their obligations abroad.

There was little English money in the colonies and the provincial substitute was the draft or bill of exchange. The Charleston merchant or factor in order to establish a balance with his English "merchant" or banker made shipments of produce directly to him and also directed his other correspondents in various parts of the world to remit the proceeds of shipments made to them to his "merchant" in England. Against the balance thus established he drew bills of exchange for his expenses or he sold his bills to his provincial customers. Bills thus drawn were sold for cash or for credit when bills were in little demand. "The method of doing business here," wrote Laurens, "is to load the ship with goods and for the amount of cost and charges to draw as soon as the bills of lading are signed upon some person in England at 30 to 40 days payable in London."[29] But a punctilious dealer like Laurens made it a point never to draw upon his European correspondent until after the vessel had sailed unless some special advantage would accrue to the owners of the ship.

Bills sometimes, perhaps always, stated with a great deal of particularity the services or goods for which payment was made, as the following bill, drawn by Governor Grant of East Florida in favor of Henry Laurens shows:

£500   St. Augustine 10 Decem 1767
Thirty days after sight of this first Bill Pay to the
Order of Henry Laurens Esq. five hundred Pounds Sterling
value of him in account for Provisions to be
bought at Charles Town for five hundred Greek Settlers
to be imported into this Province by Doctor
Turnbull in January next according to advice
received from him from Mahon and place

[29] Laurens to William Penn, Dec. 24, 1767.

the same to Doctor Turnbull's ac-
count without further advice from—
                    Your most humble Servant
To   James Grant.
Sir William Duncan Baronet
          London.

Laurens found that Governor Grant had drawn the bill for £100
too much, whereupon he defaced it and drew a bill upon Sir William Duncan payable to the order of John Drayton, Esq., in
Charleston, at forty days sight, for the exact amount due him for
the cargo of provisions.[30]

Trade with the West Indies brought in a great number of
bills of exchange; for the West Indian merchants made remittances in rum, sugar, Negroes, hard money and bills of exchange,
for the provisions and salt meat sent from Carolina for the slaves of
the sugar plantations. Bills, along with hard money, were considered a surer basis for purchasing Carolina produce than rum
or Negroes which must first be sold before they could be turned
into cash. Bills upon America (that is on the ·merchants in the
other American colonies) were not so quickly negotiable as bills
on the West Indies, because trade with the northern colonies was
not so flourishing.[31]

Bills of exchange sold normally at 700 per cent, that is a bill
for £100 sterling commanded £700 currency, and exchange had
been at 7 for 1 for more than fifty years before the Revolution.
The actual exchange value of sterling and provincial paper, however, usually varied according to the balance of the trade.[32]
In general, bills were selling at a premium from 1763 through
1765; for the successful issue of the war with France had
opened new fields for investment, especially in Georgia and East
Florida, and Negroes were being poured in to develop the country, which resulted in the planter's imports greatly exceeding his
exports. High premiums were common. In 1764 Laurens attempted to get 852 for one of his bills and succeeded in getting
775, which was a premium of 10 5/7%.[33]

[30] To Ross and Mill, ana to Sir. Wm. Duncan, Dec. 26, 1767.
[31] Laurens to Martin & Stevens, Feb. 14, 1763.
[32] P. R. S. C., XXXII, 402.
[33] To James Pennman, Nov. 21, 1767.

From 1766 through 1772 bills sold commonly at a discount. First of all, the prohibitive duty in South Carolina of £100 currency on the importation of Negroes for the three years from 1766 through 1768 created flush times for the planter and he was able to keep the merchant indebted to him, which was always the case when the value of the planter's produce exceeded his imports. Shortly after the slave trade was reopened in 1769, came the Non-Importation Agreement not to import British manufactures and Negro slaves until the disputes occasioned by the Townshend Acts should be satisfactorily adjusted (July 22). A few expressions culled from the correspondence of Henry Laurens show the situation of the merchant during this period: "In arrears for rice, cannot stir without borrowing"; "Have abundance of stg. money yet cannot extricate myself from debt"; "Owe vast sums for rice and other commodities—not able to sell a bill upon London for many months together & upward of £20,000 currency in arrears"; Have been two or three times on the point of determining to sell part of my negroes to raise cash in order to support that credit which until lately I have ever maintained."

The highest rate of discount quoted by Laurens during this period was 651, equivalent to 7 per cent, and bills sold currently at 665, equivalent to 5 per cent discount. Sometimes a merchant resorted to the expedient of giving credit in order not to have the appearance of selling at a great discount. For instance, Laurens informed Reynolds, Getly & Company on February 15, 1772, that exchange was at 679 and that he was giving a credit of three weeks on a bill he was drawing in order to draw at three per cent discount. He considered this better than drawing at the current discount of 5 per cent, since by allowing the credit he saved himself two per cent.[34]

The troubled political situation on the eve of the Revolution brought about a scarcity of bills and a rise of exchange. For example, on January 19, 1775, exchange was at 735; on August 19, it was at 749, equivalent to a 7 per cent premium; and the following day at 805, equivalent to a 15 per cent premium. Such

[34] To Reynolds Getly & Co., March 12, 1770; to John Tarleton, Nov. 22, 1770.

violent fluctuations as these over a short period, and even from day to day, must have occasioned heavy losses.[35]

Bills were frequently protested in such cases as these: when the drawee doubted the credit of the drawer, or the drawee had become a bankrupt, or when a bill came in after the accounts had been closed between merchants, or when a drawee had not received the goods against which the draft was made. Apparently the ordinary charge for noting and protesting a bill was 15 per cent; but on one occasion at least Laurens charged for what he called "a short and small disappointment" a commission of 5 per cent. These charges seem high. For instance, we find Laurens charging £6 currency for noting and protesting a bill for £7-19s-3d. sterling, and besides there were other charges payable to a sea captain for receiving and remitting the money.[36]

In Europe the interest on a bill of exchange was due from the time the acceptance arrived at maturity, and the acceptor held it at his peril; but in South Carolina, said Laurens, "the infant state of commerce and negotiation will not bear such vigorous Proceedings and nothing is more common than for negotiable notes & Bills to be withheld and pass from hand to hand months after they become due."[37]

[35] Laurens to Reynold Getly & Co.; to Thomas Tarleton; to James Laurens, Aug. 20, 1775.
[36] To Adam Bachop, March, 1768; ibid., Oct. 26, 1769.
[37] To John Graham, Oct. I, 1770.

CHAPTER IV

THE RETAILERS

I

Before entering into any detailed description of the business of the retailers, let us first consider the general character of business in colonial America as represented in the commercial world at Charleston. We have already seen in dealing with the Charleston factor that his business was characterized by its variety, that he pursued many different employments which would now be exercised by as many different classes of business men. Yet by the middle of the eighteenth century specialization was far advanced in the professions, the trades, and among the business men and merchants. Some professions, however, were still in an itinerant stage. Dentistry, for example, was a travelling occupation, for the colonial dentist was still under the necessity of working in several places in order to make a livelihood.

Almost all travelers seemed to be of the opinion that colonial Americans had bad teeth—yellow, discolored, decayed—which is little wonder since the best of them had dental service at their disposal for only a few weeks or months in the year. The colonial dentist bore a striking resemblance to his modern successor both in the matter of language and claims. A Dr. McGinnis who made a stay in Charleston in 1770 after first visiting Philadelphia and Baltimore was to be consulted in all disorders of "the teeth, gums, sockets, ulcers, cancers, abscesses, fistulas, suppurations, and inflammations of the gums." He made artificial teeth "fixed or grafted on stumps, from a single tooth to a complete set." He made sound black teeth white "without giving the least pain" and extracted teeth "with great ease and safety." His "Antiscorbutick Dentrifice" was the "most efficacious remedy ever offered the public for preserving the teeth." Other dentists advertised pills for the toothache, and brushes and powder suitable for the teeth.

A tradesman was commonly a jack of several trades or combined some other occupation with a trade in order to make a living. Handicraftsmen often conducted small shops in connection with their trades. A shoemaker might have a general store or a saddler operate a tavern and sell in connection with it groceries and liquors. A jeweler depended principally upon selling jewelry and perhaps hardware, but so much of the trade was conducted by barter that he found it necessary in order to attract customers to keep other articles at times, such as shoes, bridles, striped strouds, beer and cider.

There seems to have been no strict line of demarcation between the wholesale and retail trades, and a business man was classified according to his principal interest. The great retailers, whose most profitable business it was to sell on charge accounts to the planters, frequently sent out in their boats commodities in wholesale lots for the plantations. The wholesale dealer was a specialist only in a limited degree. He might deal principally in European goods, slaves, and wine, but he accepted for sale anything his correspondents might consign to him. For this reason he sometimes had to resort to retail dealings in order to get rid of his stock. He also sent off his "merchandizes" to the vendue master, who could legally charge only two and one-half per cent commission, to be sold either wholesale or retail; and he often had to accommodate his planter customers by selling them commodities in small quantities. Some of the wholesale dealers advertised their merchandise to be sold either wholesale or retail.

There were no banks and drug stores of the modern sort. The merchants, as we have seen, were the bankers of those days, and surgeons, barbers, grocers, and even confectioners prepared and dispensed medicines as pharmacists do today. The wholesale dealer frequently carried a special line of "chemical and galenical preparations and drugs." He kept family medicines including such familiar compounds as "female pills," "female elixirs," "balsam of life," "tincture of sage to lengthen life and keep off the decay of age," and he sold "phials, gallipots, pestles, scales and weights" and other materials for the practitioners of "physic and surgery." He also fitted out boxes of medicines for plantations and ships.

The larger retail stores seem to have kept a line of merchandise similar in variety to the big department stores of today. It was then as Charles Fraser described it at a later time. At one counter could be seen the planter purchasing "hoes, axes, plows, saddles, his osnaburghs and Negro cloth; whilst at another in the same store a lady was bargaining for her laces, her satins, and her muslins."[1] The chief retail stores were naturally much nearer the water front than they are today. Broad, Elliot, and Tradd streets were principal business districts, instead of King, which was then chiefly the resort of hucksters, peddlers, and tavern keepers.

Considering the low estimation in which women generally were held in the eighteenth century, they played an important part in the business life of the low country. It was not uncommon for women to "elope" from their husbands in these days when divorces were few, and the "eloping" wife was advertised for in almost identical terms as the runaway slave. In the advertisements the husband forewarned all persons not to harbor or entertain his fugitive wife or give her credit in his name, and masters of vessels were cautioned not to "carry her off the province" lest they be proceeded against "with the utmost rigor of the law."

Many women followed the lines of business in which we would naturally expect to find them. They kept haberdashery stores, ran boarding houses and dame schools, taught dancing, etc. The institution of slavery which gave them control over trained slaves also gave them an opportunity to follow occupations from which they otherwise would have been excluded. Women were able to continue the business of their deceased husbands, operate plantations, keep up a saddlery business, run ferries and keep stables in connection with lodging houses. Anne Hawes, according to her advertisement in the *Gazette of the State of South Carolina* for April 21, 1789, carried on the painting, glazing, and paper hanging business "on reasonable terms for cash or short credit," and hired out Negro painters by the day. The story of Eliza Lucas and her superintendence of her father's plantations is familiar history, and there were some lesser Eliza Lucases whose plantation activities gave them rice and indigo accounts in the books of the

[1] Charles Fraser, *Reminiscences of Charleston*, (1854) 12-13.

merchants. Ann Timothy after her husband's death continued
his paper, the *South Carolina Gazette,* under the name of the
Gazette of the State of South Carolina in the troubled period following the Revolution. She was appointed printer to the state, on
March 1, 1783, in "consequence of the services rendered to it by
her late husband." None of the several papers published in South
Carolina after the war came up to the standard of Timothy's
Gazette, which reflected the interest of its editor in the social,
economic, and political well-being of the province; but Mrs. Timothy edited a very good paper and she improved it by making it a
bi-weekly, publishing it every Monday and Thursday.

II

There were retailers of many grades and varieties in the
Charleston District, the two most important classes being apparently the country factors, merchants who carried on business,
mostly retail, in the city; and country merchants who carried on
business, largely retail, in the country and who were essentially
agents of the Charleston factors in much the same way that the
Charleston factors were agents of the British merchants.

Ideally, from the point of view of the British merchant and
his Charleston factor, the retailer was to take no part in the import trade. He was to receive his stock in trade from the Charleston factor and act more or less as the latter's agent. Lord Sheffield,
who was thinking only incidentally of the humble retailer, gives us
in his pamphlet *Observations on the Commerce of the American
States* the ideal program of the wholesale merchant in the southern
provinces.[2] According to Sheffield, the trade of the country was to
be carried on by British merchants who formed connections at
home. They carried out cargoes of assorted goods to be sold by the
package unopened, to the retailers, who exchanged the goods for
produce, which was turned over to the British merchants who
shipped it off. The wholesale merchant was not to be concerned at
all in retailing goods. His chief function was to organize the whole
trade of the country in such a way that he would be able "to

[2] John Sheffield, *Observations on the Commerce of the American States,* pp.
266-267. This pamphlet was published in 1784 when the United States was still
economically a colony of Great Britain.

monopolize supplies in wholesale to the country merchants" and have "the sole command of the shipping business." He was the agent or partner of the British merchant, judging to whom it was safe to give credit; he should be able by his presence on the spot, and the backing of his government, to compel punctual payment.

This ideal program was almost realized in the Chesapeake district, especially in Virginia where the navigable streams of the country gave the British factor direct access to the few shopkeepers of the country and to the planters who were the chief wholesale purchasers. The representatives of the British merchants were able to monopolize the trade of the country to such an extent that it was commonly said that they used to meet annually at Williamsburg and fix the price of tobacco; it is not improbable that they regulated to some extent the price of imports. In the country south of Virginia there was no fixing of the price of rice and indigo by British factors. The shoal channels of the streams did not permit ocean-going vessels to penetrate the country. Consequently ports developed on the available harbors; and inland and coastal trade was organized in a more complicated way, causing the emergence of a class of middlemen at Charleston and in the Charleston District and preventing the absolute dominance of business by the British factors. At Charleston there were more native merchants than in Virginia and Maryland, because business conditions were more like those in Philadelphia, New York and Boston. Some of the most extensive merchants bore Huguenot names, and the Huguenots were finding in South Carolina a field for the exercise of those business talents which in France had made them important out of all proportion to their numbers.[3]

Perhaps the most influential of these middlemen were the country factors, so-called by Henry Laurens, and perhaps it was a term generally applied to them. The country factors were merchants who kept retail stores, mostly on the wharves, where they exchanged merchandise of various sorts for country produce. They also sold country produce on commission for their customers disposing of it in Charleston or shipping it to New York, Philadelphia, the New England towns, and the West Indies. For

[3] A. H. Hirsch, *The Hugenots of Colonial South Carolina.*

example, Crouch and Gray, Carolina and New England factors, loaded vessels on commission from the "Northward" and the West Indies, and advertised for sale country produce, liquors, coffee, sugar, men's white and colored silk hose.[4]

The stock in trade of the country factor was derived principally from the places whence they shipped produce, and from the wholesale merchants to whom they sold produce. They seem not to have kept within what Lord Sheffield considered the retailer's sphere, and their business cut athwart the trade of the wholesale merchants in several ways. In the first place, they frequently imported their stock in trade directly from the West Indies and the "Northward" colonies and even from England itself. And they sometimes owned shares in the vessels that brought them goods.[5] In the second place, they had an extensive clientele among the planters and back country farmers and frequently sold in wholesale quantities. Like the great merchants, they sometimes had money to lend, with land and slaves as security, and in this way they were able to get a financial hold on their patrons. Lastly, they were owners and operators of boats and coasting vessels and competed for freights with the wholesale dealers.

The most important fact in connection with the country factor was that in an age of barter he was able by means of extensive retail trade to come into possession of a considerable share of the produce of the country and to influence to a certain degree the price of rice and indigo. There are several allusions in the correspondence of Laurens to a control of the rice market by combinations of factors and planters. For instance, Laurens wrote to William Freeman on the 24th of May, 1768: "Bought up 600 barrels of fine Rice for our Ship Ann before departing for Mepkin. My Back was scarcely turned upon Charles Town before there was a total stoppage of Sale agreed upon by Planters & Factors & in a few days the market opened again at 60/ per C Cash, without much choice of quality."[6]

The factors referred to here may have included men engaged in the foreign factorage business. But Laurens as a factor for

[4] S. C. Gaz., Sept. 17, 1773.
[5] Laurens to Freeman, June 4, 1771.
[6] For further illustration of this point see chapter on rice.

British firms was interested in buying rice and other produce as cheaply as possible and he had to buy within certain limits. As an independent trader he was interested in loading his own vessels for as high a freight as possible. So the combination of planters and factors that took rice off the market until the merchant offered a certain price interfered seriously with his business; for high priced rice meant little demand for freight and consequently a low freight rate. On the other hand, the interests of the country factor and the planter were identical. Neither owned more than a few shares in the vessels engaged in the foreign trade, and both were interested in selling rice as high as possible.

The necessary equipment for carrying on the country factor's business was a wharf or space on a wharf, with stores where country produce exchanged for goods might be stored, and boats for the "accommodation of friends in the country." John Morley, a country factor, had commodious stores on Colonel Beale's wharf, and combined a factorage business in indigo, rice, and lumber with a carting and wood-selling business, supplying masters of vessels with firewood and water. In an age when wood and coal measurers were important city officials the firewood business was lucrative, since firewood was in demand for the use not only of families, but for the many ships which put into port each year. The planter living along the streams in the vicinity of Charleston found it profitable to employ a part of his slaves in cutting and transporting firewood to the city; there the country factor who specialized in furnishing wood, water, and provisions to the vessels bought it of him outright or sold it for him on commission. John Morley did business on short credit, that is he expected his customers to pay him every three months. He advertised to sell firewood, lumber, staves, shingles, etc., at five per cent commission or at seven and one-half per cent, making himself liable for losses and bad debts. He owned and employed in his business the following schooners "well founded and esteemed of judges to be as profitable vessels as any in the coasting trade": John, 220 barrels of rice; Ann and Martha, 110 barrels of rice; and one-half Cannon Brothers, 150 barrels of rice; Morley made use of thirty or forty slaves in his business, including twelve boat-men and three patroons.[7]

Country factors sometimes kept ordinaries, inns, houses of entertainment, using the social contact thus gained to forward their business interests. Some of them were vendue masters. Public vendue sales were common in America and the West Indies. Goods were advertised to be sold in small lots on vendue days, Mondays and Fridays or Tuesdays and Thursdays, the days the newspaper came out. A number of people gathered and goods were sold to the highest bidder.

There was a feeling of social superiority on the part of big merchants and planters toward the retailers who did business on a petty scale, a good example of which is given in a letter of Laurens to Richard Oswald on July 7, 1764. Oswald, one of the richest of the British merchants, who owned a factory at Bance Island in Africa from which he exported slaves to the West Indies and the southern colonies, sent out two gentlemen, Messrs. Ratsel and Gervais, to South Carolina in 1764 to spy out some western land with a view to establishing plantations there. Oswald wrote to Laurens, who had a general oversight of his affairs in South Carolina, proposing that the two men set up first as merchants and afterwards become planters. To this proposal Laurens replied as follows: "As to their entering into any retail trade in these Parts, I cannot admit of it, would be mean, would lessen them in the esteem of People whose respect they must endeavor to attract. They are no Planters—easily perceived, they have understanding and industry enough to make very good ones in a short time, under tuition or assistance of a capable overseer for one or two years & when once they are set down in a creditable manner as planters they may carry on the sale of many species of European and West Indian goods to some advantage and with good grace."

[7] *S. C. Gaz.*, Mch. 8, 1770. The word patroon was commonly used in colonial Carolina meaning, among other things, the master of a coasting vessel. The Standard Dictionary defines patroon: a coxswain or master of a galley or coaster in the Mediterranean, deriving the word from L. patronus—the master of a slave. Murray's New English Dictionary defines patroon: the captain, master or officer in charge of a ship, barge, or boat; the coxswain of a long boat—now rare. Examples of the use of the word in this sense are given for the years 1769, 1775, 1789.

This class distinction which marked the plantation society was not a New World growth due to the institution of slavery which allowed men to conduct business on a large scale; it was the transplantation of an idea essentially bound up with European feudal society, which in some forms still persists in men's minds. In the nineteenth century Thackeray was depicting the same sort of snobbery among the schoolboys of Old England. He shows us in Vanity Fair George Osborne, the son of a broker, who is taught by his associates to feel socially superior to William Dobbin whose father is a grocer and sells soap and candles.

The trade territory outside of Charleston was organized by means of village and crossroads' stores. These were owned sometimes by planters who farmed on such a large scale that it paid them to charter vessels and send their produce directly to England to eliminate the heavy charges of the Charleston factors, or by lesser planters who were in partnership with Charleston merchants. As the back country trade developed, planters who owned or came into possession of locations along the main routes of travel into the city became prosperous by trafficking with wagoners. The plantation called Ferguson's Swamp contained such a location. It was situated on the Congaree Road, forty miles from Charleston and nine from Moncks Corner. There a planter with twenty-five or thirty Negroes could cultivate about a hundred acres of land, run a tavern for the accommodation of wagoners, and sell them at his own door the surplus produce of his plantation.[8] An especially good stand was at a bridge leading from the western part of the province to the capital. The toll of the bridge was vested by the legislature in the owner of such a plantation for a period of as much as twenty years. Here wagoners must pass on their way to the city and the planter could sell them rice, indigo, corn and other provisions, and also run a tavern and store for their accommodation. Another favored location for the planter-merchant was at the forks of two rivers or on the bluff side of a river, where in addition to plantation activities, a store and tavern could be run and a ferry operated to advantage.

[8] See Advertisement of Blake Seay White in *S. C. Gaz.*, Sept. 9, 1778.

Most of the village and crossroads stores seem to have been branches of larger firms in Charleston established as feeders to the business of the great exporting and importing merchants, who found it necessary to have competent partners or agents to look after their extensive business interests in the country. Charleston firms advertised their wares in branch stores in nearby villages such as Moncks Corner, Dorchester, Jacksonburgh, Bacon Ridge, where trade was drawn to the community centers by selling goods at Charleston prices; they also advertised in back country villages like Camden or Granby and even in the ports of Georgetown and Beaufort.

The country store was run in conjunction with other employments. Probably the minimum requirement for this business was a plantation, a few boats, and some storehouses. The principal business of the storekeeper was to sell a varied assortment of goods, groceries, hardware, and Negroes on credit to the planters and by barter to the backcountrymen and to buy in the fall of the year rice, indigo, and other produce, usually on commission, for some Charleston firm. The fall of the year, particularly the month of September, was a season of unwonted business activity. While the crop was being made it had been all outgo and no income for the planter or farmer. Now he brought his produce to the storekeeper, settled with him by a balancing of accounts, supplied the needs of his family, bought his supply of Negro clothing and shoes for the year, purchased plantation equipment and additional Negroes to enlarge his plantation operations, if it had been a good crop year and his credit warranted this undertaking. Many Negroes were kept busy filling the storehouses with produce to await shipment by boat or wagon to the city. A plantation or plantations were operated by the storekeeper because they were good investments; the plantation also served as a depository for new Negroes, some of whom were not in a condition to put upon the market upon their arrival. And while the crop was being made and business was dull the plantation gave employment to the storekeeper.

The growth of the backcountry trade is well illustrated in the development of the business of Joseph Kershaw. In the year

1758, the Charleston house of Ancrum, Lance, and Loocock sent their agent, Joseph Kershaw, who had been an efficient clerk for James Laurens and Company, to the Wateree River to establish a country branch of the firm; in this each of the partners, including Kershaw, was to have a joint concern. The result was the locally well known Pine Tree Store of Kershaw and Company at Pine Tree Hill, now called Camden, at the head of navigation on the Wateree River.

Five years later, in 1763, Kershaw had built up so extensive and prosperous a trade that he took into partnership his two young clerks, Eli Kershaw, his brother, and John Chesnut, who had been an apprentice in his store, relinquishing to them two-thirds of his share in the concern. He himself took charge of the store at Pine Tree Hill, now operating under the firm name of Kershaw, Chesnut and Company; Eli Kershaw and Company were to run a store at a place called Rocky Mount, in the Cheraws, at the head of navigation on the Pedee River; John Chesnut and Company took the direction of the store at Granby, at the head of navigation on the Congaree.[9] When the partnership thus founded was dissolved, on December 8, 1774, the Charleston partners retiring from the business, the store at Camden was worth £15,054-6s.-6d.; that at Rocky Mount £9,628-1s.-11d.; and that at Granby £8,102-0s.-7d.[10]

The property of the Camden firm consisted of storehouses, store of goods, mills, wagons, horses and about one hundred valuable Negroes—coopers, millers, bakers, wagoners, jobbing carpenters, boatmen, and field slaves employed in carrying on the business—and many thousand acres on Wateree River which were put on sale in convenient lots of from one hundred to two hundred acres to suit purchasers of all ranks.[11] The property at the Cheraws consisted of a valuable plantation called Liberty Hill,

[9] Districts were called by the names of the Indian tribes that had once occupied them: Thus the region of the upper Pedee was called the Cheraws, the region in the neighborhood of Columbia the Congarees, etc. For boats of 70 tons the Wateree was navigable to Camden; the Congaree to Granby; for boats of lesser draught the Pedee was navigable to a place called at different times Rocky Mount, Chatham, Cheraw. Drayton, *View*, 30-31.
[10] Kirkland and Kennedy, *Historic Camden*, 375; Kershaw Papers.
[11] Advertisement in *S. C. Gaz.*, July 11, 1774.

and other lands on the Pedee, a stock of goods, storehouses, mills, and about fifty valuable Negroes.[12]

After the dissolution of the above mentioned partnership, Joseph Kershaw did not lose his Charleston connection. He established in Charleston a house under the name of Kershaw and Company, near the Exchange, where all sorts of produce from the back-country were sold. He also had a "concern" in the firm of George Ancrum, Jun., and Company, a successor to the house of Ancrum, Lance and Loocock. He was furthermore a partner in the following firms that had stores in Camden: Kershaw and Wyllie, Kershaw and Hoyle, and John Wyllie and Company.[13] Thus a successful venture in back-country trade had raised an obscure country trader to the rank of a great Charleston merchant.

Joseph Kershaw came from the West Riding, of Yorkshire, England, and was probably selected by the Charleston firm as their representative because he had learned flour milling in the old country. As early as 1760 Ancrum, Lance and Loocock were advertising "Fine Carolina Flour," in the manufacture of which they were "concerned," which probably came from Kershaw's mills on Pine Tree Creek.[14] Kershaw also operated saw and grist mills, a bakery, a tobacco warehouse, and a distillery. Camden became the center of a valuable back-country trade in tobacco, flour, ship bread, deerskins and indigo, which were transported to Charleston both by land and water.[15] There were boats on the Wateree large enough to carry fifty or sixty hogsheads of tobacco, and Kershaw was dispatching in 1786 about forty wagons a day to Charleston.[16]

Although Camden was hardly more than a straggling village at the time of the Revolution, Kershaw was petitioning as early as 1765 for the establishment of a fair at Pine Tree Hill, which the assembly did not allow, "because no benefit or advantage could arise to the province therefrom."[17] It was not until 1774 that Joseph Kershaw, Eli Kershaw, John Chesnut, William Ancrum,

[12] Gregg, *Hist. of the Old Cheraws*, note p. 119.
[13] *S. C. Gaz.*, June 4, 1772; *Gaz. of the State of S. C.*, Oct. 30, 1783.
[14] *S. C. Gaz.*, July 5-12, 1760.
[15] E. Watson, *Memoirs*, 297.
[16] Washington, *Diaries*, 37; Kirkland and Kennedy, *Historic Camden*, 14.
[17] *S. C. Gaz.*, Mch. 30-Apr. 6, 1765.

and Aaron Loocock, "the proprietors of Camden," were empowered to hold fairs, "2 in each year, to continue 3 days."[18]

Both of the Kershaws were what would have been called in biblical times the founders of cities. A village grew up at Pine Tree Hill after the coming of Joseph Kershaw, and the change of name to Camden, in honor of Lord Camden, one of the defenders in Parliament of colonial rights, is attributed to him. Eli Kershaw, with his brother Joseph and others, laid out a village on the Pedee called at first Cheraw, but afterwards rechristened by Eli Kershaw, Chatham, in honor of the elder Pitt.[19]

The relations existing between the Charleston merchants and their country agents were similar to those existing between the Charleston merchants and the big English houses. The Kershaws and Chesnut were both factors of Ancrum, Lance and Loocock and also independent traders, buying country produce on account of their partners and on their own account. They received some of their stock in trade from Great Britain through the hands of the Charleston merchants and some from Charleston. Like the Charleston merchants, they acted as bankers both for their customers and for their partners, lending and borrowing money, taking and collecting notes and bonds, buying money, and at the end of the year settling with their correspondents by a balancing of accounts.

III

The back-country trade was carried on chiefly by that direct exchange of goods for produce called barter; the plantation trade by that indirect exchange of goods for produce called credit. In the former case little or no money was required, in the latter case business could be done with an astonishingly small amount of cash. A Beaufort Merchant's Account Book deposited at the Charleston Library shows just how little cash might be received in the course of a year. This firm did business in September, 1786 amounting to £1,263/11/2 and received in cash £48/17/0; did business in October amounting to £698/17/4 and received in cash £10/14/7.

---

[18] *Council Journal*, 1773-1774, Oct. 8, 1774.
[19] Gregg, *Hist. of the Old Cheraws*, 118-119.

And these entries are typical of the account carried on throughout the year.

The plantation was the chief field for both the retail and the wholesale trade, since the back-countrymen produced their food, manufactured their clothes, made their liquor at home, and relied on the outside world chiefly for such articles as nails to build their houses, iron for the fashioning of tools, salt to cure their provisions, and perhaps a small amount of European manufactures. Nevertheless, the back-country trade was important enough to cause the same merchant to conduct a store within the city gates for his planter customers where he advertised goods seven for one, eight for one, nine for one, according to whether they were sold for cash, short credit, or long credit; and another store without the city gates for the convenience of back-country customers where goods were advertised for sale in exchange for country produce.

The planter spent his surplus for European and East Indian manufactures for his family; for high grade flour, which came from the northern colonies, mostly from New York and Philadelphia, that of the back-country not suiting his fastidious taste; for groceries, liquors, and perhaps some vegetables, although during this period cabbage, turnips, beets, carrots, onions, and Irish potatoes were grown in the vicinity of Charleston in sufficient quantities to supply the market; and most of all, for more Negroes to till more land, and quantities of Negro cloth.

The manufactures of Great Britain and other commodities consumed in Carolina ranged in value from about £250,000 to £400,000 annually, which does not seem a great quantity for two provinces, except when one considers that by far the greater part of these goods were sent to South Carolina to be circulated chiefly among the people of the plantation district, where the population did not exceed thirty thousand souls; almost all of them went to the tidewater section of the two provinces, for the back-country people supplied their wants mainly with home manufactures.

What some of the items in the plantation trade were we are told by Governor Glen, who in the middle of the eighteenth century felt "concerned," he wrote, to find imported into the province "quantities of Fine Flanders Laces, the Finest Dutch Linens and French Cambricks, Chintzs, Hyson Tea, and other East Indian goods, Silks, Gold and Silver Laces, etc." Glenn remonstrated with the people on account of their "Extravagance and Luxury" and reminded them that by pursuing the "maxims of Discipline, Industry, & Frugality" the "Dutch from low beginings climbed up to be high & mighty states; and that by following the contrary methods the commonwealth of Rome fell from being Mistress of the World."[20] But this wise admonition seemed not to have been heeded, for Hewatt says of the years after 1763 that "intercourse with Great Britain was easy & frequent" and that "all novelties in fashion & dress were quickly introduced"; "even the spirit of luxury & extravagance, too common in England, was beginning to creep into Carolina." "Almost every family," he says, "kept chaises for a single horse, and some of the principal planters of late years have imported fine horses and splendid carriages from Great Britain."[21]

Such items as horses and carriages were probably sold to the planters by the wholesale dealers; the other items were sold to him either by the Charleston retailer or the country merchants on an annual charge account and paid for in the fall of the year with produce. That there was no strict line of demarcation between the wholesale and retail business is illustrated by the fact that, while the plantation trade was largely in the hands of retailers, even groceries bought for the use of the planter's family, such as flour, sugar, onions, apples, rum, were bought in quantity because of the slow and uncertain means of communication.

Liquor was a great item in the plantation trade. Almost every retail store in Charleston kept rum; and wines, mostly from Portugal, and rum, mostly from the British West Indies, were sent out to the plantations in large quantities despite the high duties on them. It was an age when drunkenness seems to have been expected of gentlemen in Europe and America, when overseers were paid part of their wages in rum, and when quantities of liquor were used on the plantations as medicine for the slaves. The

[20] Carroll, *Collections,* II, 227.
[21] Hewatt, *Hist. of S. C. and Ga.,* II., 293-294.

slaves, particularly those in Charleston, managed to get hold of rum for other than medicinal purposes. Grand juries throughout the period were complaining that the morals of slaves were being debauched in the dram shops. Yet it was against the law for the keepers of taverns, houses of entertainment, or retailers of strong drink to sell or deliver such drinks to slaves without the consent of the owner or person having charge of them. Despite the law, "even at noonday," wrote Stranger in the *South Carolina Gazette* of September 24, 1772, "the dram shops are crowded with negroes."

The retailers were probably excluded effectually from the business of furnishing the plantations with slaves from Africa. That was the particular business of the Charleston factors, who sold Negroes from Africa either direct to the planters or through his agents, the country merchants. But the retailers did a flourishing business selling Negro clothing, for Negro clothing was one of the great items of expense in the planter's bill.

In those days when farming was done almost altogether by man power, perhaps the amount spent for Negro clothing was greater than that spent for agricultural tools. Certainly the clothing for one Negro came to no great figure. In the West Indies slaves were clothed once a year, the men with a shirt and trousers of osnaburg and a hat; the women with a shirt and petticoat of osnaburg and a hat.[22] In Carolina where the climate was colder, well disposed masters gave their slaves once a year a suit of coarse woolen cloth, two rough shirts and a pair of hose;[23] but the poorer planters had thirty or forty slaves to clothe, the great planters several hundred, and the aggregate of small amounts spent for Negro clothes made an appreciable total. For example, Henry Laurens ordered at one time for his two plantations, Mepkin and Wright's Savannah, seven hundred yards of Negro cloth. All of the Negro's clothing and probably most of his shoes were imported from England before the Revolution. After the war the planters patronized to some extent the rising manufactures of the northern states. Henry Laurens, on June 12, 1787, sent the fol-

[22] MacPherson, *Annals of Com.*, IV, 147.
[23] Schoepf, *Travels*, II, 147.

lowing plantation order for shoes to William Bell of Philadelphia, indicating in each case the number of pairs of shoes to go to each plantation:

The bundle contains 226 Shoe measures in 4 classes, viz.
81 for Bluffside with two additional Pairs for Sam will be 83
    for Small's side 60
    for Newton 77
    for City people 8
& over to spare of a large Size 12

226 measures............................pairs of shoes......240
Put into hands of some honest shoe maker to make strong black Shoes with Straps exactly to each measure, and each measure to come within its Shoe, particular orders not to pinch the shoe in the Instep, our friends at Bethlehem most likely to serve faithfully.

During the latter part of the colonial era the rigors of slavery were softened by certain concessions to the Negroes. In addition to their monotonous diet of rice or Indian corn, which they had to grind into meal in crude hand mills, and of salt meat, they were sometimes given fish, a little tobacco, and summer clothing. A planter's bill copied from a Charleston merchant's Account Book of 1764-1766 shows the amount spent on Negro clothing as well as the fact that this particular planter was investing in cotton summer clothing for his slaves:

14 June—	Jonah Collins D^r.	to Store sold him & sent per Gaillard's
Scotch Oznabrugs 140 Yds-4/9		26/2/6
Cotton check 34 Ells./43		21/11/8
Cotton Holland 32½		20/6/3
Irish Linen .... 24 Yds		14/2
White Plains .... 95 Yds		55/8/4
I Bbl Sorted Nails		
Ale	24/10	
24 gal. W. I. Rum		34/16/1
		£308/16/0

The newspapers in the fall of the year when the planters were buying a new clothing supply for their slaves fairly bristled with advertisements of the various kinds of Negro cloths on sale at the retail stores and the warehouses of the wholesale dealers. An occasional variation in the enumeration extending from "osnabrugs" to "white plains" was caused by the advertisements of "stripes and Scotch camlets for Negro wenches gowns" and "Fearnought blue waistcoats and Dutch caps, proper for Boat Negroes."

The law prescribed the only kind of clothing that might be lawfully worn by ordinary slaves, namely: "Negro Cloth, Duffils, Kersies, Osnabrugs, blue linen, chect linen, coarse garlix, coarse calicoes, check cottons or Scotch plaids." More latitude, it seems, was allowed as to the clothing of livery men and waiting boys. The constable who found slaves wearing any other sort of clothing than that prescribed by law was required to seize the garments and appropriate them to his own use.[24] The law in regard to Negro clothing, like other laws concerning Negroes, was difficult to enforce. We find a grand jury in 1773 complaining that the law for "preventing excessive & costly apparel of Negroes & other slaves in this Province, (especially in Charles Town) is not being in Force; as it would in great measure prevent the Robberies that are so frequently commited by them, in Order to support & maintain the present Extravagance of their Dress, which mode we conceive to be beyond their Means & Stations of Life to obtain."[25]

[24] "Stranger" in *S. C. Gaz.*, Sept. 24, 1772.
[25] *S. C. Gaz.*, May 24, 1773.

CHAPTER V

THE NEGRO AS A FACTOR IN BUSINESS

I

Having traced in outline the trade organization through which business on the plantation, in the back country, in the port towns, and in the West Indies was bound to the merchants of Charleston, let us return to the city and take under consideration a very peculiar species of merchandise, of strangely protean character, man one day and an article of merchandise the next, as circumstances required. The Negro, as we have seen, was one of the important articles of exchange between Carolina and the West Indies. He was, although an object of commerce, the most important of all articles of merchandise from an economic point of view. He made the fortune of the British merchants and their Carolina factors; because of him the rice and indigo fields existed; but he was able even in colonial times to assert in the face of all public sentiment to the contrary that he was essentially a human being capable of learning trades and carrying on business successfully. By his participation in almost all lines of business in the low country he came to be an immensely complicating factor in the business and social life of Charleston.

We have already seen how the great merchants at Charleston virtually monopolized the foreign slave trade, the smaller factors having to content themselves with the slaves that came into their hands through their business connections with their West Indian or "Northward" correspondents. The great merchants alone had the capital necessary to house hundreds of slaves, to put them on sale, and to distribute them to the planters of Carolina, Georgia, and Florida. The great merchants engaged largely also in the domestic slave trade, of which, however, they had no monopoly; for all classes of business people sold country Negroes, and slaves were put up for sale at almost any sort of place—the grocery store, the shoemaker's, on the auction platform of the vendue master, at the race course between the heats of the races, in the public Negro yard, on the plantation, at the retail stores, and at the wholesale warehouses of the big importing merchant.

The great merchants, who did a large credit business, no doubt had many slaves returned to them by planters who could not meet their obligations; but the demand for "seasoned" Negroes was great. After 1763 when many new plantations were being "settled," great gangs of "new" Negroes from Africa were purchased, and it was necessary that the planters have trusty experienced slaves to incorporate with the "new" Negroes to teach them the English language and plantation work. Even a few trained slaves among a gang of ignorant ones were invaluable. The country-bred Negroes of South Carolina dreaded very much being sent away, especially to the wilds of Florida. Ships going to the southward with "seasoned" Negroes had to be watched closely to keep the slaves from escaping. Henry Laurens, in forwarding a "parcel" of Negroes to St. Augustine in 1768, wrote his correspondent that he gave the slaves "some clothes to go away chearfully, as well as because such was necessary for them"; and that he had been at a little expense to keep them on board ship lest they should escape.[1]

The great development in plantations going forward sent up the price of slaves, and "seasoned" Negroes sold for extravagant prices, especially in good crop years. Before the war with France slaves without any particular qualification sold as high as £220 currency. In 1768, a banner crop year, Henry Laurens wrote to one of his good customers for slaves in East Florida that "common plantation slaves, likely & young" had sold at a recent large sale at prices ranging from £490 to £550 currency, and that he had been obliged to give for a "proper" man to "manage rice and indigo" the sum of £600 currency.[2] In 1772, another good crop year, "Stranger" wrote in the *South Carolina Gazette* of September 17, that slaves who were tradesmen, cooks, seamstresses, etc., were bringing as high as £1,000 currency.

The newspapers were full of advertisements of "seasoned"

[1] To Doctor Wm. Stork, Jan. 28, 1768.
[2] To James Penman, Feb. 9, 1768.

Negroes, who were listed along with other domestic chattel, advertisements like the following being not uncommon:[3]

To be sold on Ashley River
upward of one hundred Negroes among whom are many valuable tradesmen; about 200 head of tame cattle, 100 Sheep, and a large number of hogs; Likewise a thorough-bred English Stallion, rising six years old, and other horses. Conditions of sale—Cash for all sums under 50 pounds, and for above 3 mos. credit and security.

In spite of the many "seasoned" Negroes in the market the great merchants found it necessary to advertise for Negroes to fill their orders. In the *South Carolina Gazette* of February 16-23, 1765, Henry Laurens advertised for "two Negro carpenters, two coopers, three pair sawyers, forty field negroes young men & women, some acquainted with indigo making, and all with the ordinary course of plantation work," for which he offered good prices in cash or bills of exchange upon London. Indeed Negroes were so much in demand in the period after 1763 that they were purchasable only for cash or upon bond with interest from the date of sale; good security had to be given before the "property was altered," a phrase recurring again and again in the advertisements and referring to the fact that Negroes were commonly sold in gang lots.

II

Because the Negro was valued in proportion to his ability to perform work it paid the white man to teach him any trade he was capable of learning. This was done almost from the first and by the latter half of the colonial period Negroes were employed in almost every branch of business, even jewelers were advertising their slaves for fancy prices because they could fashion rings. The fact that Negroes were in demand for every kind of work caused a system of hiring out slaves to be evolved in the southern colonies and in the West Indies. This system was the subject of a law in South Carolina as early as 1712, the preamble of which reads: that "Several owners of slaves are used to suffer their said slaves to do what and go whither they will and work where they please, upon condition that the said slaves do bring their aforesaid masters

[3] *S. C. Gaz.*, Jan. 16-23, 1762.

as much money as between the said master and slave is agreed
upon, for every day the said slave shall be permitted to employ
himself, which practice hath been observed to occasion such slaves
to spend their time aforesaid, in looking for opportunities to steal,
in order to raise money to pay their masters, as well as maintain
themselves, and other slaves their companions, in drunkenness &
other evil courses."[4]

Slave owners of all classes were engaged in the business of
hiring out Negroes, from the shiftless and indolent owner of a
few slaves who hired them out and lived on their wages, to the
owner of many hundred slaves who took advantage of the opportunities offered in the city to employ his surplus slaves profitably.
It was no novelty to find a merchant adding to his advertisement
of broadcloth, brocades, and silks a postscript saying that he had a
few Negro carpenters for hire.   Henry Laurens wrote a letter on
July 2, 1775, to his brother James, one of the great Charleston
merchants, who was in London for his health, in which he enclosed
a list showing what disposition he had made of his brother's slaves
in Charleston that were able to work.   The list was as follows:

Auba (& Wally to attend her Child) hired to Mr. Thomson Schoolmaster
at £90 per An. from 12 June 1775.

Betty allowed by M[r.] Thomson to stay with her Mother till she is brought
to Bed & able to go to Service.

Statira—the 28 June to the Reverend M[r.] Tennant for easy Service in the
House at £60 per An.

Ishmael—brought in 30/. Said he had earned as a porter. I gave him
the money together with a reprimand which he thought a good couplet—
he is to go to service the 3[d.] July, with Rob[t.] Pringle Esq at £7 per Month.

George—the 29 June hired to M[r.] Lody £7 per Month

Cato—to go to M[r.] Phipse the 3[d.] July £6 per month.

Chloe—to work out at a Stated Washerwoman's & bring in her wages
weekly 30/ per week & maintain Stepny . . . I shall hire Frost I mean
prentice him to a Tayler, or send him to Mepkin—her wages to commence
3[d.] July.

[4] Cooper, *Statutes of S. C.*, VII, 363.

The Negro let out on hire was expected to earn his food and clothes and turn in to his master at least a shilling per day. He was regarded as capital out at a very high rate of interest, but an unstable investment because of the frequency of loss sustained through the "elopement," sickness or death of the Negro. The average hired Negro was expected to bring in annually to his master from fifteen to twenty per cent interest. Sometimes Negroes instead of finding employment for themselves or having their masters find it for them, had their services put up at auction to the highest bidder. The German traveler Schoepf attended such a sale in 1784 in Wilmington, North Carolina, where he saw a whole family consisting of a man, his wife, and three children hired out for £70 a year, and individual slaves for sums ranging from £25 to £35, the annual hire depending upon the slave's age, health, and capacity for work. The hirer of a slave gave bond immediately for the payment of stipulated sums at stipulated dates; these sums were due whether the Negro ran away or became incapacitated through sickness or was a total loss to the hirer on account of his death.[5]

An important part of the revenue of the city of Charleston was derived from badges or licenses issued to the master of slaves or to the free Negroes who let out their services on hire. In 1783 the following sums were required for badges or tickets good for a year: For a butcher, 40/; carpenter, bricklayer, fisherman, blacksmith, wheelwright, pump or blockmaker, cabinet maker, painter, glazier, and gold or silversmith, 20/; for a taylor, tinman, tanner, or currier, 15/; for a mariner, cooper, shoemaker, barber, hatter, ropemaker, turner or any other handicraft tradesman, 10/; and for all others the sum of 5/.[6]

The free Negro was a problem. He comprised a small class in the midst of an overwhelming number of slaves, a considerable percentage of whom attempted to run away from their masters at the first opportunity, if one may judge from the large number of advertisements of runaway slaves in each issue of the gazettes. A

[5] *Travels*, II, 147.
[6] Ordinance for better ordering and governing of Negroes; *Gaz. of the State of S. C.*, Dec. II, 1783.

grand jury in 1767 presented as a grievance "the bad practice of free Negroes and Mulattoes being suffered to pass to and fro without any certificate or badge of their being free, by which means runaway slaves were suffered to pass as free."[7] A grand jury of 1770 made a similar complaint and presented as a grievance the want of a law to incapacitate free Negroes, mulattoes, and mestizoes in the future from acquiring any real property in the province.[8] Complaints like these resulted in a city ordinance in 1783 by which every free Negro above the age of fifteen years was obliged to obtain a badge from the city treasurer, for which he or she paid five shillings, and to wear it "suspended by a string or ribband, and exposed to view on his breast." To appear in public without the badge or to fail to give notice of a change of residence to the city clerk subjected the Negro to a fine of £3 for each offense. A slave who was found wearing a free Negro's badge was publicly whipped not exceeding thirty-nine lashes and was put in the stocks for at least one hour. Free Negroes occasionally acquired considerable property. The Duke de Rochefoucauld-Liancourt reported on his visit to Charleston in the 1790's that there was a free Negro in the township of St. Paul who possessed plantations and two hundred slaves.[9]

III

The widespread employment of Negroes as tradesmen both in Charleston and on the plantations, which were communities in themselves often employing blacksmiths, carpenters, coopers, tailors, and other tradesmen, prevented any great development of the mechanic arts among the whites. The mechanic, seeing only black people perform manual toil, became a sort of aristocrat himself and looked upon physical labor as the badge of slavery. Timothy Ford noted with astonishment in his diary that he saw tradesmen going about the streets of Charleston followed by Negroes carrying their tools. "Barbers," he said, ". . . are supported in idleness & ease by

---

[7] *S. C. Gaz.*, Nov. 2-9, 1767.
[8] *Ibid.*, June 25, 1770.
[9] *Gaz. of the State of S. C.*, Dec. 11, 1783; La Rochefoucauld-Liancourt, *Travels*, I, 602.

their negroes who do the business; & in fact many mechanicks bear nothing more of their trade than the name."[10]

Mechanics finding themselves out of employment on account of the competition of Negro tradesmen, began to emigrate to the northern colonies where wages were lower but where no social stigma was attached to labor, and this exodus of workmen caused a still greater increase in the wages of mechanics. In the 1790's the Duke de Rochefoucauld-Liancourt reported that carpenter's wages at Charleston for white people were $2.50 per day and for Negroes $1.50 per day, which were enormous wages for those days.[11] Merchants had to import such common and necessary articles as plantation tools and Negro shoes which might have been made as well as home. In 1787 Henry Laurens was sending as far as Philadelphia to enquire about having hoes mended and was writing to his correspondent that mechanic work in Charleston was almost double the price in Philadelphia.[12]

Yet the mechanics never ceased to be an important class in the society of the low country during the colonial period. When England made laws that injured the business of the colonists and they retaliated by forming non-importation associations to resist what they regarded as unwarranted impositions of the mother country, the mechanics at Charleston formed a progressive party under the leadership of the discontented planters. The committee for the enforcement of the non-importation association in 1769 consisted of thirteen mechanics, thirteen planters, and thirteen merchants.

In the period before 1740 John Laurens, the father of Henry, who began his career as a saddler became the largest merchant in saddlery goods in the province. In the later period the mechanic who had capital to do business on a large scale was able to maintain his position. Such a one was Thomas Elfe, a cabinet-maker in Charleston from 1768-1776. Elfe did work for some of the most prominent people as well as for some of the most lowly. He made new articles and mended old, sending out bills ranging all

[10] *S. C. His. and Gen. Mag.*, XIII, 142.
[11] *Travels*, I, 282.
[12] To Wm. Bell, Oct. II, 1787.

the way from that of Charles Strothers, in June 1771, for a child's cedar coffin priced £2, to that of Francis Young, in August 20, 1771, for a mahogany chest of drawers and book case with "Chineas Dores," amounting to £205. Except for articles of trifling value, Elfe received for his work the notes and bonds of his customers payable at a designated time, rather than ready money. The greater part of the materials for his trade he obtained from England on credit, for which he made remittances in bills of exchange bought from the Charleston merchants. He derived his income from various sources: partly from the rent of tenements in Charleston and from the produce of his plantations; but principally from the employment of handicraft slaves in his trade and from hiring out handicraft slaves, for the best of whom he received £12, £15 and £20 per month. At his death in 1776 his estate was appraised at £38,243/16/2. He owned twenty-nine slaves, thirty-five head of cattle, thirteen hogs, two boats, two carts and thirteen cedar posts. Some of his trained slaves were valued as follows:[13]

> Liverpool the Painter £700
> Jack—Joe—& Paul ....£750 each
> Hector £700
> Luke £1,000

Thoughtful people among the merchants and planters were alarmed at the situation in regard to mechanic employment in Charleston; but the practice of employing Negroes as tradesmen was so much to the advantage of an influential economic class that laws designed to better the situation were laxly enforced, if enforced at all. A grand jury in 1742 presented as a grievance: "The want of a law to prevent the hiring out of negro tradesmen, to the great discouragement of white workmen coming into this province." Laws were made limiting the number of slaves a master might keep in Charleston, with a view to keeping the Negroes in check until white servants and mechanics might be introduced. The law in force in 1786 provided that no master or

[13] Account Book of Thomas Elfe, Cabinet-maker; Inventory Book, 1776-1778, pp. 77-78.

mistress of a family should keep or subsist in or about his or her house for their daily attendance more slaves than four to the head and one to each white person in the family (exclusive of children), under penalty of being doubly taxed; but the purpose of the law was defeated by a clause which provided that no person whatever was to be permitted to keep more than two slaves to work out for hire "except of any mechanic or handicraft trade."[14]

No Negro was permitted to carry on any handicraft trade of his own in a shop or to learn a trade from another slave, and every mechanic was required to have one white apprentice to every two Negroes.[15] Judge Champion, writing in the *Charleston City Gazette* of September 29, 1785, reminded the planters that it was their business to encourage the mechanic arts in all its branches and invite "Manufacturers to reside among them until their numbers decreased the price of their work." He suggested that this might be done by taking off all taxes on handicraft business and exempting mechanics from all taxes except those on land, Negroes, and money at interest. The laws, however, were steadily relaxed in the interest of the slave owner at the expense of the white mechanic. In 1772 a master who hired out his slaves without a license or badge was subject to a fine of £10 and the employer of the slave to a penalty of £5. In 1783 for a like offense the owner of the slaves was fined £3 and the employer twenty shillings "for each day the unlicensed slave was employed above the wages agreed upon for his or her work."[16] By 1790 the city council of Charleston had abolished entirely the badges or licenses issued for the employment of slaves on hire because the tax had been found "to be burdensome & unequal." By this time the mechanic class must have been greatly reduced by migrations to the North where the mechanics found compensation for the lower price of labor in the cheaper cost of living and a higher rank in the social scale than was possible where the white man had to compete for a livelihood with hordes of slaves.

[14] "Stranger" in *Gaz. of the State of S. C.*, Aug. 3, 1786.
[15] *Ibid.*, Dec. 11, 1783.
[16] "Stranger," *S. C. Gaz.*, Sept. 24, 1772; City Ordinance, *Gaz. of State of S. C.*, Dec. 11, 1783.

IV

While the mechanics were being forced to flee to the North on account of Negro competition in business, a humbler class of white people was being crowded out of employment by the slaves who monopolized the market business "[In Antigua] the negroes are the only market people." "Nobody else dreams of selling provisions," wrote Janet Schaw in her *Journal of a Lady of Quality*.[16a] The market was perhaps the greatest single field for the employment of Negroes at Charleston.

The business of fishing was carried on principally by Negroes, mulattoes, and mestizoes, and fishermen were the only class of slaves who could lawfully own vessels. This law seems to have been frequently violated. "Stranger" writing in the *South Carolina Gazette* of September 24, 1772, says that in violation of the law many slaves are permitted to keep boats and canoes whereby opportunities are offered them to receive, conceal and dispose of stolen goods and, "*at their pleasure,* to supply the town with fish or not." Licensed fishermen were required to register with the city clerk the dimensions of their boats, the tackle, and the number of hands employed on board, with their names and to whom they belonged. Failure to make such entry within a specified time subjected the fisherman to a corrective punishment of thirty-nine lashes and to having his license withdrawn.

The planter who employed his slaves to sell provisions, fruit, garden stuff, etc., in the public markets was required only to furnish them with tickets specifying the quantity and quality of market stuff offered for sale. Negroes were strictly forbidden to sell in the public markets any provisions not received from, or the produce of, their master's plantations or estates in the country. They were also forbidden to buy anything in order to sell it again or to sell upon their own accounts under penalty of forfeiting the goods offered for sale. This regulation was extremely hard to enforce on account of the difficulty of determining whether the commodity offered by a Negro for sale was the produce of his master's plantation or whether it had been forestalled by the Negro who was under contract to find employment and turn in a stipulated sum to his master each day. "Stranger," after citing

[16a] Note p. 88.

this market law in an article in the *South Carolina Gazette* of September 24, 1772, makes this observation:

What regard is paid to this regulation may almost every day be observed, in and near the Lower Market, when poultry, fruit, eggs &c, are brought thither from the country for sale. Near that market, constantly resort a great number of loose, idle, disorderly negro women, who are seated there from morn 'til night, and buy and sell on their accounts, what they please in order to pay their wages, and get as much more for themselves as they can; for their owners care little how their slaves get the money so they are paid. These women have such a connection with, and influence on, the country negroes who come to that market, that they generally find means to obtain whatever they choose, in preference to any white person; thus they forestall and engross many articles, which some few hours afterwards you must buy from them at 100 or 150 percent advance. I have known those black women to be so insolent as even to *wrest* things out of the hands of white people, pretending they had been bought before, for their masters or mistresses, yet expose the *same* for sale again within an hour afterwards, for their own benefit. I have seen country negroes take great pains, after having been spoken to by those women, to reserve what they chose to sell to them only, either by keeping the articles in their Canows, or by sending them away, and pretending they were not for sale, and when they could not be easily retained by themselves, then I have seen the wenches as briskly hustle them about from one to another that in two minutes they could no longer be traced.

The market situation set forth by "Stranger" was frequently complained of throughout this period by the Commissioners of the Markets in their public notices and by the grand juries. For example, a grand jury in 1770, complaining of a general supineness and inactivity in magistrates and others whose duty it was to carry the Negro acts into execution, recommended the amendment of the Negro law "so as to prevent idle slaves interfering with poor honest white people's supporting themselves." This was due (in the opinion of the grand jury) in some measure to such slaves "being suffered to cook, bake, sell fruits, dry goods, and other ways traffic, barter &c in the public markets & streets of Charles Town."[17]

The man with a small capital and a few acres of land could not hope to supply the market as cheaply as the planter with his

[17] *S. C. Gaz.*, Jan. 25, 1770; For the commissioners' notice see *ibid.*, Oct. 15-22, 1763.

thousands of acres and numerous slaves. He felt humiliated when he attempted to sell his produce in the market and was jostled by insolent slaves. If he remained in the low country he became a member of that dejected and hopeless class called in derision even by the slaves "poor buckras" and "poor white trash." A sentence from the *Travels* of the Duke de Rochefoucauld-Liancourt gives us a glimpse into the condition of these people. He wrote: "In the neighborhood are a few small plantations, the property of white people who keep no slaves, and who of 50 acres, which forms the necessary qualification of an elector, cultivate about 20 with their oxen. This class is poor, and, by what I have been told, seems not to deserve much respect."[18]

The more energetic among the white people "in low and indigent circumstances" began to emigrate to the West. They helped people the up-country of South Carolina; they went to western Georgia where lands could be easily obtained; ultimately many of them found their way to Kentucky and Tennessee. Their exodus was accelerated by the hard times that came after the Revolution; and the low country, left almost entirely to the planter and his slaves, had to face the problems and dangers of the chaotic time in our history known as the Critical Period without the aid of an energetic and virile middle class that had a stake in the future of the state.

[18] *Travels*, I, 601.

CHAPTER VI

THE IMMIGRANT BUSINESS

I

What the Charleston factor might or might not do with propriety forms a curious study in the economic roots of respectability in colonial Carolina. Personally he had little or no concern in selling goods directly to consumers. In eighteenth-century Charleston that sort of business, as we have already seen, with its accompaniment of haggling over prices and intimate personal relations with all sorts of persons, even slaves, was considered degrading and was relegated to an inferior order of business man—the retailer. The Charleston factor might not with dignity sell goods by the yard; but to deal in slaves and indentured white servants was a highly honorable employment. Furnishing African slaves for the plantations was the most lucrative single branch of commerce in the country, and the business of dealing in immigrants and indentured servants was profitable at a time when there was in Great Britain a class of abject, rootless, landless white persons worse off than serfs who could not be ejected from the soil or than slaves who were cared for by their masters on account of their economic value.

The most valuable part of the import business of Charleston in the eighteenth century was the traffic in white and black people. The traffic in white people may be subdivided as it concerns itself respectively with free immigrants and indentured servants, the distinction between these groups being that immigrants, having sufficient worldly goods to pay their passage to America, received grants of land upon their arrival and usually passed immediately to the frontier. The indentured servants, to reimburse the shipmasters who had transported them, were sold at public auction like African Negroes, and were under contract for terms of service varying from two to seven years.

In general the frontier of the southern colonies was peopled more rapidly than that of the colonies north of the Chesapeake region, with the exception of Pennsylvania, and there were physical, social, and military factors to account for this difference. In the North the convergence of the mountains nearer to the sea and the lack of extensive inland navigation limited the quantity of available lands, while the presence of the French on the Great Lakes, on the St. Lawrence and in Canada acted as a further check.

Slavery in the tidewater country of the South acted as a further stimulus to the western exodus, for the masters of slaves owned most of the land along the seaboard and only a few white persons were needed on the plantations. Slavery also caused the South to be weak from a military point of view, and South Carolina was the weakest of the British-American colonies with the exception of the infant colony of Georgia. In 1761, the white population of South Carolina was about thirty thousand; the number in the militia was only about six thousand men, counting one person in every five of military age. The black population was 57,253, a great portion of whom were Negro men who were imported in preference to Negro women because they were more able to perform the hard labor of the rice plantations. In 1760 Lieutenant Governor Bull tried in vain to raise one thousand men to go against the Cherokees, and feared to send out all the troops that were raised because to draw a great number of men from the settled part of the province where the Negroes greatly exceeded the whites was a dangerous procedure.[1] The fear of Negro insurrection is reflected in the presentments of a grand jury in 1765, when the nearest Indians were living two hundred miles from Charleston, complaining that there was no law requiring the inhabitants to carry arms to church with them on Sundays.[2]

The intercolonial wars had revealed clearly the great weakness of South Carolina, and the British government, influenced by considerations of military security as well as by the economic motive of increasing production and enlarging trade, began to encourage immigration by giving the new-comers desirable lands on

[1] P. R. S. C., XXIX, 90-91, 188.
[2] S. C. Gaz., Oct. 31, 1765.

111

easy terms, an¹ certain political privileges; and special inducements
were offered for the importation of indentured servants.

The great evil of land monopoly in South Carolina, whereby
a few people acquired title to many thousand acres of land, was
struck at by the requirement that all owners of lands granted by
the Lords Proprietors should take possession and begin cultivation
within a reasonable time or forfeit their claims; in the future lands
were to be granted only in proportion to the grantee's ability to
cultivate them. The allowance of fifty acres, formerly granted to
those who came to settle the wilderness, was increased to one
hundred for the. master or mistress of a family; fifty acres were
allowed for every white or black man, woman or child of which
the family consisted when the grant was made. The land was
rent-free for two years, after which a quit rent of four shillings proclamation money was due for every one hundred acres.
Every grantee who fulfilled the terms of his grant by clearing and
cultivating three acres per year for every hundred acres granted
was entitled to another grant on the same terms. Townships
of twenty thousand acres each along the rivers Altamaha, Savannah, Santee, Pedee, Waccamaw, Wateree, and Broad were laid
out in such a manner that all the inhabitants were to have access
to a river; and every parish of one hundred families was given
the right to send two members to the assembly.³

In 1761 Governor Boone had been instructed to recommend
to the assembly in the strongest terms the passage of an act giving
suitable encouragement to all who should import white servants
into South Carolina. With this policy in view he was authorized
by the British government to grant one hundred acres of land,
free of quit rent for ten years, to all white servants, men and
women, who after completing their terms of service should become
free settlers in the province. The assembly of South Carolina did
its part by enacting, on July 25, 1761, a law giving £4 sterling
toward paying the passage of every poor Protestant adult that
should come to settle South Carolina; there was an additional allowance for provisions and tools.⁴ The effect of these measures was

³ *P. R. S. C.*, XXIX, 162-169.
⁴ *Ibid.*, 165, 188.

soon felt. Ramsay informs us that the greater part of the back part of South Carolina was peopled after 1763, that in the decade following the Peace of Paris five settlements were made, one hundred and fifty miles to the westward, "beyond all that had taken place in the preceding hundred years."[5] Lieutenant Governor Bull tells us that the up-country was settled mostly by emigrants from the northern, colonies, and there were geographical reasons why this should have been true, for the approach to upper Carolina was easier from the north through the mountain valleys than from the east across sand-barrens.

Nevertheless many Europeans found their way to the backwoods of Carolina through the port of Charleston. On August 20, 1764, Lieutenant Governor Bull wrote to the Board of Trade that the act of 1761 for encouraging poor Protestant immigrants had been so effective that nearly six hundred persons had been brought over, largely within the past twelve months.[6] The gazettes chronicled the arrival up to the Revolution of indentured servants and other immigrants in groups varying in number from thirty-five to four hundred. Though South Carolina gave no bounty on the importation of immigrants after 1768, the Scotch-Irish continued to pour into the province, many of them being ignorant of the fact that the supply of lands had been exhausted. The *South Carolina Gazette* of December 24, 1772, has this remarkable announcement: "Saturday arrived the Pennsylvania Farmer from Belfast; Sunday Lord Dunluce from Larne; Tuesday the Hopewell from Belfast and Free Mason from Larne filled with Irish Passengers, above one thousand Souls."

Under the stimulus of immigration Charleston became the resort of various nationalities; its population, cosmopolitan and keenly interested in trade, reminded the traveler of Marseilles and Amsterdam. There were of course English of all classes, with Irish, Scotch, Welsh, Swiss, Germans, French, Dutch, Africans, and refugees from Acadia and the West Indies. The cosmopolitan character of the population is reflected in the various national clubs founded: In 1729, St. Andrew's Society (Scottish); in 1733, St.

[5] Ramsay, *History of South Carolina*, I, 5.
[6] *P. R. S. C.*, XXX, 186.

George's Society (English); in 1737, the South Carolina Society (French Protestants); in 1766, the German Friendly Society; in 1774, the Friendly Society of St. Patrick; and in 1791, the Hebrew Orphan Society. As Paine said, Europe, and not England alone, was becoming the mother country of America.[7]

The new settlers came chiefly from northern Europe, because it was the settled policy of the British government to permit liberty of conscience to all persons except Catholics; South Carolina also, like the other provinces, gave bounty money only to "poor Protestants." They came mostly from Ireland and Germany because social injustice was most rank in those distressed countries. C. M. Andrews gives a succinct statement of one of the causes of the discharge of the population of Europe into America during the eighteenth century, at so alarming a rate as to threaten depopulation of certain sections of Germany and Ireland. The feudal aristocracy had given place to a capitalistic aristocracy which controlled voting, made laws, and determined the policy of the government. Everywhere there was an unjust distribution of wealth and politicians were in keen pursuit of riches when the poor were living on the verge of starvation. England, says Andrews, was "a land of two nations, one privileged, wealthy, and honored, divinely invested, as it were, with the right to rule; the other unprivileged, poor, and ignored, . . . predestined . . . to be ruled." Manufactures, trade and commerce were considered more important than agriculture, and Merry England was becoming a land of pale-faced factory workers instead of a land of healthy and, in some degree, independent farmers.[8]

The British legislation that took bread out of the mouth of the Irish peasant by placing high tariffs upon Irish linen and cattle in order that the English manufacturer and the English farmer might prosper had its reverberations in America. "It is reported," says the *South Carolina Gazette* of March 26, 1772, "that 15,000 families intend to remove during the course of the current year from Ireland to America, and that, if proper Encouragement is given, five thousand of them propose to settle in this Province."

[7] *Charleston Yearbook*, 1883, 392.
[8] *Colonial Background of American Revolution*, 188-192.

A news items from Baltimore in the *South Carolina Gazette* of November 22, 1773, says: "3,500 from Londonderry have left that port within one year and come to seek in our back extensive & happy territory peaceful & comfortable existence from the oppression of Great Britain. Let the deplorable state of that once happy prosperous land fill Americans with apprehensions and rouse them with animated warmth to resist every attempt of Parliamentary Tyrrany."

II

The merchants and ship owners of Great Britain sent immigrants and indentured servants to America very much as they shipped European and East Indian goods or Negro slaves. The relative profits on the several lines of business can be pretty accurately gauged by the commissions paid the British factors at Charleston. On the "Guinea business" the factors received ten per cent, which netted them, after various expenses attendant on the sale of Negroes were paid, about eight and one-half or 9 per cent; on other kinds of business, including the immigrant business, they received five per cent.

The essential features of the immigrant business may be traced in the case of a large body of French Protestants transported to South Carolina in 1764. In the fall of 1763, about a thousand of these people who were leaving France on account of their religion arrived in England from the country around Bordeaux. A contract to transport a part of this company to South Carolina was given to Messrs. Torrans, Gregg and Poaug, a partnership composed of John Gregg, merchant of London, and the firm of Torrans and Poaug at Charleston. In January, 1764, Gregg sent out one hundred and twenty-seven passengers to Charleston for whom Torrans and Poaug collected bounty from the public treasury, paid freight and demurrage, and furnished provisions with accommodations until the immigrants were established in their new home. On July 23, 1764, John Gregg presented his account to the Lords Commissioners of Trade and Plantations as follows:

John Gregg his Account Current with Torrans & Poaug of Charles Town.[9]

By Bounty rec[d]: on 127 Passengers, the remainder of 132 landed being under 2 y[rs]: viz: 104 at £4 and 22 at £2 is £460 stg. at 700 per cent £3220/0/0

Deduct our Commission for receiv[g]: and Settling the Bounty at 2½ per cent 80/10/0

£3139/10/0

By so much received from the Owners of Ship for 14 days Subsistence of butter & beef as per calculation £72/0/0
By Ballance due Torrans & Poaug 1191/19/3

£4403/9/3

The Board of Trade finding that part of the balance arose from expenses incurred by Torrans and Poaug for maintaining the French after their arrival in Charleston, directed Lieutenant Governor Bull to recommend to the assembly to make provision for this part of the expense; the assembly accordingly appropriated £500 sterling for this purpose.[10]

Immediately upon their arrival the French petitioned for the bounty granted upon family rights, presenting at the same time to the Governor and Council receipts in full for the payment of their passage money and certificates of membership in good standing of some Protestant congregation, duly signed by a minister, church-warden, or elder. These two matters were of the utmost consequence. If the passage money had not been paid, the immigrant became willy-nilly an indentured servant, since, under the law of South Carolina, importers, in case of persons unable or unwilling to pay their passage, might take out indentures before a justice of the peace binding such persons to serve the importers or their assigns five years. All that the Governor and his Council were expected to do in such cases was to prevent the immigrant from being cheated or imposed upon. This law in the early days must have been of particular encouragement to those villains in Europe who made it a business to entice ignorant people on board their

[9] P. R. S. C., XXX, 176-178; 181.
[10] P. R. S. C., XXX, 185.

ships or kidnap them, for shipment to America. It is well to re-member, however, that when this law was in force serfdom was the common lot of a large proportion of the inhabitants of Europe.[11] A certificate of Protestantism was equally important. Otherwise the immigrant was deported, in case he had paid his passage money, or he was shipped off to some colony where Catholics were tolerated, perhaps to Maryland or to the wilds of Florida, in the hope of finding a sale for his indentures there, which was an extremely unpleasant and perhaps fatal experience for the immigrant and a losing business for the merchant.

Upon taking the oath of allegiance, the French Huguenots received warrants entitling each individual to lands varying in amount from one hundred to four hundred and fifty acres according to his family rights. Then the process of removal to the wilderness began: the men went first under the protection of a company of rangers commanded by Captain Patrick Calhoun, to put up buildings, while the women remained in Charleston. Their new home was a tract of twenty thousand acres of land laid out in a square plat, one side of which fronted the Savannah River. About eight hundred acres were reserved for a town, which was to consist of three hundred tenements, with gardens. There was also a reservation for a common, and a glebe of three hundred acres for a minister of the Established Church. The new township was called Hillsborough, in honor of the President of the Board of Trade, and the town was named New Bordeaux for the old-time home in France from which many of the settlers had come.[12]

The British government transplanted this group of French Protestants to America for the purpose of introducing the culture of silk and wine. Efforts to promote silk culture began with the immigration of the first French Protestants into South Carolina in the seventeenth century, and were renewed at intervals for more than a century. Indeed there was good reason to hope for the success of these ventures in silk and wine in South Carolina and Georgia. The climate was mild, not unlike that of Southern

---

[11] Cooper, *Statutes of South Carolina*, III, 621.
[12] *P. R. S. C.*, XXX, 185; *Council Journal*, 1763, pp. 116-122.

Europe; grape vines and mulberry trees, on which the silk worm fed, were growing wild; and the governors were sending in reports that silk of the finest sort could be raised and wine and olives produced. Besides, the remarkable success attending the introduction of the indigo industry in the middle of the eighteenth century encouraged similar undertakings.

As early as 1722 Parliament passed a silk bounty act, and the bounty law enacted in 1769 to encourage the cultivation of silk in the southern provinces gave a bounty of twenty-five per cent on all raw silk imported into Great Britain from America between January 1, 1770 and January 1, 1777; of twenty per cent from 1777 to 1784; and of fifteen per cent from 1784 to 1791.[13]   In 1766 the assembly of South Carolina appropriated £1,000 for the establishment of a silk filature in Charleston, and another factory for spinning silk was set up at Hillsborough.[14]   This legislation produced meagre results.   Silk was produced successfully on Silk Hope Plantation, on the Cooper River, and at Hillsborough.   As much as ten thousand pounds of raw silk were exported in one year, manufactured in Great Britain and returned to the province. But the silk industry could not flourish where labor was dear and population sparse.   Small profit could be made on silk compared to what could be made on rice, indigo, and hemp.   And the French Protestants imported to introduce the culture of silk soon turned to the more profitable crops.

The same lack of success attended the production of wine and for the same reason.   The penniless immigrant could not afford to invest his labor in a crop from which there could not be any return for three years.   Vines were imported from Champagne, Burgundy, and Portugal, bounties were given and the assembly appropriated money to purchase vines; it was all in vain.   Perhaps the most extensive vineyard was one on the Broad River of sixteen hundred vines founded by one Sherba, a German, who obtained in 1771 the bounty offered by the Society in London for Encouraging Arts and Manufactures.[15]

[13] MacPherson *Annals of Com.*, III, 488-489.
[14] *S. C. Gaz.*, June 23-30, 1766; *P. R. S. C.*, XXXII, 397-398.
[15] *P. R. S. C.*, XXXIII, 262-263.

III

Contemporary records give abundant testimony of the inhuman treatment of immigrants by the merchants and shipmasters. The bounty given by South Carolina on the importation of immigrants was about equivalent to the expenses of their passage, and people were persuaded to embark in such numbers that the ships coming to Carolina were overcrowded and many immigrants arrived in such a starved and weak condition that they died in Charleston before they could be transplanted to the wilderness.

Four hundred Germans from the Palatinate were transported to South Carolina in 1764. They had been persuaded to embark for America by the false promises of Lieutenant Strumpell, and when Strumpell arrived in London and found he could not keep faith with his charges he abandoned them. Of the first embarkation of these Germans, twenty died on the voyage.[16] The *South Carolina Gazette* for June 22-29, 1767, appealed to the citizens of the province to come to the aid of three hundred Irish lately arrived, almost every one of whom was confined to his bed with fever. The editor stated that he saw in several rooms "two and three score at a time,—many dying, some deprived of their senses, young children lying entirely naked whose parents had expired a few weeks ago."

Henry Laurens, one of the largest slave merchants at Charleston, who retired from that business because of the barbarities practised by some of the participaters in that trade, wrote to his friend William Fisher, a merchant of Philadelphia, on November 9, 1768: "Yet I never saw an instance of cruelty in ten or twelve years experience in that branch equal to the cruelty exercised upon those poor Irish. Self-interest prompted the baptised heathen to take some care of their wretched slaves for a market, but no other care was taken of those poor Protestant Christians from Ireland but to deliver as many as possible alive on shore upon the cheapest terms, no matter how they fared upon the voyage nor in what condition they were landed."

Yet a way was opened for even the poverty-smitten immigrant to retaliate upon the inhuman dealers. In 1767, Torrans and

[16] *Council Journal*, Dec. 14, 1764, 385; *P. R. S. C.*, XXX, 234.

Poaug, who applied to the treasurer in behalf of two Irish merchants, owners of the ship *Nancy*, for payment of the passages of Irish Protestants lately arrived, found that the bounty money was withheld by order of the governor because the Irish had set forth in a petition that they had been treated with inhumanity, pinched in provisions and water, and so crowded together that it was probably the cause of their sickness. The Committee of Investigation decided that these complaints were well founded and the bounty money was permanently withheld.[17]

In the winter of 1767, the ship *Pearl* brought into Charleston fifty indentured servants from Glasgow, who were consigned to Henry Laurens. The crew was almost in mutiny on account of the ill treatment they had received at the hands of the ship's officers, and the servant passengers filled the town with "most violent complaints" of the ill usage they had received upon the voyage. They complained to lawyers, they applied to the governor and his council and to members of the assembly. They swore they would go to law, wrote Laurens to the ship owners "and that diabolical Court the Admiralty as Pauper without Money,—could split their Complaints into 20 different Institutions, each of which would cost your Captain of your Ship at least £50 stg.—perhaps treble the Money where two or three of them would combine to swear well that they were kidnapped (as all the Irish alleged they were) and inhumanely treated besides."

Naturally, Laurens was much embarrassed. He "saw clearly that Capt. Buchanan had been a little too strict with those people and had unwarily struck some of them—but it did not appear that he had ever used them barbarously, or in such a manner as even deserved censure." However that may have been, Laurens found himself insulted in the streets by the Irish, who demanded either their bounty money granted by the province or to be set at liberty. Laurens was so harassed that he returned to the treasury the bounty money that he had collected on forty-eight of them and set them at liberty; for nobody would purchase the indentures of any of the servants. Then he went back to the treasury and collected the bounty for the importation of poor Protestants to settle

[17] *Council Journal*, July 7, 1767, 204-299.

in the province, and thus a cargo of indentured servants became bona fide immigrants. It was cases like this, as well as the fact that most of the lands of the province had been taken up, that caused the assembly to discontinue the bounty to poor Protestants after 1768.[18]

IV

On account of the prevalence of slave labor there was not a great demand in South Carolina for indentured servants, although in the first part of the colonial period numbers of the settlers of the back country belonged to this class. Fear of Negro insurrection caused the enactment of a law in 1712 requiring that there should be one white man to ten Negroes on every plantation; but presentments of the grand juries and complaints appearing in the gazettes from time to time gave evidence that the law was frequently evaded.

Upon the arrival of ninety Irish servants from Belfast whose indentures were advertised for sale in the *South Carolina Gazette* of January 14, 1764, to gentlemen who were obliged by law to have one white servant to every ten slaves upon their plantations, the editor remarked that the due observance of the law "is intended to be enforced very soon by upwards of fifty informations." By 1772 this requirement had been relaxed and the law demanded only that every settled plantation should have a white person thereon, in default whereof, the owner was subject to a fine of £10 for every month such plantation should be without such white person.[19] In spite of the fact that coasting schooners were directed by law to be provided with white patroons, the Provost Marshall, William Pinckney, gave notice in the *South Carolina Gazette* of April 30, 1771, that he was determined to prosecute owners of coasting schooners whose vessels had no white persons on board. He observed that because of violations of the law, plantations along the Ashepoo River were frequently robbed "to the great damage of the proprietors." There was perhaps a greater demand for white apprentices in Charleston than on the planta-

[18] Laurens to Pagan Brown & Co., Mch. 16, 1768; to Henry Cunningham, May 25, 1768.
[19] Stranger in the *S. C. Gaz.*, Sept. 24, 1772.

tions; for tradesmen were required to have one white apprentice to every two Negroes.

In South Carolina where persons of social rank could evade distasteful legislation with impunity and Negro slaves were imported in vast numbers, dealing in indentured servants was not a profitable business. Henry Laurens' experience is probably typical. He used the following expressions to his correspondents in regard to the indentured servant business: "Not worth their hominy to me"; "Do not know what to do with Servants—afraid they will hardly yield money enough to pay for their food"; "I fear they will soon dispose of themselves by running away into the country from whence it will not be worth bringing them back again." Laurens wrote to William Penn at St. Augustine in 1768, in regard to some servants he was forwarding for Rolle's settlement on the St. Johns, that he gained most by the servants who ran away. This statement, however, had reference as much to the visionary character of Rolle as to the fact that the Charleston merchant lost money on indentured servants because the cost of maintaining them until he could find a sale for them exceeded what the indentures and the provincial bounty would come to.[20]

White servants continued to arrive in large numbers in the sixties; but the numbers fell off in the seventies, partly because of the discontinuance of the provincial bounty. In 1766, two hundred Palatine servants arrived from Rotterdam, among whom were "millers, bakers, brewers, masons, smiths, carpenters, joiners, coopers, tailors, weavers, and potash-makers." In the fall of the same year about five hundred Palatine servants came over in the ship *Britannia*. As late as 1772 the indentures of a few families and single persons were advertised in the *South Carolina Gazette* of October 8 by Edwards, Fisher and Company.[21]

Merchants and shipmasters were obliged to declare upon oath that to the best of their knowledge none of the servants imported by them were either "what was commonly called Native Irish or persons of known scandalous character or Roman Catholics."

[20] To Alex. Gray, Jan. 26, 1768; Reynolds Getly & Co., Mch. 19, and 21, 1768; to Wm. Penn, Oct. 1, 1768.
[21] *S. C. Gaz.*, and *Country Journal*, Jan. 14, 1766; *S. C. Gaz.*, Oct. 20-27, 1766.

Notwithstanding the phrase "known scandalous character," colonial governors were strictly instructed not to give their assent to any provincial laws for the imposing of duties on the importation of felons from Great Britain into South Carolina, because such laws were in conflict with an act of Parliament (passed for the purpose of preventing "Robberies, Burglaries and other Felonies and the more effectual transportation of Felons"). Considering the savage and unequal laws concerning crime in the eighteenth century, this piece of official selfishness was probably lucky for the so-called "criminal," and certainly lucky for the naked province he was deported to populate. It would be extremely interesting to trace the history of some of these social outcasts transplanted to an environment more favorable to the development of genuine virtue, where the twin evils of great wealth and great poverty did not exist.

Apparently it was optional with the merchant whether he sold the indentures of white servants upon commission or bought them outright of the importers and resold them upon his own account. It was a precarious business either way. Indentures of undesirable servants were sometimes given away, and sometimes sold for as little as £4 sterling payable in twelve months, the price depending upon the length of service contracted for and the quality of the commodity. On the other hand, healthy white servants, mechanics, ploughmen, unencumbered with large families and without the stigma of a prison term, indented from three to four years, were sold for prices ranging from £40 to £50. However, the cost of maintaining white servants until a sale could be found for them, and the ever present prospect of their escaping to the frontier, from which it was almost impossible to recover them, made the risks involved in this business very great.[22] Merchants advertised the indentures in the newspapers along with other commodities such as flour, rum, and dry goods, and a merchant's suggestions to his correspondents for the return cargo of a ship might include servants listed with liquor and European goods.

The average indenture in South Carolina was from three to

[22] Laurens to Reynolds Getly & Co., Apr. 15, 1768; to Wm. Cowles & Co., Feb. 18, 1768.

five years and the law required that where no contract had been entered before the arrival of the servant in the province the term should be five years. Upon the expiration of their term of service servants were entitled to a certificate of their freedom; and masters refusing such certificates incurred a fine of forty shillings for each refusal.[23]

[23] Cooper, *Statutes of S. C.*, III, 15.

CHAPTER VII
THE FOREIGN SLAVE TRADE
I

In the eighteenth century the British were the greatest slave traders in the world notwithstanding Lord Mansfield's decision, in 1770, in the celebrated Somerset case, which put an end to the trafficking in slaves out of British ports, and the leading part subsequently taken by England in the movement for abolishing the slave trade. In the year of Mansfield's decision, however, one hundred and ninety-two ships sailed from British ports bound for the coast of Africa to import slaves into British-America and the rest of the benighted world. A few years later the poet Cowper gave imperishable expression to the sentiment that the air of England was too pure for slaves to breathe in the familiar lines:[1]

> Slaves cannot breathe in England! if their lungs
> Receive our air, that moment they are free;
> They touch our country, and their shackles fall.

The share of the slave trade which fell to the British lion may be roughly indicated by estimates made for the year 1768, when ninety-seven thousand Negroes were supposed to have been carried from Africa by Europeans:[2]

By British vessels	53,100	59,400
By British vessels	53,000	59,400
By British-American vessels	6,300	
By French vessels		23,520
By Dutch vessels		11,300
By Portuguese vessels		1,700
By Danish vessels		1,200
		97,100

[1] But the shackles did not fall when the slave reached England. They fell only if the master attempted to change his status, e.g., from that of domestic servant to that of an article of merchandise and the case came before the English courts which did not recognize slavery as legal. Catterall, *Judicial Cases Concerning American Slavery*, I, chapters I and II.

[2] MacPherson, *Annals of Com.*, III, 484.

Carrying off Negroes at this rate soon almost depopulated the African coast. In the latter part of the eighteenth century Negroes were being sought at a distance of three hundred miles into the interior of the continent and there was a prospect that this lucrative branch of commerce would soon cease for lack of material. In the 1780's it was estimated that about sixty-two thousand Negroes were exported from Africa annually. Of these England carried off forty thousand, France twelve thousand, Holland six thousand and Portugal four thousand. There were still Spanish and Danish settlements on the coast but they were carrying on little Negro trade.[3]

As the supply of slaves from Africa declined, the sentiment that slavery was a great moral evil began to gain headway in Europe, and Englishmen began to suggest that South Carolina follow the example of their own country and abolish slavery, which was interwoven into the fabric of the economic life of the South. The result of this was that Southerners were early put on the defensive concerning the institution of slavery. They resented especially such suggestions from England much as they later resented the proposals of northern abolitionists. In 1786, when an English correspondent of Laurens recommended to him the example of his own country respecting slavery, Laurens replied that the English attitude in regard to slavery was "similar to that of a pious, externally pious Man's prohibiting fornication under his own roof and keeping a dozen mistresses abroad."[4]

London, Bristol, Liverpool, Manchester, Birmingham throve upon the slave trade. During the later colonial period, however, Liverpool surpassed all the other English cities and became the principal port in that branch of business. In 1709 Liverpool had only one vessel employed in the slave trade; but in 1730 the removal of duties upon the trade brought the city into the field with such energy that by 1760 she was sending out seventy-four vessels of 8,178 tons, and by 1773 one hundred and five vessels of 11,056 tons. The Revolutionary War greatly injured the Liverpool slave trade and in 1779 she employed only eleven vessels of 1,205

[3] Charleston *Morning Post*, June 24, 1786. Other estimates are found in MacPherson, *Annals of Com.*, IV, 152.

[4] To Edward Bridgeon, Feb. 13, 1786.

tons. With the end of the war she returned to the business with renewed zeal sending out in 1783—eighty-five vessels of 12,294 tons, in 1790—ninety-one of 17,917 tons, and in 1792—one hundred and thirty-two of 22,402 tons. Perhaps she reached the high watermark in 1801 when she employed in the slave business one hundred and fifty ships with a capacity for 52,557 slaves, according to the reduced rating of five slaves to every three tons burden required by the parliamentary act of 1788.[5]

Newport, Rhode Island, had the reputation of being a sort of American Liverpool. Acceptable statistics of the American slave trade are lacking, but the few scraps of business at Charleston falling to the American slaver from the master's table during the colonial period may be indicated by a notice in the *South Carolina Gazette* of July 26, 1773, which states that from November 1, 1772, to the present 6,471 Negroes have been imported into Charleston, viz:

From the West Indies (in 26 vessels) 700
From the Northern Colonies (in 6 vessels) 40
Directly from Africa in 33 vessels 5,731

6,471

In 1784 South Carolina placed a duty of £3 sterling on Negroes imported from Asia and Africa and a duty of £5 sterling was placed on those from any other part of the world, but Negroes imported from any part of the United States after a residence of six months were allowed to come in duty free.[6] This legislation, which discriminated against the British in order to favor the American trader, as well as the fact that great numbers of Negroes had been destroyed in South Carolina and Georgia during the war, must have had the effect of increasing the slave business of Newport and other northern towns.

[5] MacPherson, *Annals of Com.*, IV, Appendix No. 4; Phillips, *Amer. Negro Slavery*, 32.
[6] Cooper, *Statutes of S. C.*, IV, 608; Ships bringing slaves into Carolina from Africa were usually British. See also E. Donnan, *Documents Illustrative of the History of the Slave Trade to America.*

II

For nearly half of the sixty-one years between 1702 and 1763 Great Britain was engaged in wars in which the colonies were involved. From 1739 to 1763 there was continuous war with the exception of a breathing spell of six years between 1748 and 1754, and these conflicts interfered to some extent with the slave trade into South Carolina. The period after 1763 is characterized by freedom from war and devotion to business which brought South Carolina an expansion of trade and a prosperity such as the province had never experienced before. More slaves were imported into South Carolina than ever before in its history and they were sold for higher prices; in the course of a decade the price of slaves doubled. For the nine years from 1756 to 1765 an average of 1,894 slaves per annum were imported, the great majority of these probably coming in after the tide of war had turned in favor of Great Britain, 3,740 being imported in 1760.[7] After 1763, when a great agricultural development was going forward in South Carolina, Georgia and East Florida, under normal circumstances, from one thousand to two thousand more slaves per annum were coming into South Carolina than in the period before the French War. What was generally true of this period is expressed in a letter of Lieutenant Governor Bull to the Board of Trade. He wrote: "Though by our annual importation of 3 or 4,000 Negroes the balance of trade may lie against us, yet we cannot be considered in debt as the negroes remain part of our stock and are the means of increasing our riches."[8]

In general the policy of the British government in regard to the slave trade into South Carolina was to permit only such legislation as did not interfere with the business of the British merchant except where the welfare and safety of the province were concerned. The British merchant usually favored a provincial duty on the importation of slaves because he was interested not only in selling slaves but in making collections for slaves sold. The duty was a check on the planter's avidity for slaves and made him more able to pay for the slaves he purchased. The annual ex-

[7] S. C. Gaz., July 6, 1769.
[8] P. R. S. C., XXXII, 401.

pense of maintaining the provincial government in normal times before the Revolution was about £20,000 sterling, one-half of which was raised by duties on imported Negroes payable by the first purchaser.[9] The vast majority of these Negroes were imported direct from Africa and colonial governors were specifically instructed not to approve laws imposing duties payable by the importer on Negroes imported into South Carolina because such laws were a great discouragement to the British merchants trading to the coast of Africa.[10]

Normally the duty on grown Negroes from Africa was £10 currency, payable by the first purchaser. The General Duty Law of 1751, which was in force except for brief intervals until the Revolution, provided for a duty of £10 on all Negroes four feet two inches in height and £5 and £2½ respectively on smaller ones. On the other hand, higher duties were allowed on slaves brought in from the other colonies. This was done not only to restrict the intercolonial slave trade and at the same time encourage that of the British merchant, but also because of prejudice in South Carolina against Negroes from other places than the coast of Africa. It was believed that Negroes from the Spanish colonies incited others to escape, and that slaves from other English colonies had been sent away by the courts of justice for crimes or by private individuals for their bad qualities, particularly roguery. During the first part of the eighteenth century a duty of £30 currency was laid on all "seasoned" Negroes imported into South Carolina, which duty was increased to £50 in 1772 and to £60 in 1771.[11]

The General Duty Law of 1751 expired in 1761 and was not revived for several years, with the result that there was a period of free importation of Negroes from Africa from 1761 to 1766. This must have injured the business of the British merchant, for the Charleston factors favored a revival of the General Duty Law of 1751 and it was through their co-operation that a law was passed on August 25, 1764, laying an additional duty of £100

[9] Moore, *Materials for History*, 185.
[10] Cooper, *Statutes of S. C.*, III, 738-747.
[11] Cooper, *Statutes of S. C.*, III, 57,743; Laurens to J. Burnett, Sept. 7, 1771.

.currency upon all Negroes imported into the province for a period of three years beginning January 1, 1766. The £110 duty thus laid on Negroes from Africa amounted to a prohibition.[12] The two-fold purpose of the law, which was to lessen the danger of insurrection resulting from the importation of so many savages from Africa, and to allow the British merchants to collect outstanding debts, was defeated. The merchants, anticipating the prohibitive duty in 1766, poured vast numbers of Negroes into Charleston in 1765. In a little more than six months after the first of January 5,082 slaves had been imported, which had cost the planters about £177,870 sterling, and by the end of the year Lieutenant Governor Bull was reporting that above eight thousand had been imported, which was nearly equal to three years' importation.[13] On the approach of the Christmas holidays, when the slaves were given a few days for festivity, Bull became apprehensive of Negro insurrection and ordered the militia and patrols to be on guard constantly for fourteen days before and after Christmas. He also hired forty-seven Catawba Indians, who were a terror to the Negroes, to track the runaways who had taken refuge in the swamps.[14]

When the slave trade was reopened in 1769 after three years' abstinence, the merchants were writing to their correspondents that great sales were expected. One of the greatest crops in the history of the colony had been made for which high prices had been received: but the planters "did not discover that eagerness for buying" that was expected of them. They had begun by this time to realize the full import of the Townshend Acts, passed in 1767, which laid duties on tea, glass, paper, lead and painter's colors in order to maintain the British civil service. Some of the northern colonies had entered into non-importation resolutions by which they agreed to import only certain specified British manufactures until the Townshend Acts were repealed. The strict enforcement of the Navigation Acts, especially through the agency of naval officers unacquainted with custom house law and procedure,

[12] Cooper, *Statutes of S. C.*, IV, 187-188; Laurens to John Knight, Aug. 24, 1764 and to John Moultrie, Jan. 28, 1768.
[13] *S. C. Gaz.*, June 22-29, 1765; *P. R. S. C.*, XXX, 300.
[14] *P. R. S. C.*, XXXI, 20-21; *ibid.*, 300-301.

had embroiled some of the Charleston merchants in quarrels with the king's officers. Although the planters were "full of money" and many of them out of debt, they were cautious on account of their apprehension concerning the new taxes. Nevertheless, the great number of about five thousand slaves was imported into South Carolina in 1769, which, however, averaged only a little more than £27 sterling per head, whereas the great importation of 1765, which exceeded that of 1769 by about three thousand Negroes, sold on an average for about £35 sterling per head.[15]

In the mid-summer of 1769 South Carolina, like the other colonies, decided she was unconstitutionally taxed through the Townshend Acts, and entered into resolutions of non-importation by which no slaves were to be imported until there was a satisfactory settlement of the matters in dispute with the mother country. Peter Timothy wrote in the *Gazette* of March 29, 1770: "But for the General Resolutions entered into by the Inhabitants of this Province, it is computed that the British Merchants would have drawn from us this year,—no less a sum than £200,000 stg. for the article of slaves alone, purchased chiefly with British manufactures. Can there be a more Glaring Instance of the Impropriety of attempting to tax Britons in America?"

The non-importation association was broken up in South Carolina too late to affect appreciably the number of importations from Africa in 1771; but in 1772, 4,865 Negroes were imported and were selling in the autumn of that year for more than double the price they commanded ten years before.[16] And the year 1773 was a sort of *annus mirabilis* in the annals of the Carolina slave business. In the *South Carolina Gazette* of June 28, 1773, is an announcement that "Upward of 3,800 (Negroes) have been imported here since the beginning of May, yet they are all sold, and the demand for them continues, which proves a rapid increase of wealth and Inhabitants in this Province." By mid-summer the enormous importation of slaves had created such an extraordinary demand for corn that the exportation of it was prohibited in

---

[15] Laurens to Ross & Mill, Dec. 24, 1768, Mch. 11 and 31, 1769; To Smith & Baillies, Sept. 17, 1768; *S. C. Gaz.*, Sept. 27, 1773. Timothy's figures for Negro importation—4,865; Bull's—5,438 in *P. R. S. C.*, XXX, 300.

[16] *S. C. Gaz.*, Aug. 20, 1772; *ibid.*, May 31, 1773.

Georgia, where more than a thousand Negroes had been purchased. By September 27, forty-two Guineamen had arrived in
Charleston bringing about 8,050 slaves; the fiscal year of the
province ended November 1, when the slave business was about
over for the year.[17]

In the *South Carolina Gazette* of May 31, 1773, 1,365 Negroes were advertised for sale by a half dozen firms: 65 by Miles
Brewton; 175 Whydah and 155 Sierra Leone Negroes by Pow-
ell, Hopton and Company, protégés of Henry Laurens; 190 by
Inglis and Lloyd; 480 by Roger Smith and Alex. Inglis; 160 by
Edwards, Fisher & Co.; and 140 by John Simpson & Co. 1015
of these were advertised to be sold in Charleston on June 8 and
350 on June 7.

Both McCrady, the state historian, who has collected a mass
of highly informative material concerning the Revolutionary era,
and Elizabeth Donnan, who contributed a scholarly article on the
"Slave Trade into South Carolina before the Revolution" to the
American Historical Review for July, 1928, make a curious error
in regard to the number of Negroes imported into South Carolina
in 1773. Both errors are based on a statement appearing in the
South Carolina Gazette of May 31, 1773, to the effect that the
greatest quantity of Negroes imported in one year was 7,184 in
1765, "which is 4,457 less than have arrived the present year."
McCrady adding these two sums makes the statement that by
May 31, 1773, the annual importation had reached the figures of
11,641. Miss Donnan, thinking perhaps that 11,641 were
enough, in all conscience, for one year, gives 11,641 as the whole
importation for the year 1773.[18] If either of these statements
were true, they would represent the year 1773 as being even more
remarkable than it was; for they would make the canny Scottish
and British merchants send into South Carolina unprecedentedly
large numbers of slaves in the cold winter months when they would
unquestionably have lost a goodly portion of their merchandise
through the diseases engendered by change of climate; on this ac-

[17] *Ibid.*, July 26, Sept. 20 and 27, 1773.
[18] McCrady, *S. C. under Royal Government*, 380-381; Miss Donnan gives the *Gazette* of May 31, 1773, as a reference for these figures.

count it seems to have been the custom not to send any large number of Negroes to the Carolina market until the first warm days of spring.

The figures for the slave importation given in the *Gazette* of May 31 contain an error which was corrected in the *Gazette* of June 7, which carries the following notice: "In the second paragraph of our last Monday's Charles Town Intelligence, relative to the Importation of negroes, for less read more"; which would give the wholly reasonable number of 2,727 Negroes imported by May 31. The *Gazette* for September 20 contains this paragraph:

The number of slaves imported here since the First Day of Nov. last, now amounts to 7,507—6,768 of them in 39 Guinesmen directly from the Coast of Africa. The Ship, Hawke, Captain Ralph, of Liverpoole, took a Pilot on Board last Wednesday, off the Bar, but has not yet got in: This ship will make the 40th, and is said to have upwards of 300 Negroes on Board.

The *Gazette* for September 27 reports:

On Wednesday arrived here the Hawke, from Africa, with about 250 Slaves consigned to Messrs. Robert, John and James Smyth; the Nancy with 120 more, to Messrs. Edwards, Fisher, and Company; and on Saturday, The King George with about 160, to Miles Brewton, Esq—These arrivals have increased the number of Guinesmen to 42 and the number of Negroes imported to about 8050.

The fiscal year for the province ended on November 1 and it is not likely that any great number of guineamen arrived in October. Laurens regarded the Negro business as practically closed after September.

The *South Carolina Gazette* contains no statistics for the year 1774; but a statement in the issue of September 19 that "No less than 27 cargoes of Slaves arrived here this year directly from the Coast of Africa, besides many smaller parcels from the West Indies &c. by which the colony is supposed to have been brought into debt not less than £200,000 stg." leads naturally to the supposition that the importation for the year 1774 was about the same as that for 1769, that is about five thousand.

The information given above as to the number of slaves imported from year to year is taken from two sources: From statistics given by Peter Timothy, editor of the *South Carolina Gazette,* in his newspaper; and from reports made by the governors to the Board of Trade, mostly from Lieutenant Governor Bull's reports. Timothy and Bull usually vary in their reports by several hundred Negroes, which may be accounted for by the fact that Bull's figures are from Christmas to Christmas in accordance with instructions from the Board of Trade; while Timothy reckons from November to November, which was the fiscal year in South Carolina; or Bull's figures may represent the total importation into South Carolina and Timothy's the figures for Charleston, the import trade of Beaufort and Georgetown being trifling. For example, Bull says for 1765 "that above 8,000 have been imported this year," while Timothy gives 7,184 imports for this year. Similarly, in 1770, Bull says: "Since the 1st of January 1769 there were 5,438 negroes imported, and sold for about £200,000 sterling" while Timothy says 4,612 Negroes were imported in 1769.[19]

Efforts to arrive at the exact number of slaves imported within a given year by counting the number of Negroes arriving in the various slave ships as given in the newspapers or by counting the number of slaves advertised for sale by the merchants in the *South Carolina Gazette,* which had a circulation extending through North and South Carolina, Georgia and Florida, gave unsatisfactory results, that is, the total obtained in this way always falls short of the figures given by Bull and Timothy. This discrepancy may be accounted for by the fact that many slave cargoes were never advertised in the newspapers, but were consigned to Charleston merchants to be forwarded to some merchant in Georgia or East Florida. These cargoes were brought into port, often paid import duty, in case there were no coasting vessel ready to receive them, and were counted in the Charleston importation, but were frequently not advertised in the newspapers. Also it was the custom upon the arrival of African cargoes not only to advertise them in the *Gazettes,* but to send out what were called expresses or messengers into the country as far as Georgia and North Carolina with handbills advertising the slaves. From Savannah, in turn, ex-

[19] MacPherson, *Annals of Com.,* III, 503-504; *S. C. Gaz.,* Sept. 27, 1773; *P. R. S. C.,* XXX, 300.

presses were sent as far as St. Augustine.   Henry Laurens definitely counted upon certain firms in Georgia to handle slave cargoes for him.   In 1767 and 1768 when slaves could not be sold in South Carolina except under the incubus of a prohibitive duty, he was apparently doing a very good business by directing slave cargoes which would otherwise have gone to Charleston for destinations in Georgia.   The South Carolina law favored inter-colonial traffic in slaves by allowing a drawback of three-fourths of the duty upon slaves upon their exportation.[20]

However much the slave trade into South Carolina may have been interrupted by prohibitive duties and by political disputes with the mother country, the merchants of Great Britain managed to prosecute a highly profitable business.   There were 23,743 slaves imported into Charleston in the decade ending in 1766, and in the twenty years extending from 1753 to 1773, 43,965 Negroes were brought in.   The foundations were being laid deep and strong for the peculiar civilization of the South, wherein the prosperity and welfare of the white man are inseparably linked with the prosperity and welfare of the black man, and to which the black man has contributed his special gifts of song and story with those homely homespun virtues naturally adhering to a people of the fields who earn their bread in the sweat of their brows.

By way of résumé it may be said that after 1763 three or four thousand Negroes were imported annually into South Carolina. From 1756 to 1765 the average annual importation was 1,894; in 1765, 7,184 were imported in anticipation of the prohibitive duty on slaves extending from 1766 to 1769, which practically closed the traffic in slaves for three years.   Upon the resumption of the slave trade in 1769 only 4,612 were imported, the traffic being appreciably influenced by the disputes between England and the colonies over taxation.   1770 and 1771 were off-years in the slave trade on account of the resolutions of non-importation into which South Carolina had entered because of the Townshend Acts.   In 1772 the colony made up for two years of abstinence by importing 4,865 slaves; and in 1773 the climax of slave importa-

[20] Laurens to Clay and Habersham, Oct. 26 and Nov. 25, 1767; to Smith and Baillie, Oct. 22 and Jan. 15, 1768; Cooper, *Statutes of S. C.*, III, 743.

tion was reached when the number brought in was more than 8,000. In 1774 there was a considerable falling off in the slave importation, only about 5,000 being brought in; and by 1775 South Carolina's accession to the Continental Non-Importation Association cut off practically all slave importations until the disputes with the mother country were settled by a long and costly civil war.

III

By the middle of the eighteenth century the African slave trade was no longer carried on by royal companies chartered by a sovereign giving to certain favored subjects a monopoly of the slave trade in certain regions. The last of these companies—the Royal African Company, chartered by Charles II, in 1662, the membership of which included the Queen Dowager and the Duke of York—had been broken up legally in 1752 when the Royal African Company was divested of its charter which entitled it to a monopoly of the trade in the regions from Salee, on the Moroccan coast, to the Cape of Good Hope; but actually some time earlier by the inroads made on its business by the encroachments of the private traders; and the action of the British government which opened the trade to companies of merchants regulated by law was merely legalizing what had been actual practice.[21]

Certain English cities were empowered by law to engage in the slave trade, for example, Manchester and Birmingham; but slave ships were authorized to set sail for Africa from only three ports: London, Bristol, and Liverpool. The slave dealers left England with a cargo of British manufactures which they bartered at the company's factory or factories on the coast of Africa for slaves, it being the chief business of the merchants at the factories to procure slaves for the ships in their concern, or the dealers might buy slaves from the independent black merchants at a slightly lower figure. The English government did its part by furnishing, at the expense of the English taxpayers, men of war, forts and castles guarded by soldiers, and by sending out governors to protect and promote the slave business.

[21] Anderson, *Origins of Com.*, III, 175; DuBois, *Suppression of the African Slave Trade to the U. S.*, 4-24.

Slaves exchanged for goods were branded, as men brand horses and cattle, in several places: one brand indicated the race or tribe of the slave, an important matter, for some races brought much higher prices than others; other brands, perhaps, distinguished the purchases of the different customers. Descriptions of runaway slaves in the colonial newspapers show that slaves were frequently identified by means of their brands. The following advertisements are typical of numerous advertisements appearing in every issue of the gazettes, usually prefaced by the words "Brought to the Workhouse":

"A negro wench named Kate of the Coromante Country— With her Country Marks on her stomach, and on both her arms."

"A negro man of the Guinea country—had his country Marks on his left Breast, and all over his Belly, and is branded on his Back, but it Cannot be made out."

Bills of lading for slaves sometimes, perhaps always, expressed the brand, as shown in the following bill of lading for slaves, shipped in 1766 to a Charleston firm to be forwarded to Georgia:[22]

Shipped, by the grace of God in good order and well condition'd by James [surname illegible] in and upon the good ship call'd the Mary Borough, whereof is master, under God for this present voyage, Captain David Morton, and now riding at anchor at the Barr of Senegal, and by Gods grace bound for Georgey, in South Carolina, to say twenty-four prime Slaves, six prime women Slaves, being mark'd and number'd as in the margin, and are to be deliver'd, in the like good order and well condition'd, (the danger of the Seas and Mortality only excepted) unto Messrs. Broughton and Smith, or to their Assigns; he or they paying Freight for the said Slaves at the rate of Five pounds sterling per head at delivery, with Primage and Avrage accustom'd,—In Witness whereof, the Master or Purser of the said Ship hath affirm'd to three Bills of Lading, all of this tenor and date; the one of which being accomplish'd, the other two to stand void; and so God send the good Ship to her desir'd port in safety, Amen.

Marked on the Right Buttock
O
O

Dated in Senegal, 1st February, 1766.
David Morton.

[22] Brooke, *Liverpool as it was During the Last Quarter of the Eighteenth Century*, 235.

The slave ships were crowded to capacity and the mortality among the unfortunate Negroes must have been frightful in the early days. Even in the last quarter of the eighteenth century, when measures had been taken to protect the Negroes, it was said that the purchaser of twenty new Negroes was lucky if fifteen of them were alive at the end of three years, so great were the hardships they were called upon to suffer in the middle passage. The nations found at length that inhumanity did not pay even in pounds, shillings, and pence. The Portuguese, who carried twenty thousand slaves a year to their colony of Brazil, were giving in 1788 a premium for every slave that arrived alive; the French were also giving premiums for the delivery of slaves alive; and the English in the same year by act of Parliament decreed that only five slaves could be carried to every three tons burden of the vessel. A premium of £100 to the master of the vessel and £50 to the surgeon was allowed in case no more than two in one hundred slaves died on the voyage, and half those sums if the loss did not exceed three in one hundred. Because humanity paid in handling valuable human cargoes from Africa, the Negro was much better treated en route to his American destination than the poverty stricken white European emigrant.[23]

The West Indies were a sort of clearing house for slaves. Here the Guineamen usually halted and the ship's surgeons prepared the Negroes for market by rubbing their skins with oil and closing their wounds and scars with mercurial ointment and other drugs, after which they were sorted into classes. The first class contained the healthy and prime slaves; the second class, the weak and puny, with those under age and the superannuated; and the third class, the refuse, consisted of those whose energies were so depleted that no art could make them appear passable. Refuse Negroes sometimes sold as low as a dollar a head since most of them died in a short time. Doctors sometimes made a practice of buying the most promising of them, treating their ailments, and later putting them on the market. Carolina merchants seemed to count upon having a few refuse Negroes in every "parcel" that

[23] MacPherson, *Annals of Com.*, IV, 164-166.

came from the West Indies, who remained a long time on their hands before a purchaser could be found.[24]

Frequently cargoes of slaves were advertised as being "prime" because they were picked out of several cargoes in the West Indies. The nearness of Charleston to the great slave mart of the West Indies was of real advantage to the retail merchants who did not have extensive connections with the great English firms and who therefore received few or no slave cargoes from Africa; they were, however, able to participate in the benefits of the lucrative trade in "new" Negroes by sending for small "parcels" to the West Indies to sell along with their other commodities. The great factors also supplemented their stock of African Negroes by receiving remittances from their West Indian correspondents in the form of "new" Negroes. For "seasoned" Negroes of the West Indies, however, there was little or no demand in Carolina, and a prohibitive duty was placed on their importation, it being assumed by the Carolina dealers that there was something wrong with an exported "seasoned" Negro.

Frequently the captain of a slaver acted as a merchant and disposed of his cargo, having received general instructions as to the terms of sale and houses where slaves could be best sold; or he might be guided by the advice of some trusted Charleston factor. For many years after Laurens retired from active participation in the slave trade, he capitalized his thorough knowledge of the Carolina market and received a commission from certain British firms for advising masters of ships how slave cargoes might be disposed of to the best advantage. The Guinea captains were described by Peletiah Webster in his Journal as "a rough sort of people but somewhat caressed by the Charleston merchants on account of the high profits of their commissions."[25]

Generally, however, the slave cargoes were consigned to some merchant or factor in partnership with the English firm which had sent out the slaves, and frequently the Charleston factor was part owner of the slave ship. Sometimes the cargo was turned over to some Guinea factor who was under definite contract to dispose

[24] Ibid., 146-147.
[25] Webster, Journal of a Voyage to Charleston, 1764, p. 144.

of the Negroes on commission for one or more English firms. Torrans, Gregg, and Poaug, mentioned in connection with the Immigrant Business, was an example of the first kind of method, Torrans and Poaug constituting the Charleston branch of the firm. Laurens, who was in business by himself during the period after 1763, acted mostly in the capacity of a commission merchant, being suspicious of the involvements of a partnership.

The Guinea factor or merchant did not confine himself to slaves, but did a general importing business, commingling in his advertisements slaves with other commodities, as the following advertisement shows:

To be sold at Charles Town upward of 46 healthy likely negroes, all well cloathed, Just arived after a Passage of 5 days from New Providence
Lloyd & Meyle
who have to dispose of, a few pipes of choice Madeira Wine & some Mahogany Plank.

The gazettes announced the arrival of slave ships at any season of the year; but the big slave ships did not begin to come in before spring, often as late as April, thus saving the dealers the expense of additional clothing and diminishing the chance of losing slaves through change of climate. Also winter cargoes did not usually fetch so good a price as those arriving at other seasons. "If they come later than October," says Laurens, "they should have a warm Jacket and Breeches." He regarded the season for selling Negroes as practically over by September. Special care was necessary, too, on the part of the purchaser of Negroes arriving in the winter. James Habersham, who contemplated buying some slaves in Charleston for Governor Wright of Georgia in the winter of 1772, wrote to the governor that he hoped the slaves would "go tolerably reasonable" since the season for buying Negroes was not very favorable, and he expected "to have them brought round within Land in a warm decked vessel" for "they must be treated carefully at this season of the year."[26]

The prices which Negroes brought depended, among other things, upon whether they were sold for cash, short credit or long credit. Short credit usually meant from one to six months, long

[26] *Col. of Ga. His. Soc.*, VI, 216.

credit meant a year or more. Those who paid cash got their
slaves about ten per cent cheaper than those who received credit,
even if the credit was only for two or three months. Negroes
were paid for in produce—usually in rice and indigo—in bills of
exchange on England, and in cash.

The common method of selling Negroes before 1732 was for
payments of rice on time, the rice being valued at about 37/6 per
hundred-weight, the casks going for nothing. If the planter
failed to make payments, the ten per cent interest per annum allowed on the debt added considerably to the factor's commission;
for he was under contract only to remit the rice when he received
it. After 1732 the planters became more prosperous and the British
merchants more strict in their demands. The factor was required
to make good all bad debts, to remit two-thirds of the purchase
price of the slaves in twelve months and the other one-third within
two years after the date of the sale.[27]

In the prosperous years after 1763 a new kind of installment
payment for Negroes was introduced into Carolina from the West
Indies. It was referred to by Laurens as "the modern method of
remitting in the bottom." Laurens, who began to contract his
slave business about 1764, was accustomed to have cargoes of Negroes consigned to him which he sold for a known commission of
five per cent upon sales and five per cent upon returns, and he
agreed to remit a certain per cent of the proceeds of the sales at
certain stipulated periods. By this method the factor earned a
commission of eight and one-half to nine per cent after all the
expenses of the sales were paid. Laurens sold Negroes for cash,
for three months credit, or for as much as twelve and fifteen
months credit, on the planter's bond bearing interest at eight per
cent. He was thus acting simply as a factor transacting business
for a definite commission.

The Carolina slave market was not so dependable and steady
as the West Indian. Carolina slaves subsisted chiefly on home
grown provisions and Charleston exported besides quantities of

[27] See article in *S. C. Gaz.*, for Mch. 9, 1738 quoted by McCrady in "Slavery in
the Province of S. C.," *Amer. His. Assoc. Annual Rpt.*, 1895, 655 *et seq.*

provisions to the West Indies. The West Indian slaves lived altogether upon imported provisions, and supplies for their maintenance
could be drawn from all the American colonies from Massachusetts to Georgia. In Carolina when there was a large crop of
rice and plenty of provisions were raised, large sales of Negroes
were expected. In bad crop years the reverse was true. Laurens
described the Carolina market as "either high or too low to live
by." In the West Indies prices did not vary greatly because if a
good market for Negroes was not found in one island, the merchant ship could go to another with a chance of doing better;
hence a stricter method of remittance grew up by which the English merchant received his money earlier and oftener.

The new terms of remittance, not suited to the Carolina market, were forced upon the Charleston merchants by the English
dealers. A stated price for each cargo was fixed and the factor
undertook to sell the Negroes at so much per head and to remit
specified sums at such times as were agreed upon, such as 3-6-9 or
3-6-12 or 3-6-15 months. Under the new method a merchant
who used good judgment in disposing of his slaves and was a good
debt collector, could gain in good crop years from twelve to seventeen per cent upon the sum which he remitted to England,
whereas by the old method nine per cent was the highest commission possible; but an element of speculation had entered the
business. In poor crop years the planters could not meet their
obligations and the factor who was under contract to remit stood
a very good chance of losing.

What particularly recommended the new method to the English merchants was that payments for slaves began at once. The
slave ship after discharging its cargo of human freight went up the
"freshes," that is the fresh water part of the Cooper River, to
undergo repairs before attempting another voyage and to be ex-
empt from attacks by the worms, which were so destructive to the
ship's bottom in salt water. There it remained for two or three
months while the factor was laying up a cargo of rice, indigo, and
deerskins for the return trip to England, the balance on account
of the first payment being paid in bills of exchange. And thus

bills in the bottom, as the English merchants said, kept the wheel in motion.[28]

Other considerations affecting the sale of slaves as set forth in advertisements were: the place from which they were imported and the tribe to which they belonged; their physical condition; their age; and the length of time they had been en route to their destination.

Slaves direct from Africa were always preferred to Negroes from the West Indies or the other American colonies. There was a prejudice against even "new" Negroes who had halted at the West Indies for any length of time before being exported, and the merchant always explained in his advertisement of West Indian slaves that they were prime slaves picked out of a large cargo, or sometimes out of three large cargoes "lately arrived from the coast."

In the eighteenth century the people of the southern provinces were becoming well educated in the geography of Africa. Whydah Negroes were advertised in the newspapers; Negroes of the Coromantee and Fantee[28a] Countries; from Angola, Sierra, Leon, Senegal, Guinea; Negroes from the Windward and Grain Coast, from the Rice Coast, and from the Gold Coast. Janet Schaw says in her *Journal of a Lady of Quality* that it behooves the planter to consider whence he purchases his slaves; those from one coast are mere brutes, fit only for the fields, while those from another are bad field Negroes, but faithful house servants.[29]

An article in the *Gentleman's Magazine* for October, 1764 (vol. 34), entitled "Negroes, their importance, with rules for Chusing them" informs its readers that Congo Negroes are comely and docile, but not hardy enough for the labor of the fields, they should therefore be kept for household business, or taught the mechanic arts, and they will then turn them to very good account; that the Papaws from the Gold Coast are the best for field labor; that the Coromantee will never brook servitude,

---

[28] For the terms of contract between the English merchant and his Charleston factor see: Laurens to John Knight, June 12, 1764; to Richard Oswald, May 24, 1768; to Henry Bright, Aug. 25, 1768; to Ross Mill & Co., Aug. 17, and Sept. 2, 1768.

[28a] The word "Fantee" probably means "Bantu."

[29] P. 128.

though young, but will either destroy himself or murder his master.

In Carolina where the demand for field slaves was very heavy, the words "Gold Coast" and "Gambia" were synonyms of quality. "Gold Coast Negroes" in blazing letters were the introductory words of many advertisements, and in the advertisements of other Negroes one runs across such descriptive expressions as "remarkably fine negroes, such as are usually imported from Gambia." The Negroes of Sierra Leone and along the Gambia River were partly civilized and operated plantations on which were cultivated corn, pepper, tobacco of an inferior kind, and rice, which was said to be superior to that of Carolina. Sometimes Negroes from these regions if employed about the Negro factories or in the homes of English business men in Africa, could speak English and such slaves upon their arrival in Carolina were specially advertised and were kept separate from the other Negroes in the Negro yard, because they brought higher prices. In one instance, at least, Negroes of this description were apprenticed to a shipwright for five years upon their arrival, and were advertised for sale on that understanding.[30]

The physical condition of the slave was an important consideration to the purchaser. In the advertisements of slaves the following descriptive adjectives were repeated over and over: "prime," "likely," "healthy," "choice," "healthy and likely," "young and lusty," "all in good health and have had the smallpox." The smallpox was such a scourge in colonial times that an epidemic of it often put a stop entirely to the slave merchant's business, and there were very strict laws requiring slave ships to submit to quarantine before landing cargoes. Therefore, whether a slave had had the smallpox or had been exposed to it was a very serious matter, and one finds advertisements ending with the statement that most of the slaves for sale have had the smallpox in their own country. As a health precaution, it was forbidden in 1785 to bring Negroes ashore without decent clothing, or to continue them on shore longer than from sunrise to sunset.[31]

[30] MacPherson, *Annals of Com.*, IV, 141; *S. C. Gaz.*, June 22, 1769 and Dec. 3, 1772; *Gaz. of the State of S. C.*, Jan. 13, 1785.
[31] *Ordinances of the City Council of Charleston*, Sept. 1, 1785, p. 31.

The author of "Negroes, their importance, with rules for Chusing them," mentioned above, tells us that Negroes should never be bought old, for such slaves are always sullen and unteachable, and frequently put an end to their lives. Also the old could not give their masters the length of service naturally expected from a young slave. The preferred ages were between sixteen and twenty-five, and youths below the age of sixteen were preferred to old Negroes because the expectancy of service from the latter decreased with the increase of their years. A particularly attractive cargo was one that consisted chiefly of boys and girls, young men and young women.

One finds frequent references in the advertisements of slaves to the length of time the slave ship was en route to its destination. Since death and disease were frequent occurrences on the voyage from Africa, this point was of special significance. The length of time taken to make the trip from the coast of Africa to Carolina evidently shortened with the years. For example, in 1763 Miles Brewton advertised a cargo of slaves arrived from Gambia "in a short passage of 6 weeks"; but in 1772 he announced a cargo of slaves brought from the same country in thirty days.[32]

Laurens gave the following general directions to some young West Indian correspondents who wished to forward slaves to him: "Let your purchases be of the very best kind of slaves black & smooth free from blemishes, young and well grown— the more men the better but not old—none will sell better than Gambia Slaves—if you touch any below this description let a very great bargain only tempt you & let me know the real cost of them—be sure to give them good covering & victuals & secure the promise of the Master by whom you send them to beat them with humanity & keep up their Spirits."[33]

Slaves which cost in Africa from £8 to £22 doubled and tripled in value on being brought to the West Indies and Carolina. In 1764 Laurens sold a cargo at an average price of £40 sterling per head. John Louis Gervais sold a cargo in 1772 for an average

---

[32] S. C. Gaz., Oct. 19-31, 1763 and June 18, 1772.
[33] To Lloyd and Barton, Jamaica, Dec. 24, 1764.

of "upwards of £45 sterling per head"; and in that remarkable
year in the Negro business, 1773, Laurens wrote to a correspondent that prime men were selling for £350, prime women for £290
currency, and boys and girls in proportion, which expressed in
sterling meant about £50 for men and £41 for women. And these
prices were of course not as high as those sometimes paid for individual slaves. "Stranger" writing in the *South Carolina Gazette* of
September 17, 1772, says: "Negro men brought directly from
the coast of Africa sell for £430 to £450 currency each," the
equivalent of about £60 to £65 sterling. These were of course
top-notch prices in banner years. In a less favorable season the
merchant was glad to get from £28 to £35 sterling for his Negro
merchandise.[34]

The successful slave merchant or factor had to be a person
with strong financial backing, of superior executive ability, and of
outstanding social talent. Good security must be given for the
performance of engagements and heavy bonds were required upon
delivery of valuable slave cargoes; the receiver of them must
besides have ability in the dispatch of business and an extensive
acquaintance with good customers. He also must be well known
throughout a wide territory for the planters were cautious about
bonding themselves to a little known slave dealer. Such a person naturally took his place in the highest ranks of society both
in Europe and America. Richard Oswald, one of the English
negotiators at the Peace Conference at Paris in 1783, at which
American independence was acknowledged, was one of the richest
merchants of London. He owned a Negro factory at Bance
Island in Africa and he made a good part of his money sending
slave ships to Carolina. Henry Laurens, who was afterwards president of the American Congress, was proud to act as Oswald's factor and boasted in 1764 that he had recently sold a cargo of slaves
at higher prices than anybody else in the colony. Not only was
no social stigma yet attached to the slaver, but the person who
faintly suggested that slave dealing was reprehensible was looked

[34] MacPherson, *Annals of Com.*, IV, 153; Laurens to Thomas Mears, Aug. 24,
1764; to John Halman, Sept. 8, 1772; to the same, June 25, 1773.

upon as a weak-minded sentimentalist. The typical attitude toward slaves is reflected in a controversy in 1769 between Laurens and Egerton Leigh, sole Judge of his Majesty's Vice Admiralty Court at Charleston, in which Leigh charged Laurens with being a self-righteous hypocrite who had abandoned the slave trade from "goodness of heart." Laurens passionately resented Leigh's insinuation and replied hotly that the statement that he had retired from the Negro business from "goodness of heart" was a falsehood, that he had done so because he had no partner to assist him in that arduous business. Yet Laurens, who had probably made most of his money selling Negroes, was writing to his son John in 1776: "You know, my dear son, I abhor slavery." A little later he was making plans to emancipate his slaves and was disturbed by the consideration that to do so would disinherit his children. Laurens's reaction to slavery and the slave trade makes a curious study of the individual's part in the evolution of public opinion. Perhaps the sentiment Laurens came to entertain concerning slavery was a part of that cloud on the .horizon of public opinion, no larger than. a man's hand, which, through a century, was to gather black and threatening, overcasting the whole American sky, and burst at last in a storm that swept African slavery out of existence. But not the exploitation of man by man. That in the less obvious form of economic bondage seems destined to be with us, if not like the poor for always, yet for some time to come.

In Carolina even the slave merchant could apparently add something to his social prestige by investing his money in broad plantations. Society had not yet rid itself of the feudal notion which associated nobility of rank with the ownership of land, and was still obsessed with the idea that to perform well one must perform greatly. Therefore, there was much overlapping of the two occupations of merchant and planter. The great merchant became the great planter and shipped off the produce of his plantations at a great profit because he eliminated exorbitant shipping charges. The prosperous planter invested his money in a mercantile establishment so that he might serve himself, establish direct relations with the merchant firms in England and thus free himself from the excessive charges of the Charleston merchants. In the period before the Revolution one of the largest Negro trading establishments in Charleston was that of Thomas and Roger Smith, two wealthy young planters with wide family connections.[35]

[35] Laurens to Ross & Mill, Mch. 31, 1769.

CHAPTER VIII
RICE, INDIGO, AND DEERSKINS

I

The leading exports from Charleston were rice, indigo, and deerskins, named in the order of their importance. Rice of an inferior sort was introduced into South Carolina during the last quarter of the seventeenth century, but rice growing was not profitable until the planters discovered that, although it could be grown on high lands, it throve best on the low rich soil of the inland swamps. Until the Revolution rice continued to be grown chiefly in inland swamps in those spots that could be irrigated by impounded water, although successful experiments were made as early as 1758 in reclaiming river swamp land and a few progressive planters had tide-swamp plantations. For example, Laurens wrote Francis Levett, in St. Augustine, on September 12, 1769, that he was buying land for his correspondents "capable of being kept perfectly dry or being covered with fresh water almost every spring tide." It was not, however, until the close of the war that planters began to develop tide-swamp plantations on a large scale, by felling cypress forests and building a system of dykes and sluices for irrigating the low lands along the rivers by means of the tides. It was even later that the water culture method of tending rice was generally practised, whereby floods of water absolutely under control were used to kill the weeds and grass and promote the growth of the plants, thus improving the yield of the crop and lessening the labor of the slaves.[1]

Cypress swamps usually contained the black greasy soil with clay foundation suitable for the growth of rice. The first task of the planter was to drain the swamp and then fell the trees. Thrifty planters living along navigable streams converted the trees into lumber to be used on the plantation or shipped to market; others piled them in heaps and left them to rot. On such newly cleared

[1] *Charleston Yearbook*, 1883, 397-398; Drayton, *View*, 115.

land good crops were produced the first year while the ground was still covered with the stumps of trees.

Rice was planted in March, April, and May in trenches or rows made with the hoe about three feet apart. As soon as the seed was in the ground, water was let in from an adjacent stream and most of the growth of the crop took place under eight or ten inches of water. When the rice became grassy, the water was drained off and the weeding was done by slaves who worked in a stooped position in the stagnant water. Thus the cultivation of rice was an extremely unwholesome business; not only did the Negroes have to plant and weed rice in water mid-leg-high and above, but the exhalations from the swamps caused what was known as "obstinate intermittants" or country fever. It was said that Negroes, whose natural constitutions were suited to the climate, were immune from this fever; but the combination of country fever, malnutrition, and the exhaustive labor of "manufacturing" rice doubtless wiped out thousands of African lives in order that Europe might have a cheap rice supply. Yet a rice field was a beautiful sight both in blossom time when the delicately perfumed flowers seemed to float on the surface of the water and just before the harvest when the waving grain rose high above the water.[2]

Rice had more picturesque enemies than modern cotton with its rust and boll weevils. Since it was a crop requiring embankments and cultivated by periodical overflowing, the floods themselves unless handled with good judgment were destructive, and the crawfish if unchecked could sweep away all the young rice on a fine plantation. Besides, inland swamps were subject to droughts at the very time when water was most needed. The harvest enemies of rice were the bobolinks or rice birds, who, dressed all in their streaked winter garb for their southern migration, halted at Carolina for three or four weeks in September and descended in great flocks on the rice fields when the grain was in the milk, committing great depredations. The birds arrived very lean from their long journey but soon grew very fat. Negroes were detailed

---

[2] Elkanah Watson's description in *Memoirs*, p. 52; *American Husbandry*, I, 387-397; Carroll, *Collections*, II, 196 *et seq.*

to guard the rice fields and shoot the birds, which were considered not only pernicious pests but toothsome delicacies. Some of the old cook books contain recipes for cooking rice birds.[3]

Harvesting took place late in August or early in September, while the straw was still somewhat green. As soon as the field was drained, Negroes cut the grain with sickles, laying it on the stubble to cure for two or three days, after which it was bound in sheaves and either stacked or put away in barns. The harvest season was joyous. "At this season," wrote Timothy Ford, "every thing on the plantation gets fat,—the fowls round the barn, & even the wild fowls find a rich supply of food. The rice flour mixed with chaff or cut straw forms the most luxurious feeding for hogs & horses—they are invariably fatned. The negroes are inspired with alacrity in beating & preparing the rice by the certainty of their coming in for shares with the rest of the *stock* on the plantation. For here it must be noted that what is called the clean rice is not the *merchantable* rice; for it is easy to conceive that the beating must break many of the grains in pieces; and this divides it into *rice, midlings, & small rice.* These are all separated by sieves; the first is put up in barrels for market; the second reserved for family use; & the third for the consumption of the plantation."[4]

As early as 1691 the legislature passed a law to encourage the invention of machinery for cultivating rice and preparing it for market; thereafter rice machinery was being constantly improved.[5] In 1756 Adam Pedington received a patent for a new machine for cleaning rice.[6] John Cuthbert, planter, invented certain implements for better preparing and cultivating "rice, indigo, and grain in rows by means of ploughs, horse hoes, hand hoes and pickers" and the legislature gave him a patent on his new method for fourteen years.[7] In 1768 Laurens wrote about "a poor Dutchman whom the Assembly had given £500 sterling for an

[3] Habersham to Laurens, *Ga. Hist. Col.,* VI, 132; *American Museum,* IV, Dec. 1788.
[4] *S. C. Hist. & Gen. Mag.,* XIII, 183-184.
[5] Cooper, *Statutes of S. C.,* II, 63.
[6] *Ibid.,* III, 30-31.
[7] *Ibid.,* IV, 229.

improvement on a pounding machine."[8] In 1774 Mr. William
Bellamy brought from Philadelphia the model of a machine invented by himself to be worked by water, wind, horse, or hand
by which he proposed to grind one hundred bushels of rice per day,
without breaking a grain. He also had an invention for cleaning
and brightening the grain. High hopes were raised that the
whole crop of rice might be exported by April, in case the Bellamy machines were successful. What came of his projects is
unknown. Drayton writing as late as 1800 said that in some
parts of the state rice was still beaten by the old laborious method
of mortar and pestle, which would mean that the task of a male
laborer was six pecks per day, of a female, four pecks. Drayton
also mentions two kinds of mills in use before the Revolution, operated by oxen, mules or horses: The pecker machine, which was
so-called because "the pestle struck in the manner of a woodpecker
pecking a tree"; and the cog machine, which had "a large cog
horizonal wheel turning a trundle wheel which worked upright
pestles." These machines could beat out from three to six barrels
of rice per day.[9]

In the fall of the year, after the rice crop was made, some of
the Negroes were set to work splitting pine staves and headings;
others cutting oak hoop poles for barrels. These were loaded on
ox carts and carried to the cooper shop that was in every rice
neighborhood to be fashioned into barrels. The broad-wheeled
ox cart was almost the sole mode of land transportation of the
rice planters, as the narrow-wheeled wagon was of the up-country
farmers. When the rice was ready for market, three or four
barrels of it were loaded on an ox cart and carried to the nearest
river landing to be shipped to Charleston. Planters living in the
neighborhood of Charleston sometimes carted their rice to market
instead of sending it by boat. This was the practice of Colonel
William Washington, a cousin of George Washington and one
of the great Carolina planters. Colonel Washington lived about
twelve miles from the city across the Ashley. His ox carts, each

[8] To James Grant, Jan. 28, 1768.
[9] S. C. Gaz., Sept. 19 and 26, 1774; Drayton, View, 121.

drawn by three or four yoke of oxen attended by two or three Negro drivers, could make one trip to Charleston in a day.[10]

At Charleston rice had to pass the examination of the rice inspector, after which the "poor or middling" planter sold it to a rice factor or, if rice was selling low, he put it in storage to wait for an advance in price, an expensive procedure; in the latter case, however, the storage rate was not subject to the whim of the rice factors or wharf owners, but was fixed by the provincial government. Rich planters, like Colonel Washington, who sometimes made five hundred tierces of rice on a single plantation, found it profitable to charter ships and act as their own factors in order to avoid the heavy commission and freight charges of the merchants. Some of the great planters living along streams that gave them excellent transportation weighed and coopered their own rice and sent it to Charleston where it was hoisted into overseas vessels without landing. Sometimes several planters clubbed together and chartered a ship to send produce to the European or West Indian market.

It was freight charges particularly that reduced the profits of the rice planter. These heavy charges were due to the great toll exacted by the middlemen for their services, and to the fact that overseas ships could make only one or two voyages a year. According to Governor Glen's testimony in the 1740's "rice that £100 would purchase cost the importer £200 in British duties, freight and other charges."[11] Freight charges were variable, being affected by the season of the year and the conditions of supply and demand. Naturally, freight rates were highest when there was a great demand for vessels to carry off the crop, that is, from January through May, and lowest from June to September when there was not much produce to be shipped. Thus there were great fluctuations in freight rates for rice within a year. For example, on April 4, 1771, rice sold for forty shillings per hundred weight cash and for 42/6 in bills of exchange and credit; freight to London was £3 per ton and £3/15 to Holland.[12] By June of the same year rice was selling at the boom

[10] Drayton, *View*, 141.
[11] Carroll, *Collections*, II, 268.
[12] Laurens to James McKenzie & Co.

price of sixty shillings and freight to London might be had for twenty shillings. This latter freight rate, however, was not normal but due to the abnormal demand for rice in Germany on account of crop failure.[13]

Under normal conditions after 1763 freight rates probably were no higher than forty-five to fifty shillings for Portugal; forty to fifty shillings for London and Bristol; and fifty to fifty-five shillings to Cowes and a market. The following are the highest freight rates quoted by Laurens to his correspondents in 1767, 1768, 1769:

	Portugal	London	Northern European market
1767	50/[14]	40/ to 45/[15]	55/[16]
1768	45/[17]	40/ to 45/[18]	50/ to 55/[19]
1769	50/[20]	40/ to 45/[21]	50/[22]

A large crop of rice created a strong demand for freight. In good crop years the great merchants and planters frequently chartered all the available vessels, and freight for rice was not to be had by the man of moderate means until later in the season when the market was glutted.[23] When rice prices were high, freight rates were proportionately low. On March 31, 1772, when rice was selling for the very high price of eighty shillings per hundred weight, freight for Cowes and a market (Holland, Hamburg, Bremen) was as low as 47/6 per ton; but when rice was selling at sixty shillings on April 19, 1773, no more could be obtained for the markets than 37/6.[24]

Professor Wallace in his *Life of Henry Laurens* quotes from Governor Glen's report, probably to the Board of Trade, which was published in London in 1761, to the effect that in 1746 the

[13] Laurens to Capt. Geo. Chisman.
[14] To Alex. Brown & Co., Dec. 7, 1767.
[15] Wm. Cowles, Dec. 7, 1767.
[16] Reynolds Getly, Dec. 11, 1767.
[17] James Poyas, Jan. 13, 1768.
[18] *Ibid.*
[19] Wm. Cowles, Nov. 7, 1769.
[20] *Ibid.*
[21] Wm. Cowles, Mch. 3, 1769.
[22] *Ibid.*
[23] *Col. Ga. Hist. Soc.*, V, 36-37.
[24] Laurens to Reynolds Getly & Co. and to Wm. Cowles.

freight rate per ton from Charleston to Europe was £6/10 sterling; from Charleston to the West Indies £4/10; and to the northern colonies £3/10; and that the rates in 1747 and 1748 were the same less ten shillings in each case. Assuming these rates to be normal, and they probably were for that period of upheaval, Professor Wallace joins them to Henry Laurens' statement, made on September 11, 1762, that freight rates to London were as low as £5 per ton, and makes the comment that although the freight rates were moderate enough to foster active commerce, they probably were six or eight times as high as freight rates are at present. In making this deduction, Professor Wallace seems to have lost sight of the fact that in 1762 vessels were advertised regularly in the Charleston papers to sail under convoy to Europe on account of the war with France, and £5 per ton was perhaps a cheap wartime freight. After 1763 £3 per ton for London was apparently considered a very high freight rate.[25]

The trade of Charleston, like that of most centers of agricultural districts, was seasonal. Business was brisk from January through May because rice was in great demand in the winter months in the industrial cities of Holland, Germany, and Flanders when peas and all kind of pulse were scarce, and also because at that time great cargoes of slaves from Africa were arriving and being disposed of to the planters who were beginning a new crop. From June to autumn business was dull. Few ships came from Europe and communication with Europe was mostly by way of Philadelphia, which had a constant correspondence with Charleston by sea.[26] For example, the *South Carolina Gazette* of September 10, 1763, reported "44 sail in the harbor—17 ships, 1 Billander, 6 scooners, and 10 sloops," "the greatest number ever known to be here at this time of the year." Josiah Quincy, however, who visited Charleston in the height of the shipping season wrote in his diary on February 28, 1773: "The number of shipping far surpasses all I had seen in Boston. I was told there was not so many as common at this season, though about 350 sail lay off the town, which struck me very agreeably, and the new

[25] Wallace, Laurens, 49.
[26] P. R. S. C., XXXII, 439; Laurens to Edw. Bridgen, Aug. 10, 1787.

Exchange which fronted the place of my landing made a most noble appearance."[27]

Perhaps we may attribute to the cessation from business activities for a season the taste for the fine arts which distinguished Charleston above most of the other American cities. Wealth had come through rice, indigo, and slaves. Leisure came to the upper strata of society with the summer. The planter came to town fleeing from the country fever during the "three sickly months." The merchant who had been all bustle and business a few months before had now to invent employment for his clerks and himself. As business became dull, society became gay. People attended dances, concerts, lectures, and there was much social entertaining to while away the hours until business began to mend. This was in September when the families of the planters began to return to the country and a few ships began to arrive, together with some small vessels from the West Indies, Spain, and Portugal.

The overseas vessels stayed in Charleston from one to three months, during which time the master of the vessel disposed of the slaves and other merchandise which made up his cargo, if it had been consigned to him, or he turned it over to some firm of factors. He also had to have his ship overhauled for the return voyage, for which purpose he passed up the "freshes" to save the bottom of his vessel from the worms. The merchant, for his part, paid the disbursements of the ship captain, provided a return cargo, and advertised the ship for the return journey, somewhat after the following fashion:[28]

For London
(To sail with the First of the Crop)
The Ship
Heart-of-Oak,
Henry Gunn, Master—
For freight of Rice, Indico and Deer Skins,
or for Passage, having extraordinary Accommodations.
Apply to
Edwards, Fisher & Co.

[27] P. 195.
[28] *S. C. Gaz.*, Nov. 12, 1772.

In good crop years 120,000 barrels of rice were shipped from Charleston alone, and 20- or 30,000 from Georgetown and Beaufort. And the amount of rice produced was gradually increasing as the acreage under cultivation was extended. The average of eight crops from the mid-summer of 1747 to the mid-summer of 1755 was 63,000 tierces per annum; the six crops from 1755 to 1761 averaged 68,000 tierces; the crops from 1761 to 1767— 94,000 tierces; and the crops from 1767 to 1773—124,500 tierces, which was nearly double the average before the year 1755.[29]

About sixty per cent of Carolina rice found a market in Northern Europe via the English ports; the rest going chiefly to Portugal, which was in a state of commercial vassalage to England. Small quantities were taken by Spain and Italy, but Carolina rice could not be sold without a license in France, where rice from Turkey could be bought about five shillings cheaper.

In 1769 Charleston exported to Europe 123,317 barrels of rice, and of these 24,264 barrels and 5,046 barrels went respectively to Portugal and Spain, which seem to have been the sole customers for Carolina rice in Southern Europe in that year.[30] In the New World the West Indies, particularly the British islands where the great sugar plantations were located, were the best customers for Carolina rice of the small grain kind. The British West Indies sometimes consumed more than all of Southern Europe combined. New York, Pennsylvania, and Rhode Island took off small quantities. All three of these colonies were interested in the provisions, rum, and Negro trade that bound the West Indies, Africa, and America together. Their ships often touched at Carolina to sell Negroes and to dispose of an inferior rum used in the Indian trade, and those commodities were paid for in rice and other produce. The trade of Carolina with different parts of the world can be measured with some accuracy by the rice shipments to the different countries, of which the *South Carolina Gazette* of October 10, 1771, gives the following typical example:

---

[29] S. C. Gaz., May 31, and June 21, 1773.
[30] MacPherson, *Annals of Com.*, III, 491-492.

Total shipments of rice from Nov. 1, 1770, to Oct. 10, 1771,
were .... 130,601 **barrels**
To ports in Great Britain 73,235½
To ports in North America 9,664½
To British West Indies 30,304½
To Foreign West Indies 975½
To Portugal 14,439
To Spain 1,760
To Italy 222

Certain ports in Great Britain were given the privilege of
handling rice intended for re-exportation. In 1765 the liberty
of importing rice for immediate exportation was granted by Parliament to Plymouth, Exeter, Poole, Southampton, Chichester,
Sandwich and Glasgow; and in 1772 to Bristol, Liverpool, Lan-
caster, and Whitehaven.[31]   The largest shipments of rice went,
however, to the three ports authorized to clear out vessels to Africa
for the slave trade.   These were London, Bristol, and Liverpool.
The peculiar advantage of Bristol was that large vessels could load
and unload at the quay, which was about a mile long, "without the
expense, delay, & plunder of lighterage."   About three-fourths of
the rice from Carolina naturally found a market at Cowes, the
chief port of the Isle of Wight.   The chief business of this port
was to land and reship commodities that were obliged by law to
land in a British port before they could be carried to any foreign
port.   Not only was Carolina rice forwarded to its final destination from Cowes, but the English farmer's grain in prosperous
years went to Spain and Portugal via Cowes.   Sometimes the
wharf owners of Cowes and of the lesser ports of Gosport and
Leith advertised their shipping facilities in the Charleston papers.[32]
    The price of rice was not at all stable.   In the early part of
the colonial period it sometimes sold as low as ten and twelve
shillings currency per hundredweight.   After 1760 the price
ranged all the way from twenty-five to ninety shillings.   Thirty-
five shillings was considered a poor price, forty-five shillings
average, sixty shillings excellent, and ninety shillings extraor-
dinarily good.   The price of rice was of course dependent on

[31] MacPherson, *Annals of Com.*, III, 417, 517.
[32] MacPherson, *Annals of Com.*, IV, Appendix IV.

demand and demand was often influenced by abnormal conditions. Our ancestors lived nearer the verge of starvation than we do, largely because of poor means of communication. So when bad crop years came the colonial assemblies were sometimes forced to prohibit the exportation of provisions. When the government undertook to provide for the hungry along the rice coast, rice usually sold for an excellent price. In 1766, for instance, the assembly of South Carolina forbade the exportation of rice and fixed the price at £3 current money per hundredweight. Part of the reason for the high price of rice was, no doubt, the shortage of rice and other food products.[33]

Naturally the sale of rice depended upon the crops in Germany, Spain, and Portugal, the chief European markets. There was a crop failure in Germany in 1771, and so great was the demand for rice that there was more speculation in it than ever was known before. Some of the great merchants engaged whole crops of it at sixty shillings. By the first of December rice was selling at 65/ cash and there was little demand for bills of exchange; by January, it was at 80/ and by June it had reached 90/.[34] The number of vessels in the harbor was the barometer of the market. Laurens wrote in a letter to Reynolds, Getly & Co., on February 20, 1770, that rice was down to 47/6 and probably would have fallen to 45/, but "in came 8 or 10 sail of ships and rice became scarce at 50/ and no charters were talked of."

The duty on rice in England under normal conditions was as high as 6/4 sterling, which was often as much as the first cost of the rice in Carolina; the result was that the people of Germany and Holland were able to get rice more cheaply than the English. Sometimes, however, the English farmers made great harvests and wished to take advantage of the high grain prices in the European market. The British government then provided an export bounty on grain, and, in order to give the poor at home a cheap food supply, periods of free rice importation from America were

---

[33] S. C. Gaz., June 2-9, 1766.
[34] Laurens to John Tarleton, Dec. 7, 1771; to Reynolds Getly & Co., Jan. 16, 1772; Col. Ga. Hist. Soc., VI, 143, Habersham to Wright.

allowed, lasting sometimes a few months, sometimes a year. Usually a duty of two and one-half per cent ad valorem was laid on the exportation from Great Britain of rice imported free of duty from the British-American colonies.[35] Laurens, who asserted that he shipped off nearly one-tenth of the rice crop in 1767 to "his friends" in England, said that when the British duty was laid on rice the price usually fell in Charleston about ten shillings, and when the duty was removed the price usually advanced ten shillings.[36]

The periods of free rice importation were occasions for speculation on the part of the merchants in Great Britain and America, since some of the British merchants were in a position to give advance information. Thus it was known in Charleston to a chosen few as early as January, 1768, that Parliament would in the following December, continue the exemption of rice from duty, a fact which speaks volumes for the intimate relation existing in the eighteenth century between "big business" and the English government. Early in January, 1768, Laurens was let into the secret when his correspondents in Bristol and London began to give large orders for rice. He immediately began feverishly to buy rice, which was selling the first of the year at 50/, at a month to six weeks' credit, but soon advanced to 50/ cash. He bought at this price nearly four thousand barrels for which he paid about £7000 sterling, enough to fill "10 'or 12 sail vessels, mostly large ones." "People," wrote Laurens, "who wonder at my Bustle for Rice just now will be troubled a little later by the Devil Envy."

A few other merchants must have been buying feverishly like Laurens, for by February 16 rice was selling at 60/ and Laurens was compelled to give that price for six hundred and fifty barrels he bought in August. By September the price "broke at 70/" and by November hundreds and thousands of barrels were being bought up "with uncommon vehemence" and "with little regard for quality"; and some merchants were engaging large crops to be delivered at any time before February, 1769. Laurens predicted that rice would continue at 70/ until Christmas; this

---

[35] MacPherson, *Annals of Com.*, III, 463, 521, 529.
[36] To Geo. Appleby, May 24, 1768.

prediction was not fulfilled, because the year 1768-1769 was a phenomenal crop year. From Charleston alone more than one hundred and twenty thousand barrels of rice were shipped to Europe. By December 14, rice was down to 62/6 with so many vessels in the harbor loading upon commission that the price was not likely to vary 2/6 either way until certain information arrived of exemption from, or resumption of, the duty on rice.

It took about three months for this important news to reach Charleston. When the intelligence came, on March 4, 1769, that rice had been exempted from duty, it was known, said Laurens, "to twenty different planters as soon as it was to the merchants." Nevertheless, the big crop caused rice to decline to 55/. Whereupon, little was sold because the rice factors began to lock up "such parcels" as came to town and instructed "their constituents" in the country not to send rice to market until the price advanced. The boats on the rivers were stopped and the planters and factors were waiting quietly for 60/. By March 22, the price was again at 60/, and likely to continue at that point because African cargoes began to drop in, which always created a demand for rice to be shipped to England to pay for slaves.

During such seasons of speculation the Charleston factor was in an enviable situation. If the anticipated high prices were realized, he was able to take advantage of them and load his part of the ships for profit. If the price declined, the principal loss fell on the British merchant, and in any case, the factor received a handsome commission. The great disadvantage was that at such times bills of exchange would not command rice, and the factor had to advance money from his own pocket to pay cash prices. For example, Laurens in 1769 postponed a long planned trip to England, because, as he wrote Habersham, of Georgia, he was "over head & Ears in debt for Rice bought last winter and not able to pay for want of circulation of bills."[37]

[37] Account of speculation taken from Laurens's correspondence with the following persons, in 1768: James Poyas, London, Jan. 13; Reynolds Getly & Co., Bristol, Jan. 20; Smith & Baillie, St. Christophers, Jan. 19; James Habersham, Savannah, Jan. 25; John Moultrie, St. Augustine, Jan. 28; Wm. Cowles & Co., Bristol, Feb. 8; Watson & Olive, London, Feb. 16; Reynolds Getly & Co., Feb. 19; George Appleby, Shropshire, May 24; Wm. Cowles & Co., Nov. 9; Dr. Andrew

II

Until the middle of the eighteenth century France and Spain had a monopoly of indigo production in the West Indies and furnished the European market. England herself bought annually about six hundred thousand pounds of the valuable dye needed in the textile industry, for which she paid about £150,000 sterling. This monopoly was brought to an end through the experiments of a young English girl, still in her teens, living on her father's plantation "seventeen miles by land and 6 by water from Charles Town." Eliza Lucas, who became the wife of Charles Pinckney, Chief Justice of the Province of South Carolina, and the mother of Thomas and Charles Cotesworth Pinckney, statesmen of the Revolutionary period, was the daughter of a British army officer who was governor of Antigua, in the West Indies. Colonel Lucas, on account of his wife's health, sent his family to reside in South Carolina, where he purchased three plantations, which he put under the management of his only daughter, Eliza.

Eliza was well educated and had a strong love for nature, which led her to collect plants for her friend Dr. Garden, in Charleston, the friend and correspondent of Linnaeus. She was fond of growing plants and made experiments with cotton, guinea corn, ginger, and alfalfa.

Among the tropical seeds and fruits sent her by her father to be planted for her amusement on the plantation at Wappo, were some indigo seeds. With these she experimented in 1741-1743 and found out that the West Indian indigo, which was an annual plant, was more productive than the indigo growing wild in the province. In 1743, her father engaged an expert indigo maker, named Cromwell, from Monserrat, at high wages, to come to Carolina and let his daughter see the whole process of extracting the dye. Cromwell made a mystery of the process and purposely produced an inferior dye by throwing in too much lime, in order to discourage Miss Lucas; but she detected his treachery and worked out the true process of making indigo dye. In 1744 the

Turnbull, St. Augustine, Nov. 14; Edward Brice, Bristol, Nov. 15; Wm. Fisher, Philadelphia, Dec. 14; and in 1769: Mm. Cowles & Co., Mch. 3; James Poyas, Mch. 4; Wm. Cowles & Co., Mch. 22; James Habersham, Aug. 15.

whole crop was saved for seed and given in small parcels to the
neighboring planters. Three years later 134,118 pounds of indigo
were exported from Charleston. In 1748 Parliament was petitioned by the Carolina planters and the British merchants trading
to Carolina for a bounty on indigo. In that year Carolina
indigo began its career by receiving a bounty of 6d. per pound,
and by being put on the list of enumerated goods which must go
direct to England.[38]

Indigo was grown mostly on the many islands along the coast
of South Carolina and Georgia, afterwards famous for the production of sea-island cotton. Some was produced on the comparatively high land back from the rice swamps, and a little in the
back country by small farmers, who could produce a fine grade
because they were prepared to give careful attention to the tedious
process of extracting the dye. John Hopton, a young merchant's
clerk, who made a tour of the frontier in 1769 as a part of his
mercantile education, reported many instances in the back country
of small farmers with nine or twelve working hands making £200
to £300 per hand by planting hemp and indigo. Tidewater
planters sometimes had indigo plantations in the back country.
Henry Laurens and John Louis Gervais, who obtained a grant of
thirteen thousand two hundred acres near Ninety-Six, grew indigo
successfully on a part of the tract.[39]

Indigo was found growing wild in South Carolina, but neither
the native nor the sugar island sort was so much cultivated as the
"false Guatemala" or "True Bahama," which was an annual
plant introduced from the West Indies.[40] An acre of land produced from sixty to eighty pounds of indigo and a slave could
cultivate two or more acres. Thus twenty-five slaves could manage a plantation of fifty acres and produce besides sufficient provisions for themselves and the planter's family. It was economical
to grow rice and indigo on the same plantation, much as the
Southern farmers today grow cotton and tobacco; for the second

[38] For story of indigo see *Charleston Yearbook*, 1883, 400-402; *Journal and Letters of Eliza Lucas;* Carroll, *Collections*, II, 140; MacPherson, *Annals of Com.*, III, 491.
[39] Laurens to Grant, Oct. 27, 1769.
[40] Carroll, *Collections*, II, 203; Smith, *Tour*, II, 57-58.

cutting of indigo was finished in August about the time the rice harvest was beginning, and the slaves, for whom the planter had paid a big price, could be employed in "manufacturing rice" the rest of the year, and besides have time to saw lumber, and make hogsheads and barrels, to supply the sugar colonies.[41]

A light rich soil unmixed with clay or sand was best suited to indigo. Sometimes the ground was prepared as early as December by being turned up with the plow, cleaned from weeds and grass and harrowed. The seed were sowed in the early spring, usually in April, in furrows made with the drill plow or hoe, two inches deep and eighteen inches distant from each other. The plants were ready for the first cutting in July, for the second the last of August, and for a third about Michaelmas, if the autumn were mild, otherwise the third cutting was of little value, though six or more cuttings were obtained in the West Indies. In the early stages of its growth the chief enemies of indigo were grasshoppers or locusts. Lieutenant Governor Bull said that if some means could be found to destroy these pests, one hundred and fifty thousand pounds more indigo could be made with the same labor.[42] In the later stages, it was attacked by worms, which had to be carefully picked from the plants by slaves.

An indigo plantation was an unwholesome place, because the water required to make the dye soon became putrid and bred millions of flies. The *South Carolina Gazette* of September 27, 1773, suggested that some method should be taken to compel planters after the dye had been extracted, to bury indigo weeds, which were often spread wet and stinking over the fields, for manure; that the vast quantities of flies produced by this neglect were so troublesome to cattle that they could not feed in the day, but ran about as if mad and perished in great numbers; that the inhabitants of the sea-islands, who used to furnish large supplies of meat for the Charleston market, had been obliged to buy their supply since they began the cultivation of indigo. Indigo had the additional disadvantage of being a soil exhauster. "It was commonly observed," wrote Hewatt, "that all creatures about an in-

---

[41] Carroll, *Collections*, II, 203; Smyth, *Tour*, II, 57-58.
[42] *P. R. S. C.*, XXXII, 394.

digo plantation are starved, whilst about a rice one, which abounds in provisions for man & beast they thrive & flourish."[43]

Perhaps one of the reasons why indigo never outstripped rice as the leading staple of Carolina was that while it could be easily grown it required great care and skill to prepare it for market. A successful indigo planter could not spend a year in Europe, with impunity, and leave his business in the care of overseers and the half-wild black people.

When the indigo leaves were thick and full of juice, they were cut and laid in vats or steepers for about thirty hours, care being taken to prevent the bluish farina from being rubbed off the leaves. When the water was thoroughly impregnated with the substances of the weed, it was drawn off into other vats to be beaten and the dye was precipitated by means of lime water. Various contrivances were invented for beating the water, the chief requisite being some device to keep the water in violent motion until it became a strong purple color. The sediments remaining after the water was drawn off a second time, were pressed, cut into pieces about two inches square, dried carefully in drying houses specially constructed for the purpose, and finally put up in casks for the market.

Indigo was of great value in a small package. Therefore, the "richest ships," described frequently in the gazettes, had indigo as an important part of their cargo. The *South Carolina Gazette* for February 24-March 2, 1767, describes such a ship:

> The Ship Beaufain, Capt. Daniel Curling, cleared since our last for London, has on board no less than 394 casks containing 141,009 pounds weight of nett indico (supposed about one third of the crop) besides 751 barrels of rice, 14 hogsheads and six bundles of dress'd deer skins, 17,779 pounds of hemp, 32 Barrels of Turpentine, 5 boxes of seeds, and other articles, and it is reckoned the richest ship that has sailed from this port, except the Squerries, Capt. David Mitchell, who in the year 1759, took in upwards of 200,000 pounds of indico.

Efforts were being constantly made to improve the method of obtaining the different grades of indigo. For the purpose of encouraging experiments the legislature of South Carolina offered

[43] Carroll, *Collections*, II, 255.

rewards and the Society for encouraging Arts and Sciences in England gave a medal. One of the early innovators was Thomas Mellichamp, who discovered an entirely new method of producing flora indigo, and the legislature voted him one thousand pounds currency as a reward for his discovery. His "directions for making indigo of the different kinds equal to the best French" were published in the *South Carolina Gazette* of August 16-23, 1760.[44] Moses Lindo, Inspector General of Indico, published in the *Gazette* of January 12-19, 1767, a recipe for making an indigo dye superior to the best French, "discovered and made public by him for the benefit of Great Britain and her colonies."

When indigo was brought to the market, the buyer judged of its quality by breaking it and observing the closeness of its grain and its brilliant copper or purple color; by feeling its weight, heavy indigo of every color being considered poor; by burning it, good indigo being almost entirely consumed in fire; and by testing it in water, a pure and fine indigo being entirely dissolved in water.[45]

Inspection of indigo was not compulsory as was the inspection of rice, naval stores, hemp, and other commodities. This was probably because inspection was for the purpose of raising the reputation of commodities in the foreign market, and Carolina indigo was not intended for foreign consumption. Only the best grade of rice went to Europe, and it was many years before Carolina hemp was of a sufficiently high grade for the English market, for which reason it was shipped to the northern colonies.

The inspector of indigo at Charleston from 1762 to 1772 was Moses Lindo, a Jew. Lindo had been an indigo sorter in London and had immigrated to South Carolina in 1756 in order to buy indigo for a company of London merchants. After a successful career as an exporter of indigo, Lindo was appointed "Surveyor and Inspector General of Indico" by Governor Boone, September 21, 1762. This office was without salary but Lindo received liberal commissions. He charged old customers five per cent and those employing him for the first time or after an interval of

---

[44] See also *S. C. Gaz.*, Nov. 8, 1773.
[45] Carroll, *Collections*, II, 145.

abstinence were obliged to pay a straight fee of two dollars per hundred-weight. Lindo considered it his duty not only to inspect indigo, but to detect and punish fraud in connection with it by publishing in the gazettes the names of those "who damped or purposely wetted indigo or who jumbled the 1st, 2nd, & 3rd. sorts together." The casks inspected by Lindo were distinguished by a special seal consisting of a crown and the letters G. R.[46]

Charleston was the natural market for the indigo grown in the Charleston District, just as it was the natural market for rice grown along the rice coast. In ordinary years five hundred thousand pounds of indigo were exported from South Carolina; in banner years from one million to a million and a half pounds. But there were scarcely more than a half dozen years from 1748 to 1775 when a million or more pounds were exported. The *South Carolina Gazette* for June 21, 1773, gives the following account of the number of pounds of indigo exported from Charleston from 1748 to 1773:

1748....151,049	1757....726,535	1766....599,116
1749.... 93,099	1758....372,478	1767....587,272
1750....120,030	1759....911,957	1768....464,905
1751.... 33,616	1760....475,847	1769....387,004
1752.... 13,029	1761....255,467	1770....483,094
1753.... 17,437	1762....251,689	1771....564,133
1754.... 55,559	1763....404,083	1772....516,709
1755....193,803	1764....450,989	1773....794,150
1756....399,542	1765....467,725	

In 1774 and 1775 Charleston exported more than a million pounds of indigo, from which it may be inferred (by estimating the exports from Beaufort and Georgetown) that possibly a million pounds reached England in 1757, 1759, 1773, 1774 and 1775.[47]

Hewatt's statement that after learning the nice art of making indigo as well as the French, the Carolina planters were able not only to supply Great Britain but to undersell the French in several of the European markets, is extravagant in view of

[46] S. C. *Gaz.*, Apr. 27-May 4, 1765; *ibid.*, Aug. 25-Oct. 1, 1764.
[47] S. C. *Gaz.*, Dec. 26, 1774; *Ibid.*, Feb. 20, 1775.

the fact that England was using as much as six hundred thousand pounds of the dye in the middle of the eighteenth century, and her annual consumption of indigo was increasing with the development of her textile industry. England continued to import French and Spanish indigo; for the finest grade of indigo, the French or Hispaniola, required for its growth the rich soil of the sugar islands and was little grown on the loose sandy soil of Carolina.[48] Because French indigo sold from eighteen pence to two shillings higher than Carolina, English dealers sometimes packed their best grades of Carolina and East Florida dye in serons, or French casks, warranted them to be genuine Spanish or French dye and passed them off on the English mercers.

There was of course a phenomenal development of the indigo industry in Carolina; for indigo was comparatively more valuable than rice. No swamps had to be cleared and drained for its cultivation. A bounty instead of a duty was placed on its importation into Great Britain, and the British government placed a tariff of /2 per pound on foreign imported indigo before 1763 and after 1763 a tariff of /6 per pound for its protection. Fortunately there was always a steady market for a drug produced in so few countries.[49]

As early as 1748 indigo brought nearly half as much money into South Carolina as deerskins, which ranked second in importance to rice, the crop of that year being valued at £16,465 sterling, while deerskins brought £36,000 sterling. In 1769 the 380,570 pounds of indigo shipped from Charleston brought £66,599/15; and in 1775 the 1,150,662 pounds shipped from Charleston must have brought in at least £200,000 sterling, counting 3/6 for the average price of the crop. In 1769 indigo formed sixteen per cent of the total value of Carolina exports to England; and in 1775 it formed about thirty-five per cent.[50]

The price of indigo depended on the grade. Much ordinary indigo sold for as little as a shilling a pound in England. Copper,

[48] Carroll, *Collections*, II, 140; MacPherson, *Annals of Com.*, III, 491.
[49] *S. C. Gaz.*, Oct. I, 1764; *P. R. S. C.*, XXXII, 31.
[50] *S. C. Gaz.*, Feb. 20, 1775; MacPherson, *Annals of Com.*, III, 491-492.

purple, and flora sometimes brought as high as a dollar and a dollar and a half per pound. There was of course a great deal more of the ordinary than of the higher grades, and the planter who received as much as a dollar for his dye sometimes had the event chronicled in the gazettes. There is such a notice in the *South Carolina Gazette* of December 27, 1773; it says: "13,000 pounds weight of Indico belonging to two planters, were last week sold by Mr. Samuel Prioleau, Jun. at a Dollar a Pound, to Moses Lindo, Esq; Inspector General, who had declared that the whole Quantity is equal, if not superior, to any French that, in many years of Experience he has had, has gone through his Hands, or fallen under his observation."[51]

Twenty-five shillings in Carolina, the equivalent of about 3/6 sterling, seems to have been a satisfactory price for indigo, and thirty-five to forty shillings a boom price. Moses Lindo, who as Inspector General of Indigo was exceedingly jealous of the reputation of the Carolina dye, stated that when the best French and Spanish dye sold at seven shillings per pound, Carolina of the first sort sold at 5/9, the second, at 4/2 and the third, at 2/9. Lindo seems to have been by nature and occupation a "booster" and more likely to overstate than understate the case for Carolina dye.

The indigo industry practically disappeared within the decade following the Revolution, although a little was grown as late as the nineteenth century. During the Revolution indigo was in great demand in France. It formed a much safer remittance for military supplies than bulky rice, and the indigo that escaped the vigilance of the English warships commanded a fancy price. It took the planters eight or ten years after the war to realize that they could not grow indigo without the English bounty in the face of the competition of the indigo from the East Indies. Gradually the back country turned to tobacco, and the planters to the extension of their rice fields, until, in the last years of the eighteenth century, the invention of the cotton gin caused the swift abandonment of both tobacco and rice for the more easily grown and more profitable cotton.

[51] Lindo to Ledyard in the *S. C. Gaz.*, Aug. 30, 1773.

III

By 1760 the great Charleston skin trade was a shadow of its former self. In the opening years of the eighteenth century Governor Archdale could write: "Charles Town Trades near 1000 miles into the Continent." At that time a great trade, chiefly in deerskins, was being carried on with the Catawbas, the Cherokees, the Creeks, the Choctaws, and the Chickasaws, who were living in territory now occupied partly or wholly by the present states of North and South Carolina, Tennessee, Georgia, Alabama, and Mississippi. In fact, Charleston was the center of one of the most important skin trades on the continent of North America.

The decline of the peltry trade was coincident with the occupation of the up-country by white immigrants; it was perceptible in the thirties and rapid in the fifties. Then Charleston's trade with the Creeks ceased as the merchants of Georgia became able to supply these Indians. After 1763 the Georgia Indian trade was confined to the Lower Creeks and the Indians of East Florida; but unlike that of Charleston, it was constantly increasing in the pre-Revolutionary period. In 1765, James Habersham, pioneer merchant of Savannah, could write: "Our Creek leather is now preferred in London to Cherokee, which was not the case 20 years ago."[52]

Another great blow was struck at the Charleston skin trade when the British acquired West Florida in 1763, and began to enlarge their trade with the Indians of the Southwest and to ship skins direct to Europe through Pensacola. At this time the Indian traders to the Choctaws and the Chickasaws were instructed to get their supply of goods hereafter from Mobile since it was often a hazardous business to transport supplies to them from Charleston through the frequently hostile Creek country. Moreover, the government wished to use the Choctaws as a check on the Creeks. Besides, the English were developing after 1763 new areas of trade in the Southwest at the expense of Spain. In 1767 English vessels were reported at Mobile and Pensacola loaded with Indian trading goods which they sold to the French and Spaniards; they

[52] *Col. Ga. Hist. Soc.*, VI, 36.

returned with considerable quantities of skins. By 1769 ten ships were employed in the direct trade between Pensacola and England.

In this way the skins which used to be handled by the Charleston factors were finding other outlets and after 1763 the Carolina skin trade was confined to the Cherokees, of whom Governor Bull wrote in 1770 that their trade was not very beneficial. He thought they commanded the attention of the government more upon political than commercial considerations as they formed a barrier against the incursions of the powerful Indians of the Ohio and Illinois tribes and a counterbalance against the Creeks in case of war.[53]

Yet, owing to the diversified character of the industry in western Carolina, deerskins were the most valuable single export of the back country until the Revolution. As late as 1747, when the deerskins exported from Carolina were worth £400,000 currency, a sum equal to about £57,143 sterling, they must have run rice a close second among the leading exports. The next year, 1748, the rice exports were valued at £88,393 and the deerskins, ranking second, at £36,000 sterling. After 1748, indigo easily outstripped deerskins for the second place. In 1769, however, deerskins still ranked third, though the combined exports of the back country were more than equal to the value of the deerskins, and the £18,422 sterling paid by the English dealers for Carolina deerskins that year formed a little more than four per cent of the value of the total exports to Europe.[54]

There are three periods in the management of the Indian trade. In the early days it was a monopoly of the proprietors who derived immense profits from selling skins. When South Carolina became a royal province, in 1729, the Indian trade was controlled, not by the Governor and his Council, but by the Commons House of Assembly, which appointed commissioners and an agent, responsible to the House, to look after the trade. In this period the Indian trade was left almost wholly to the control of the

[53] *P. R. S. C.*, XXXII, 403.
[54] *P. R. S. C.*, XXXI, 72; *ibid.*, XXIX, 117; MacPherson, *Annals of Com.*, III, 130. The Catawbas, who lived about 200 miles northwest of Charleston, were then surrounded with white settlers and were forced to join the Cherokees in the mountainous west.

separate colonies. Finally, after 1763, the British government, in conformity with its general policy of tightening control over the American colonies, began gradually to take over the management of Indian affairs. The Superintendent of Indian Affairs for the Southern Department (composed of North and South Carolina and Georgia), an official appointed by and responsible to the Crown, had his powers enlarged, and a more systematic regulation of the trade was attempted with a view to lessening the control of the individual colonies.

We shall concern ourselves first with the middle period. In 1760 the South Carolina Provincial Agent had a general supervision over Indian trade and traders, and the real management of the business was in the hands of a commission appointed by the legislature. This commission was composed of five men, generally Charleston merchants, who received two and one-half per cent commission on the sale of skins and two and one-half per cent on the purchase of goods for the Indian business. The chief duties of the commissioners were: to use the money appropriated by the legislature to supply the Indians with British manufactures "at a cheap and easy rate to prevent their seduction by the French and Spanish"; to sell in Charleston to the highest bidder the peltries brought from the Indian country; to fix the rate of barter at which goods were to be sold; and to render an account to the legislature once a year of the state of the public business.[55] The commissioners were required by law to give at least ten days notice in the newspapers of skins to be sold, goods to be bought, or wagons to be hired for the Indian service.[56] The *South Carolina Gazette* for November 19, 1763, contains one of their advertisements which reads as follows:

> The Directors appointed by law to carry on the Trade with the Cherokee Indians on account of the Publick, hereby give Notice, that they have occasion to hire two covered Waggons with sufficient Horses, Tackling & Drivers to carry up goods, from hence to the Factory at Fort Prince George, Keowee; and return back with Skins; and also have occasion to purchase with ready money, some pieces of blue Strouds, coarse white Linnens, small striped Flannels, Haggerheaded Duffields, Cotton Hollands,

[55] Cooper, *Statutes of S. C.*, IV, 168-188; *Indian Books, 1762-1765*, 1-5.
[56] Cooper, *Statutes of S. C.*, IV, 109.

Furniture-Checks, a few pounds of white Thread, a Cask broad-hoes, some white Seed Beads, a few pieces Ribbon, and some salt, Boxes of Paint, and Tin Sauce-Pans; Therefore desire such Person or Persons, who are willing to furnish the same, or any part thereof, to make known their respective proposals and Prices, to any of the Subscribers, in five days from Publication hereof.

Thomas Lamboll, Th^os Shubrick; Gabriel Manigault; John Savage; Thomas Smith; Directors.

The goods advertised in this way were usually paid for in certificates of proclamation money, the favorite denomination apparently being £2. The commissioners were authorized by the legislature to issue certificates for any sum of money up to £6,000, for carrying on the trade, and these certificates were receivable into the public treasury for the payment of duties and taxes. Gabriel Manigault, the cashier of the commissioners, paid out for many years, for supplies to the Charleston merchants, sums ranging in amount from £2 up to several thousand pounds.

Heavy and light-dressed deerskins and beaver were likewise advertised in the gazettes, and the merchants who bought them put them away in the packhouses along the water front where they were watched over by Negroes until the ships from England came in; for deerskins, like rice and indigo, were enumerated and could be exported only to England or a British colony; they also had to pay an export tax. An important duty of the Negroes was to air and beat the skins. As late as 1772 (December 24) the *South Carolina Gazette* could print a notice like this one: "Accidents frequently happen to carriages and many persons have their Limbs broke, (from horses taking fright) from the common practice of beating skins in the Streets and on the Bay—'Tis therefore hoped it will be discontinued."

Skins were shipped in hogsheads, and sometimes in rum puncheons. Hogsheads probably did not contain a fixed number of skins, although it may be inferred from references in the correspondence of Laurens that a hogshead contained approximately five hundred skins. For example, on August 10, 1768, Laurens shipped Cowles and Company, of Bristol, 3,400 deerskins in seven hogsheads; on September 24, of the same year, he shipped to the same firm 5,600 deerskins in twelve hogsheads.

An important duty of the commissioners was the preparation of a table showing the rates of· barter at which goods were to be exchanged for skins. In the early days the Indians exchanged valuable skins for a few trinkets, looking glasses, pieces of colored cloth, hatchets, etc. Later the savages, whose whole system of living had been changed by their commerce with the white man, refused to hunt for cheap merchandise and small trinkets. Besides, the price of skins was enhanced by the fact that wild animals grew scarce and more difficult to entrap as the hunting range became more extensive. Also competition with the French and Spanish became keener. In 1762 the general rule for settling the rates of exchange with the Indians was not to put a greater advance upon the goods than was sufficient to defray the expenses of carrying on the trade and maintaining the principal stock.[57]

While some money was used in carrying on trade in the Indian country, the standard of value was a clean, dry, well dressed and merchantable skin weighing one pound. The general rule for the rate of exchange between peltries and goods in 1763 was a pound of dressed deerskins for every six shillings current money cost of goods in Charleston; but in case goods were ponderous and perishable a higher price was required in barter. Skins weighing less than half a pound were not purchased and of course allowances were made for skins weighing more than a pound.[58]

In 1716 a gun sold for thirty-five skins; a yard of cloth for eight; a white duffield blanket for sixteen; a hoe for five; thirty bullets for one; a laced broad coat for thirty; an ax for five; a pistol for twenty; a sword for ten; a calico petticoat for fourteen. But in 1762 these prices were cut nearly in half. A yard of calico then sold for two skins; a hoe for three; sixty bullets for one; and an ounce of vermilion for one, etc.[59]

The factors and other agents for carrying on barter with the Indians were appointed by and responsible to the provincial commissioners. There were employed at the trading house at Fort Prince George one factor, two clerks, and two porters, all

[57] Cooper, *Statutes of S. C.*, IV, 170.
[58] *Indian Books*, Dec. 3, 1763.
[59] *Ibid.*, July 29, 1762; John H. Logan, *History of Upper So. Ca.*, I, 255.

white men. The factor's annual salary was £300 proclamation money, that of the clerks £140 each and of the porters £40 each proclamation money. The factor held a highly responsible position. He had charge of the trading house at the fort and it was his duty to take charge of all goods and wares sent up by the Board and barter them to the friendly Indians for skins, furs, leather and, in the early days, slaves. Slaves rather than skins were the chief staple of the Indian trade in the first part of the colonial period. Special brands were made at Charleston for stamping

skins and slaves. The one used for the Cherokee trade was —

$$\frac{C}{H}$$

cut in iron and burned into the skin of the slave. This practice was discontinued by the Board as far as slaves were concerned about 1716. But brands were still sent out from Charleston to the factors at their posts, the one in 1763 being an iron brand with the letters S. C. T. (South Carolina Indian Trade), which was branded above the necks of the skins.[60]

The factor was a bonded official and also a magistrate with authority to stop all persons attempting to penetrate into the Indian country without a license. Perhaps his most difficult task was to apprehend illicit traders and assist in their prosecution; for the provincial authorities found it every year more difficult to prevent private traders from participating in the benefits of the fur trade. The factors were enjoined by the board not to sell goods on credit because it was the policy of the board to let the Indians have just enough powder and ball for their hunts and not enough to start a war. Credit was thus the principal cause of disputes between the Indians and the traders. This excellent rule, however, was not enforced. The factors were also not to accept presents from the Indians nor trade on their own accounts.[61]

All the goods for carrying on the trade with the Cherokees were transported the three hundred miles from Charleston to Fort Prince George, Keowee, in wagons under the competent direction

[60] Logan, *Hist. of Upper S. C.*, I, 253, 257; *Indian Books*, Feb. 23, 1763.
[61] *Indian Books*, 1762-1765, 17-18.

of wagon masters. These wagons carried heavy loads over rough roads. The four wagons of Thomas Nightingale carried in the spring of 1763, 7,975 pounds of goods to Fort Prince George. The freight rate on these wagons was a matter for negotiation between the owners and the Indian commissioners. The usual price in 1762 and 1763 seems to have been £4 current money for each hundred-weight carried up, and at the same rate for each hundred-weight brought down.[62]

The route was over the old Cherokee trail, established in 1718, which ran from Charleston through Orangeburg to Fort Congarees (near the present site of Columbia) and thence north-ward over the present route of the Southern Railroad from Columbia to Greenville, to the heart of the Cherokee country. One of the halting stations was called Ninety-Six, because it was ninety-six miles from Keowee, or Fort Prince George, the end of the trail.

The chief objects of British policy in regard to the Indian trade after 1763 were, first, to avoid the expense attendant on a variety of provincial establishments and to bring about a more efficient management of the trade than was possible while it was under the direction of the jealous provincial governments; secondly, to check the decline of the fur trade by preserving the hunting grounds of the Indians, as in the establishment of the proclamation line beyond which settlements were not to extend; and thirdly, to win the friendship of the Indians by putting a stop to the frauds and licentious conduct of private traders, which was a principal cause of disaffection among the tribes. These results were to be secured by increasing the power of the Indian superintendent, who was appointed by and responsible to the Crown. Although the regulation of the Indian trade was still left to the colonial legislatures and the Indian superintendent made reports to them, the superintendent was given a seat in the provincial councils. While free trade among the Indians was granted to all duly qualified and licensed traders, it was the special duty of the superintendent to see that the abuses practised by unscrupulous traders met with

<hr />

[62] *Indian Books*, Nov. 24, 1763, III; *ibid.*, July 5, 1762.

suitable punishment, and that settlements beyond the proclamation line were prevented.[63]

To accomplish these objects a stricter organization of the Indian business was necessary. In the Southern District two deputies were appointed to the superintendent; one to manage the affairs of the Choctaws and Chickasaws and the small nations on the Mississippi, the other to transact business with the Cherokees, the Creeks, and the Catawbas. Commissaries were established in the different nations "to diffuse trade among the Indians and to check the enormities of the traders."[64]   Under the new management Edward Wilkinson, who had been for many years factor at Fort Prince George, was appointed to take charge of the stores at that place. Wilkinson organized the firm of Edward Wilkinson and Company and in 1769 when the co-partnership expired, he advertised for sale the following stores in the Cherokee Nation: one at Estatoe near Toogola, one at Sugar Town, one at Toxaway, one at Estatoe, one at Tusheege, and the main store at Fort Prince George. "The purchaser," the advertisement ran, "may have the supplying of three experienced traders, one at Cowee, one at little Chote, and one at Toque; and also may engage the Factors who are now in our employ, to continue at the above mentioned stores."[65]

Particular stress was laid under the new management on the regulation of traders, many of whom were despicable creatures and lived as vagabonds. Governor Boone described them as being "of the refuse of the earth, who stick at nothing to obtain temporary advantage and who frequently provoke the Indians by injustice to throw the whole province in confusion."[66]   Under the new regulations the principal traders were responsible for the conduct of their subordinates. By this time it had been realized that it was

[63] *Council Journal,* 181; *P. R. S. C.,* XXIX, 259-263. To such lengths did provincial jealousy go that it was commonly said that the Cherokee War with South Carolina could not have continued so long had not the Indians been supplied with provisions and even ammunition from Virginia and Georgia. For many years John Stuart was Superintendent of Indian Affairs for the Southern Department and Sir William Johnson, for the Northern Department.
[64] *Col. Rec. N. C.,* VII, 839; *Indian Books,* Nov. 24, 1766.
[65] *S. C. Gaz.,* Aug. 1, 1768, and Feb. 2, 1769.
[66] *P. R. S. C.,* XXIX, 397, XXXI, 319.

useless to forbid the traders to give credit; so they were permitted to give limited credit for as much as thirty pounds weight of Indian dressed deerskins and all debts due by the Indians above that sum were considered as not recoverable. Neither was a trader to credit an Indian with more than five pounds of gunpowder and twelve pounds of bullets in one hunting season. These regulations were not enforced, for in 1773 the Creeks and Cherokees ceded to South Carolina and Georgia millions of acres of land to wipe out their indebtedness to the traders.

CHAPTER IX

ILLICIT TRADE AT CHARLESTON

I

The British government by enforcing efficiently its revenue laws and apprehending respectable smugglers at Boston produced a train of events that culminated in a war of rebellion involving the whole American continent, or that slender coastal portion of it inhabited by British colonists, and finally resulted in the loss to the empire of its American provinces. But in the far South at Charleston there was little smuggling, and the smuggler here was not the respectable person that he was at Boston. Nevertheless, a number of the great Charleston merchants threw in their lot with the Americans when the crisis came, rather than support the British Empire, which most of them regarded as the rock of their prosperity. This may be explained in part by the fact that the British government in its efforts to discover and destroy illicit trade pursued methods and employed agents that inflicted injury on the fair trader and thus created a lack of respect for British authority and a spirit of resistance to British law.

In the period following 1763 the British government found itself face to face with two stubborn facts. In the first place, there was a national debt of £148,000,000 incurred mostly by wars waged in the seventeenth and eighteenth centuries, about half of it representing the cost of the recently concluded Seven Years War. In the second place, there was a vast amount of smuggling carried on in every part of the empire, but especially in the North American colonies. These two facts gave rise to the two intricately interwoven colonial problems of major importance during this period; one the political problem of collecting a tax in America; the other the business problem of executing the laws against smuggling and thus providing additional funds for the current expenses of government and for the establishment of a sinking fund for the reduction of the national debt. But first of all it was necessary to revise the navigation and trade laws and make a program that could be carried through successfully, assessing duties collectible and profitable.

Remedies were applied where violations of the law had been most flagrant. The most profitable trade of the northern colonies was with the West Indies, both British and foreign. The Yankees were the colonial ocean-carriers. They loaded their vessels with British manufactures and home-made liquor, strong and fiery, distilled from imported molasses and sugar, one of the New England brands of rum being appropriately called "Kill Devil." They visited Africa and purchased slaves with these commodities. On their return voyage they touched at the Spanish West Indies, an excellent market for slaves, which could be exchanged for gold and silver in bullion and coin, cochineal, medical drugs, live stock and mules. Live stock and mules were acceptable on the plantations in the British West Indies, and there a rather high priced undutied sugar and molasses could be purchased, but not enough to supply the demand; so they might proceed to the French West Indies to buy molasses for the distilleries back home laden with a duty of six pence per gallon, or they might simply smuggle their commodities in and smuggle the molasses out and save themselves a six pence. The course they pursued is obvious. Cheap foreign molasses became, as John Adams phrased it, an ingredient of American independence. It was notorious that these American colonies had carried on a great smuggling trade during the war with the French West Indies and it was believed that English arms would have triumphed earlier in the Caribbean but for supplies furnished to the enemy from America through the Dutch and Danish Islands and through the Spanish Port of Monte Christi. It was this situation which caused the illustrious Pitt to declare that he would employ the whole force of the British navy rather than allow this illicit trade to continue. But the English government had considered some of this trade so essential that it had been carried on during the war by means of flags of truce.[1]

The new revenue laws passed in 1764 were designed to make this lucrative trade with the West Indies, hitherto of so little profit

[1] Anderson, *Origins of Com.*, III, 83-84.

to the British exchequer, a real source of income; and colonial trade outside the empire was to be made to contribute its quota of revenue. Therefore, these duties were to be reduced and collected. Instead of a duty of 5/6, foreign clayed sugars were to pay 2/, foreign molasses and syrup /3 per gallon, instead of /6. There was a duty on foreign goods reshipped from England to the colonies and Oriental and French dry goods paid duties for the first time. Wine from Madeira paid a very high tariff, while Spanish and Portuguese wines imported through Great Britain paid low duties. A small duty was placed on coffee and pimento shipped from one colony to another. The indigo industry was encouraged by raising the duty from /2 to /6 on foreign indigo imported into the empire.[2]

Already the machinery for the collection of duties had been made more effective by the act which authorized naval officers to act as deputized customs officials and assist in the apprehension of smugglers. Early in 1764 war ships were arriving at the colonial ports to assist in the enforcement of the acts of trade. Governors and naval commanders were receiving special instructions to suppress smuggling, and officers residing in England were notified that absenteeism in the customs service would be no longer tolerated. It began to look as if the trade of the North, particularly that of New England, would be ruined, for it was largely by the illicit trade that the New Englanders received the gold and silver which they remitted to England for manufactured goods.

What was a matter of bread and butter to New England was a matter of serious annoyance and loss to the South. South Carolina, in particular, had been an almost ideal colony, manufacturing little, importing much, exporting raw materials in great demand in the mother country, and buying quantities of slaves which the British merchants sent out. In regard to smuggling the colony's record was excellent, because there was little temptation in the South to carry on illicit trade.

In the middle of the eighteenth century Governor Glen informed his superiors in England that no country in America had less illegal trade than South Carolina, but that it would be difficult

---

[2] 4th George III, Cap. XV.

to prevent such trade because of the great number of rivers and
creeks and the small number of officers of the customs. He
recommended that the number of custom officers be increased and
that adequate salaries be paid them "which they may live upon."
Lieutenant Governor Bull reported in 1764 that he had been informed by customs officers and merchants of established character
that "some little illicit trade" was carried on but "in inconsiderable
degree," that there had been "few suspicions and fewer Instances
of Persons having carried on such trade here."[3]

It was with pride that the citizens of Charleston referred to
the fact that they were not smugglers. Henry Laurens made it
his boast that he had never engaged in illegal trade, and the editor
of the *South Carolina Gazette*, Peter Timothy, an ardent patriot
during the Revolution, remarked in his paper of April 6, 1769,
that the number of coasting schooners in the harbor had been
reckoned last Monday and their number found to be sixty-seven
—"not one of them employed in illicit or contraband trade." Nevertheless, the Board of Trade was alert and charged the governors
strictly to report all cases of smuggling, however inconsiderable,
to detail methods to combat it, and to recommend measures to
prevent it.

During the war with France the difficulty of getting evidence
to convict smugglers and the inadequate customs staff—only one
collector and two searchers being at Charleston, and one searcher
each at Beaufort and Georgetown—lured some into smuggling,
especially in the busy season when the crop was being carried off.
The illegal trader usually loaded his vessel with rum and molasses,
put in at some navigable inlet where there was no customs officer
and brought the contraband by night in small pettiaugers to
Charleston, where he disposed of his cargo and reloaded with
military stores, provisions, and supplies for the Indian trade, which
he carried to Pensacola and Mobile and disposed of at a huge profit
to the French settlers, using the Spanirds as intermediaries. In
this way the French received supplies which enabled them to retain
the good will of the Indians, and it was reported that it was they
who instigated the Creeks to murder the English traders in Geor-

[3] Carroll, *Collections*, II, 232; *P. R. S. C.*, XXX, 210-216.

gia during the war and encouraged the Cherokees to continue their war against South Carolina.[4]

To put an end to such traffic, so far as South Carolina was concerned, an act was passed June 10, 1760, prohibiting for three months the exportation of provisions and all goods and ammunition necessary for the Indian trade except under certain strict regulations: both seagoing and coastal vessels were required to give bond not to take on any smuggled goods after clearing out. The evil continued, however, and resulted in stricter regulation of the coastal trade. In 1762, upon complaint of General Amherst that the enemy were being supplied with provisions from some of the English colonies, another act was passed by the South Carolina legislature requiring coasters to renew bond every year and imposing a penalty for leaving the province without clearing out at a port of entry. The governor was authorized to deputize officers at places on rivers and creeks, with power "to seize, inform, and prosecute" offending vessels.[5] British officials soon encountered opposition in the performance of these duties. Governor Boone, formerly governor of New Jersey, wrote to the Board of Trade on January 9, 1763: "Opposing illicit trade and bringing to condemnation a vessel concerned in it rendered me obnoxious to the commercial people of the northern provinces, and my discountenancing it by every means in my power has by no means made me acceptable to the trading part of this colony."[6]

This was the situation when the new British regulations were being published in the *South Carolina Gazette,* and the British war-ships were taking their stations along the Atlantic coast to see that the laws were enforced. This new imperial program was not viewed with any great degree of alarm by the Charleston merchants; but a new and unforeseen development took place. Naval commanders soon showed themselves unfit for the business of enforcing the customs. They seized indiscriminatingly on ships engaged in the West Indian trade and almost put a stop to the lucrative trade to the Spanish West Indies which England had

[4] *P. R. S. C.,* XXX, 210-216; *ibid.,* XXIX, 42, 44-45; Cooper, *Statutes of S. C.,* IV, 109.
[5] Cooper, *Statutes of S. C.,* IV, 109-111; *ibid.,* 173-175.
[6] *P. R. S. C.,* XXIX, 307-308.

promoted for a century and which Spain had guarded the coast to prevent. The very life of Charleston trade was attacked when naval officers began to seize vessels engaged in the coastal trade. Seagoing vessels carried on a great deal of the inland trade in the wealthy plantation districts of South Carolina and Georgia. Charleston merchants who had branch stores in the country sent out supplies to them in decked pettiaugers to protect the goods from the weather. In the same type of vessel indigo, rice, and lumber were transported to Charleston, the boats usually carrying one hundred barrels of rice and passing along the sea coast because they drew too much water to make the entire trip by the inland waterways.

By provincial law such vessels were required to give bond every twelve months and were not obliged to enter and clear at the custom house every voyage, which might have caused them to lose a fair wind and lie windbound two or three weeks. By the new British regulations seagoing vessels laden with rice not provided with the proper papers were liable to seizure and libel in the court of admiralty, and imperial law superseded the provincial. Thus naval commanders, who were accustomed to conform absolutely to the letter of the law, seized on such coasting vessels; and the owners, even if the libels were dismissed in the admiralty court, were put to great expense as well as loss of time.[7]

It took an incredibly long time to gain the ear of the British government and rectify a simple error like this, and meanwhile planters, merchants and boat owners in general were liable to have the most ordinary course of their business interrupted by imperious naval commanders. It was not until January, 1766, when the petitions of the British merchants praying for the repeal of the Stamp Act were before Parliament, that Charles Garth, agent for South Carolina, presented a memorial to the Board of Trade "requesting its interposition to secure the coastal trade of the Province of South Carolina from being molested by Captains of His Majesty's Ships of War for not complying with regulations of the Act of Navigation."[8]

[7] *P. R. S. C.*, **XXX**, 273-276.
[8] *P. R. S. C.*, **XXXI**, Garth to B. T., Jan. 21, 1766.

II

While public opinion in the colonies was inflamed against the mother country on account of the efficient execution of the revenue laws, another blow was inflicted on colonial business by the passage of the Stamp Act, and some of the resentment that found vent in mob violence against the execution of this act probably had its origin in the earlier source of irritation. The Stamp Act, however, was resented on its own account. It seemed an unwarranted extension of the powers of Parliament at the expense of the provincial assemblies; it provided for the further increase of taxes at a time when the taxes collected under the revenue acts were more than the Americans were accustomed to pay; and finally, it came to America in the worst possible time psychologically. A period of economic gloom had succeeded a period of prosperity. The war with France had put in circulation a great deal of money to support fleets and armies, and American produce had been in great demand at good prices. Peace under any circumstances would have brought a cessation of war-time prosperity, but with the coming of peace three successive blows produced abnormal depression.

In the first place, in order to remove the "Gallic peril" from her borders and secure her American colonies, England had demanded Canada from France instead of the West Indies with which the colonies had close trade relations. Thus peace gave security to the northern colonies but also lessened trade to the West Indies. To the South, however, peace brought little diminution of the valuable West Indian trade, for by an act passed in 1764 South Carolina and Georgia were allowed, on the payment of slight duties, to export rice to parts of America southward of Georgia, in order that they might retain markets entered when England had occupied certain of the West Indies during the war. The second blow came with the revision of the trade and navigation laws and the establishment of an efficient machinery for the collection of duties. But here again the South was not so vitally affected as the North. The demand on the part of the northern traders might not be so good for rice and indigo, which were exchanged for Negroes and rum so much needed in the Carolina Indian trade. Rum manufactured from molasses that paid the

3 pence duty was doubtless higher priced than customarily, but all this was made even to the indigo planters by the law which placed a tariff of 6 pence per pound on imported indigo, instead of the 2 pence as formerly. A third blow was inflicted, which affected all America alike, when the colonies were prohibited, in 1764, from making any further issues of legal tender currency, in order that creditors, who were principally the representatives of the British merchants in America, might not suffer through the payment of debts in depreciated paper currency. This law produced a money stringency shortly after the war.

On the heels of this, in a half empty House of Commons, in February, 1765, the Stamp Act was passed, which had for its purpose the raising of revenue in America by requiring stamps on official and public documents in order to defray the expense of a small standing army at a time when there was serious trouble with the Indians. Two forms of resistance were immediately organized in America to combat the Stamp Act. The circular letter sent out by the House of Representatives of Massachusetts on June 6 to the legislative bodies of the other provinces proposing a meeting of delegates from the several provinces in New York to consider the Stamp Act, which meeting took place on October 7, prepared the way for dignified and rather supplicatory intercolonial protest against the Stamp Act as unconstitutional and therefore illegal, the constitutional argument being advanced that Parliament had no right to lay taxes on the Americans to which the colonial legislatures had not given their consent. Another form of resistance was mob violence. In South Carolina this form of resistance was no less effective and no less violent than in the other colonies.[9]

The organizer of the mob in South Carolina was Christopher Gadsden, a native of the province, who, like most business men of the day, followed various lines of employment. He was a merchant, factor, and wharf owner, though he probably was not one of the great importing merchants who acted as factors for British merchants. Those men did business on a large scale and were

[9] Non-importation was also resorted to, especially in the North, but seems not to have been effective in South Carolina in 1765. See Schlesinger, *Colonial Merchants and the American Revolution, 1763-1776*, pp. 63-65.

among the wealthiest men in the province, and Gadsden upon
several occasions was twitted by his political opponents upon his
lack of success in business. His main business seems to have been
operating a wharf where the planters brought their produce. He
also acted for a long time as factor at his own wharf, buying
country produce to be shipped abroad on his own account or to be
sold to the Charleston merchants to fill their orders. Gadsden
was one of that small number of men in America who felt that
American independence of England was necessary and inevitable,
and he was willing to use the most efficacious means at hand to
bring about this desirable end. No man in America strove more
earnestly than did he to bring about the Stamp Act Congress,
and it was probably due to his efforts that South Carolina sent
three delegates to the Congress including besides himself, Thomas
Lynch and John Rutledge; it was one of the two Southern provinces represented at this meeting, Maryland being the other.

The law and order element at Charleston may be typified by
Henry Laurens. Laurens was one of the great merchants, one
of the wealthiest men in the province, and one of those whose
business relations with English firms were very intimate and cor-
dial. Laurens believed that a "graceful obedience" should be
shown to the Stamp Act until "its annihilation" could be procured
in a constitutional way. He urged petition and remonstrance
to secure repeal, but he refused to vote for delegates to the Stamp
Act Congress. He opposed non-importation of British goods as a
means of bringing pressure to bear on the merchants of the mother
country, and, like a true representative of the British merchants,
he viewed with disfavor the budding interest in colonial manufactures that sprang up with the passage of the Stamp Act. He looked
upon the mob with abhorrence and disgust and was convinced "that
six men of spirit could in the beginning have crushed the whole
show; whereas meeting with no opposition, they carried their point
with a high hand."[10]

Men of the Laurens type dominated public opinion in Charleston until the fall of 1765. Lieutenant Governor Bull reported

[10] Wallace, *Laurens*, 116-122; Johnson, *Traditions and Reminiscences of the
American Revolution in the South*, 14.

that "while the people of the province believed that the Stamp Act imposed too great a burden upon them, they were generally disposed to pay due obedience to the act and at the same time in a dutiful and respectful manner represent to His Majesty the hardships it would lay them under and pray for relief." On the arrival of ships from New England (which usually came to Charleston early in the fall), with accounts of popular demonstrations against the Stamp Act in the North, all this was changed. Then, wrote Bull, "by the artifices of some busy spirits the minds of men were universally poisoned with principles imbibed and propagated from Boston and Rhode Island."[11] Perhaps, too, the accounts in the *South Carolina Gazette* of the violent measures being pursued in the North had some influence in inciting riot at Charleston.

When the *Planter's Adventure* arrived in the harbor, on October 18, 1765, with stamps, so threatening was the attitude of the mob that the vessel did not come up to the town but halted at Fort Johnson and deposited the stamps. Then followed nine days of rioting, whipping, hanging and burning in effigy, manifestos, and a picturesque bit of mummery whereby a coffin inscribed "American Liberty" was solemnly buried while the muffled bells of St. Michael's tolled. Four houses, at least, were searched by the mob in the effort to locate the stamps. Two of these belonged to men believed to be stamp collectors; the other two belonged to Chief Justice Shinner and Henry Laurens, whose disapproval of mob violence had brought down on him the suspicion of the populace. When November 1 arrived, the day on which the Stamp Act was to go into effect, the stamp distributor and the collector had been forced to resign and no stamps were to be found in the province. Without the use of stamps there could be legally no commerce, no exchange of property, no making of wills, no giving in marriage, and no suits instituted for the recovery of debts.[12]

The port of Charleston was closed for thirteen weeks, that is from November 1 until the first week in February. Lieutenant Governor Bull found, however, that if the law were strictly

[11] *P. R. S. C.*, XXX, 281-282.
[12] *S. C. Gaz.*, Oct. 19-31, 1765.

complied with it would subject the king's forces in East and West Florida, the Bermudas, and New Providence to danger of famine. He, therefore, in December, directed the customs officers to grant clearances (indorsed by him with the statement that no stamped papers had been distributed in the province) to a sufficient number of vessels to carry provisions to these places and naval stores to the king's ship *Escort* at the Bahamas. By the first of February, about one thousand four hundred ships were lying idle in the port, freight was at an unheard of low rate, the sailors were becoming licentious, and the clamor was growing louder every day for the opening of the port. Late in January efforts had been made to force the customs officers to clear vessels without the Lieutenant Governor's permission. Bull was obliged to make a compromise, for he was apprehensive of "popular tumult, violence and even bloodshed" if the letter of the law were longer complied with. He therefore issued permits for vessels to clear for which he charged a fee equal to that which would have been required had stamps been used.[13]

Officials, being liable under the Stamp Act to heavy penalties if they carried on public business without the use of stamps, were afraid to act. Creditors who wished to commence suits against their debtors were unable to procure a process from the court for the purpose. Dougal Campbell, the clerk of Common Pleas, refused to issue writs, saying that he had been named by office in the Stamp Act and was subject to heavy penalties for disobeying its provisions. Chief Justice Shinner declared that no stamps could be obtained and adjourned court. In the spring of 1766 popular clamor demanded that the courts of justice proceed in civil cases. Arguments were heard in open court for and against opening the courts, and the four Assistant Judges (men who were often natives of the province, since the small salaries paid them did not tempt British politicians) handed down a decision, the Chief Justice dissenting, that it was legally impossible to enforce the Stamp Act and that the courts should proceed as if there were no such act.[14]

[13] *P. R. S. C.*, XXX, 277-278; *ibid.*, XXXI, 21-25.

[14] *P. R. S. C.*, XXXI, 36; "It is very necessary that some measures should be taken to curb the growing power of the assistant Judges and support that of the Chief Justice," wrote Montagu to the Board of Trade. See *ibid.*, 40.

Agreeable to this decision, a judgment was ordered to be entered; but Dougal Campbell ·refused to enter it, or to issue any process by order of the court, whereupon the Assistant Judges by letter requested Bull to suspend Campbell for not obeying the order of the court. Bull referred the letter to the assembly, which also requested him upon two different occasions to suspend Campbell, but the governor refused to comply with these requests. The assembly then passed resolutions censuring Campbell and fining him. When the matter was brought to the attention of the authorities in Great Britain, the conduct of Bull in support of the clerk of Common Pleas was approved and the fine imposed by the assembly upon Campbell for his refusal to enter a judgment on unstamped paper was remitted. While these wrangles were clogging the action of the court, the Stamp Act was repealed, and the business of the courts could go forward as usual.[15]

In the winter of 1766 people were becoming restive under the embargo. Planters had no demand for their produce and the time to prepare for the spring planting had arrived. The merchants had ceased to make remittances. When the assembly convened it was found necessary to postpone the payment of taxes on account of the "stagnation of business and trade." As an emergency measure, certificates of indebtedness were issued to the public creditors, which being receivable at the treasury for taxes and other public dues, circulated like ready money, and thus somewhat relieved the money stringency.[16]

Bad as affairs were in South Carolina, they were worse in Great Britain. For the merchants' warehouses in America were still full of goods and the country, prevailingly agricultural, could produce every real necessity. In England, however, where dependence was largely upon commerce, there was "uncommon distress." "Manufacturing plants were idle, provisions extravagantly high, and the populace hungry." Besides, the British merchants needed woefully the several million pounds they were accustomed to receive from America.

Petitions from the trading towns began to flood the King and

[15] *P. R. S. C.*, XXXI, 270; Drayton's, *Memoirs*, 49-54.
[16] *P. R. S. C.*, XXXI, 33.

Parliament, urging the repeal of the Stamp Act. The result was that the so-called "Dignity of the Crown" was sacrificed upon this occasion to the pocket books of the British merchants; the colonists went unpunished for their acts of resistance, and the Stamp Act was repealed, March 8, 1766.

III

Before colonial business had recovered from the confusion wrought by the Stamp Act, the Townshend Acts were passed. The British ministry, in sponsoring the Townshend Acts was meeting the objection which Americans had raised to the Stamp Act. Franklin had explained before a committee of the House of Commons that the Stamp Act was an internal tax forced from the people without their consent, if that consent had not been given by their representatives in the local legislatures, because it was levied on all forms of commercial writing in daily use among the people. Parliament had a right to pass laws regulating American commerce, that is it might levy an external tax, which, Franklin said, "was a duty laid on a commodity imported which added to the first cost, and other charges formed a part of the final price of the commodity." People were not obliged to pay such a tax, for they could refuse to buy the article on which it was imposed. Therefore, the duties levied by Parliament under the new laws were placed on tea, glass, lead, paper, and painter's colors imported into the colonies.[17]

One complaint under the new trade and revenue laws was that it was impracticable for Americans to secure redress for abuses which they suffered at the hands of uninformed naval officers, corrupt custom house officials, and admiralty judges, since appeal from the admiralty courts was only to England, and the delays and costs involved in such an appeal were prohibitive. Partly for this reason, but principally for the more efficient execution of the laws relative to trade, the Townshend Acts established a board of commissioners of the customs at Boston, that stronghold of the smuggling trade. This board was given entire charge of the collection of customs throughout the continent and in Bermuda and

[17] *Amer. Tracts,* II, No. I, 16-17.

the Bahamas. Four courts of vice-admiralty were set up at Halifax, in Nova Scotia, at Boston, at Philadelphia, and at Charleston, with original jurisdiction over the capture of vessels in their respective districts, the court at Boston having appellate jurisdiction over the subordinate vice admiralty courts. The jurisdiction of the court established at Charleston extended over all cases arising in North and South Carolina, Georgia, East and West Florida.[18]

The Townshend Acts were directed mostly at the commercial provinces where smuggling was great. Even the odious writs of assistance, which authorized the searching of men's private premises for smuggled goods, were not felt keenly at Charleston where there was little smuggling. It was of course a matter of serious alarm in South Carolina, where the legislative department of government had made great encroachments on the executive, that the money raised by the rather heavy duties laid under the new laws was to be used to pay the salaries of colonial judges and civil officers, thus freeing them from dependence on the local assemblies. That portion of the law, however, which was to affect the plantation provinces more directly was the provision that commissioners of the customs were to reside in American ports and that revenue cases were to be tried in courts without a jury.

The Townshend Acts were passed early in the winter of 1767, and the immediate response of New England was the organization of associations among the merchants of the port towns agreeing not to import British manufactures, with certain exceptions, until the Townshend Acts were repealed. By October 27, 1767, Samuel Adams had brought Boston to the point of entering a non-importation association.

But Christopher Gadsden, the Carolina Samuel Adams, was not able to bring Charleston and the province of South Carolina into a non-importation agreement until nearly two years later, namely, July 22, 1769. The plantation province was doubtless harder to organize on account of the scattered condition of the inhabitants as compared with the provinces where town government prevailed, but the difference was due in large measure also to the fact that public opinion was not yet ripe in the South for

[18] *P. R. S. C.,* XXXVI, 221-227.

revolt against the obnoxious laws. Much water went over the wheels in South Carolina between the enactment of the Townshend Acts and the formation of a non-importation association in the mid-summer of 1769. The harassments to which business was subjected during this period created a spirit of resentment and resistance against arbitrary and tyrannical acts of the king's officials. The result was that many even of the conservative mercantile class, who regarded the maintenance of the empire as the rock of their prosperity, joined the naturally radical planter and mechanic classes in their demand for a repeal of the obnoxious laws. The irritations and losses occasioned by the administrative methods of royal officials were an important influence in finally placing South Carolina among the provinces in active rebellion against the mother country.

The career of Daniel Moore, collector of the port of Charleston, who resided in town only six months, illustrates how a fair trader might be harassed and injured in his property under the form of law.[19] Arriving in Charleston in March, 1769, at a time when the American people were excited over the promulgation of the Townshend Acts, Moore soon became involved in disputes with the merchants and planters over taking high fees at the custom house. The port charges for clearing sloops for the West Indies were particularly high. Laurens complained that a certain little sloop paid more than a ship ten times her burden used to pay six years previously. The upshot of it all was that some of the principal merchants sued Moore upon the charge of "having demanded and taken more than was his due."

The particular charge upon which Moore was arraigned was that of having taken fees for signing indigo certificates, an offense subject by parliamentary law to heavy penalties. Witnesses of "known verity and character," in fact, some of the chief merchants at Charleston, testified on oath that Moore had received fees from them for signing indigo certificates. After a tedious trial Moore was acquitted; but Egerton Leigh, the Admiralty Judge, stated that he had "given some cause for a prosecution of this nature." Moore was required to pay the trifling cost of two

[19] Henry Laurens' expression.

pleas, while the prosecutors were ordered to pay the remaining costs, which amounted to about £200 sterling.[20]

The career of Moore illustrates at its worst the deleterious effect of two clauses in the revenue law of 1763: the one decreeing that custom officials were not liable for damages where a probable cause for making seizures was certified by the judge— this was for the protection of custom officials from damage suits in the common law courts; the other which placed the burden of proof on the owner of the seized goods or vessel, and decreed that all claimants of such goods must deposit security to cover the cost of suit. Such provisions as these on the statute books placed too great a strain on the cupidity of the enforcement officers. It became more profitable for the owner of even a fair trading vessel, guiltless of any breach of the law, "to compound matters" with the custom officials—in plain language, to bribe them not to seize his vessel—rather than to have his case brought into court from which he was not able to emerge until he had paid the utmost farthing.

When court was held, it cost from £100 to £150 sterling; the ship, at best, after a month's detention and consequent loss of freight would be acquitted upon the equity of the case and a probable cause of seizure would very likely be certified by the judge, which would throw the costs of the suit upon the defendant. This throws light upon Daniel Moore's alleged assertion a month or two after his arrival at Charleston that he could "sweat them at law with their own money," referring to the merchants and planters who were opposing his high-handed measures. Two courses only were open to the merchants of Charleston: They might either "compound matters" with the custom house officers or they might put up such a fight against the law as would compel its repeal.

The tyranny of the law may be illustrated by the rather extreme case of the schooner *Active*. The *Active* was one of a number of small schooners employed in the trade between Charleston and Winyah. It was loaded in May, 1776, with pitch, tar, pork,

[20] P. R. S. C., XXXI, 42; Laurens, *Extracts from the Proceedings of the Court of Vice Admiralty*, 42.

etc., at Georgetown, bound for Charleston. By order of Moore the vessel was seized and libeled in the admiralty court. At the trial Judge Leigh declared: "There is not the least shadow or Pretence that the said vessel has at any time been employed in any illicit trade whatsoever, whereby his Majesty's revenue can be diminished or affected or the fair Trader undermined or prejudiced." Nevertheless, the judge, in order to protect Moore, certified a probable cause for seizure, which prevented the owner from bringing suit to obtain redress, and the owner was sentenced to pay the costs of the suit, which amounted to £150 sterling, in order that he might retain his small coasting vessel that was not worth as much as £80 sterling.[21] Henry Laurens, who had never had a contest with the revenue officials before the arrival of Moore, was active, as he phrased it, in opposing the "unwarrantable measures of the rapacious Collector," and he felt very strongly that he was the object of that officer's revenge when two of his coasting vessels were afterwards seized and prosecuted.

Many South Carolina merchants and planters owned plantations in Georgia, and when they sent their vessels loaded with either enumerated or non-enumerated commodities to such plantations they were required to enter bond and give security for the landing of them according to the law. In the overseas trade, however, where bond had been given for enumerated goods either in Great Britain or America, no bond was required for non-enumerated goods. But in the intercolonial coastal trade the fraudulent shipping of enumerated goods, under the pretense of the vessels being in ballast or having only non-enumerated articles, led in 1764-1766 to acts requiring a bond also for non-enumerated goods, and in one of the acts even for empty ships.[22]

The strict enforcement of these laws requiring bond would have subjected the owners of vessels employed in the Georgia plantation trade to great hardships. If the merchants complied strictly with the law they would have had, in many instances, to send their vessels on long roundabout trips by Savannah, Sunbury, or some other Georgia port to secure the proper documents to

[21] Laurens, *Extracts*, etc., 39-40.
[22] 4th Geo. III, Cap. XV, §§23, 24, 28; 5th Geo. III, Cap. XIV, §§25, 26, and 6th Geo. III, Cap. LII, §28.

take back to Charleston. For this reason, the law relative to the giving of bond had been laxly enforced, and often vessels coming from places where there were no custom houses had been admitted to entry at Charleston without having given any bond what-ever. "The practice of the custom house," asserted Judge Leigh, had been "various, fluctuating and uncertain."[23]

In May, 1767, Laurens sent the schooner *Wambaw*, a vessel of about fifteen tons burden, to his plantation on the Altamaha, loaded with tools and provisions, which were neither enumerated nor dutiable goods. So the Deputy Collector did not require a bond before the vessel cleared, but gave the master a certificate that the schooner was bound for Georgia with provisions for Mr. Laurens' Negroes. Laurens departed for Georgia by the short overland route and directed the loading of the *Wambaw* for the return trip with shingles for ballast. Finding that the nearest port where there was a custom house, Sunbury, forty miles distant, could be reached only by a road that had been pronounced impassable by the grand jury, he sent the master of the vessel to Frederica, nine miles away, to secure a lumber bond, for the law allowed bond to be given before a magistrate or where there was no custom house by "two known British merchants."

The *Wambaw* got back to Charleston before Laurens and was seized by George Roupel, the Searcher of Customs, on the order of Daniel Moore, the Collector, on the ground that she had not complied with the law by giving bond before leaving Georgia. Laurens' brother James and his friend Gabriel Manigault, reputed to be one of the wealthiest merchants in America, acted for him in his absence. These men were approached by representatives of the Collector and were told that if they would go to the custom house and "ask the Collector as a great Favour, to admit the vessel to an Entry," he would grant it, the purpose evidently being to make an example of Laurens and break the spirit of the Charleston merchants who had been putting up a great fight against the Collector. This offer was indignantly spurned. Then a hint was given that "the chastity of the vessel" might be pre-

[23] Laurens to Wm. Cowles, July 13, 1768.

served by allowing her "to slip away in the Dark." Again this proposal was rejected.

Upon the arrival of Laurens the vessel was in a fair way of being acquitted, for it was then learned that she had given the required bond in Georgia and Judge Leigh had asserted that the Deputy Collector's action in allowing her to depart without giving bond implied she might return in the same way. But Laurens volunteered the statement that the shingles were not wholly for ballast, that he meant to sell them afterwards, which caused the condemnation of the vessel, despite the judge's declaration that "no fraud was committed or intended" by the vessel. Laurens was required to pay all the costs and charges of the suit, including the judge's fee of £277, and it cost him about £175 currency money to repurchase his vessel, which was about fifty per cent more than the vessel was worth. A few days before, a French smuggler had been seized for importing and landing foreign goods at night and had been condemned; but because the case had not been contested the costs of the prosecution had been ordered paid from the proceeds of the sale of the vessel and cargo, and even the sailors' wages were paid out of the same fund.[24]

The case of the *Broughton Island Packet*, another of Laurens' seized schooners, was on trial at the same time as that of the *Wambaw*. The *Broughton Island Packet*, like the *Wambaw*, had been sent to Laurens' Altamaha plantation with tools and provisions, for which Laurens gave the bond for enumerated goods. She returned with logs and chunks thrown in solely for ballast and was seized at Charleston for not having obtained a lumber bond in Georgia.

The judge, however, acquitted the vessel on the ground that her load, unlike that of the *Wambaw*, was solely for ballast, and he declared that she had been seized "upon a frivolous Pretense." Nevertheless, the judge ordered Roupell, who had unjustly libelled the vessel, to pay one-third of the costs, the owner to pay two-thirds, and the thrifty judge collected a fee of £216/15. Leigh was not only sole Judge of the Admiralty Court, he was also At-

[24] Laurens, *Extracts*, etc., 1-2, 42; Laurens to Oswald, Oct. 10, 1767; Wallace, *Laurens*, 137-139.

torney General, Surveyor General, member of the council, and conducted besides a private law practice, which made it inevitable that compromising situations should develop. After the trial Collector Moore expressed his determination "to overset the judge." He said that he had paid Leigh £50 for his legal opinion as to whether to seize the *Broughton Island Packet* and that the vessel had been seized in consequence of Leigh's advice; then the judge had made a poor return by acquitting the vessel and ordering Moore's associate, Roupell, to pay one-third the costs. Leigh explained that the £50 had been given him some time before by Moore as a retainer for general legal advice, and that he had told Moore plainly that he could not advise him in admiralty or criminal cases, as in the former he must act as judge and in the latter as prosecutor.[25]

Since the judge had declared that the *Broughton Island Packet* had been seized "upon a frivolous Pretense" and had made no mention of a probable cause of seizure, Laurens was able to bring suit for damages against Roupell. Leigh, who as admiralty judge had pronounced the adverse verdict against Roupell, must now as Attorney General conduct his defense. The case was decided against Roupell and Laurens was awarded a verdict of £1,400 damages, which Roupell was allowed to pay out of the public revenues.

Shortly after the *Broughton Island* case, Collector Moore decamped "in a mean pitiful manner," and there was only one merchant in Charleston who failed to sign the representation of facts relative to the Collector's conduct which the merchants forwarded to the provincial agent in London.[26] Moore's hurried exodus was occasioned by an altercation between himself and Laurens, probably over the seizure of Laurens' vessels. Laurens assured the Collector that he would lay no hands upon him, he only intended, he said, to reprimand him for his folly, but he was provoked by the insolence of the old man "to lay a finger upon his nose," which was done in a very public place, with a crowd of spectators looking on who were ready to interfere when the Collector called a

[25] Leigh, *The Man Unmasked*, 43-44; Laurens, *Extracts*, etc., 5, 42.
[26] Miles Brewton whose family was connected with that of Moore.

brother officer to his rescue. The next day the Collector appointed a deputy and left the province.[27] "Such officers in any department as that collector, and officers of his disposition," wrote Laurens, "are men who shake the affections of the Americans and drive them to a greater distance from the powers in the Mother Country."[28]

But the departure of Moore brought no improvement in conditions at Charleston. The Carolina merchants were to find from bitter experience that the collector, and others like him, were the natural accompaniments of a commercial system which gave great powers over the property of American citizens to inadequately paid admiralty judges and custom commissioners and allowed them to batten upon court fees. They were tempted to promote suits at law because it meant money in their pockets. Roupell, the searcher, nursed a spirit of revenge, on account of the £1,400 verdict rendered against him, which he attempted to gratify at the first opportunity.

In June, 1768, the ship *Ann*, owned one-fourth by William Fisher, Quaker merchant of Philadelphia, one-fourth by Henry Laurens, and the other half by the firm of Cowles and Company, of Bristol, was loaded at Charleston with rice, deerskins, and other enumerated commodities. Laurens gave bond for the enumerated articles, obtained a general permit to load, and departed for Georgia, leaving the completion of the loading of the vessel to his clerk and the shipmaster. After Laurens' departure, the shipmaster received on board some rum, Madeira wine, pink root, and cattle horns, all non-enumerated goods. When the clerk went to the custom house to clear out the vessel with a manifest containing every article of her cargo, he was told that there were non-enumerated goods on board for which no bond had been given and that the vessel was liable to seizure. Neither the clerk nor any of Laurens' friends were allowed to give bond for the non-enumerated goods, notwithstanding that it had been customary to give bond after vessels were loaded but before they sailed, as had been done the day before in the case of Captain Maitland's ship.

[27] Laurens to Ross & Mill, Oct. 8, 1767.
[28] *Ibid.*, James Penman, Oct. 13, 1767.

Laurens' contention that the *Ann* was not even required to give a non-enumerated bond because there had been a "positive agreement of the deputy collector with the merchants that when Bond was given either in England or here for enumerated articles the other Bond for non-enumerated articles should not be required" probably would not hold water; for apparently the *Ann* returned to Great Britain regularly by way of Philadelphia, and was therefore subject to the regulation requiring a bond for non-enumerated goods of vessels engaged in intercolonial trade.

Before court was held the real motive for the seizure was revealed when Roupell offered to secure the release of the *Ann* if Laurens would surrender his verdict for £1,400, which offer was indignantly spurned. When the case came up, so notorious had Roupell's motive become that Leigh required of him the "oath of Calumny," an almost unused form, disclaiming any malicious motive. Not only was the *Ann* acquitted, but the judge declared that the master of the vessel had done everything in his power to comply with the requirements at the custom house but had been hindered by the customs officers themselves, that his conduct was free from all suspicion of fraud, that he had been "trepan'd" and surprised by the customs officers for "private Reasons." Nevertheless, the judge certified a probable cause of seizure, which deprived Laurens and his partners of any legal means of redress. Laurens was ordered to pay about half the costs, which amounted to about £100 sterling, a fifth part of which was used to discharge the judge's fee; meantime the ship had lost a freight round to Philadelphia. Egerton Leigh, who tried the case, was both judge and prosecutor, and Laurens felt that had Leigh been Attorney General and any other man judge of the admiralty the *Ann* would not have been seized.[29]

Laurens judged rightly that "the integrity of his reputation" was involved in the frequent seizure of his vessels. He asked Leigh, who was his nephew-in-law, whether a publication of the abstracts of the cases he had been concerned in would be considered a contempt of court, and was told rather superciliously that

[29] Laurens to Wm. Fisher, July 5, 1768; to William Cowles & Co., July 13, 1768; Laurens, *Extracts*, etc., 42.

he might publish what he pleased. In February, 1768, he brought
out a pamphlet called "Extracts from the Proceedings of the
Vice Admiralty Court in Charles Town, 1767-1768" in which
"the several cases adjudged by Leigh as sole Judge of the Admiralty Court were laid before the public." Leigh replied on March
30, 1768, in a pamphlet entitled "The Man Unmasked," in which
he presented a weak defense smoothly written and heavily inter-
larded with many learned allusions according to the approved liter-
ary fashion of the day. The contest between Laurens and Leigh
degenerated into one of those orgies of abuse in which our ancestors
sometimes indulged. An important development came when Laurens forwarded parts of his *Extracts* to influential men in England,
the American colonies, and the West Indies. The result of Laurens' disclosures was that Moore was obliged to resign as collector
and that Leigh was given a choice of his place on the bench or the
attorney generalship. He gave up his judgeship, which was the
poorer paying position, in September, 1768, and "there was no
gentleman duly qualified in the law" found in the province who
would accept the place as sole judge of his Majesty's Court of
Vice Admiralty. The place was vacant, therefore, for about eight
months, and a vessel that had been seized in the interim was restored to the owners "for want of such a judge."[30]   Into such
odium had the custom house service fallen that lawyers declined
to be concerned "for any of the King's officers in any case relative
to Custom House duties lest they should disoblige the merchants
and planters."[31]

Naturally, during this period Laurens' correspondence is full
of references to custom house officials. He frequently makes use
of the following adjectives to describe them: rapacious, haughty,
insolent, overbearing, ignorant, wicked. He connected the present discontent in America with the tyranny of the custom house.
"The king," he wrote, "never had in this province so vile a set of
servants in the Custom House as there are at present. Not moved
by any considerations except such as tend immediately to their
interests. Upon good terms with such men whose traffic exposes

[30] *S. C. Gaz.*, Sept. 17, 1768 and May 11, 1769.
[31] *P. R. S. C.*, XXXI, 414-415.

them to the suspicion of smuggling a little."[32]   He subscribed himself a staunch friend to the British constitution; but, he said,
"Wicked and Ignorant Officers in America have alienated the
affections of the Americans from the Mother Country even more
than the Laws so much complained of."[33]   It seemed particularly
galling to him that underpaid officials were empowered by British
law to seize the property of the substantial citizen.   On January
22, 1769, he wrote to Governor Grant, of East Florida: "If
Great Britain would fix a pack upon the unbroken steed—she
should at least have employed skillful hands to make the first attempts to put it on the humerous creature."

However odious British officials might make themselves to
honest American business men, they seemed to suffer "no diminution of reputation" in the mother country.   Laurens regarded the
removal of Moore and Leigh "as earnests of future attention to
us"; but Leigh, despite an unsavory moral character, remained
Attorney General, and became a baronet in 1772; Roupell, the
searcher, was promoted to be collector of the port of Charleston.   "On your side of the water," wrote Laurens, "we find such
men, are either rewarded or permitted to purchase Honours which
wear the aspect of Reward."[34]

In 1769, about the time a non-importation association was
being formed at Charleston, Laurens was publishing a second
edition of *Extracts from the Proceedings of the Court of Vice
Admiralty at Charles Town, in 1767-1768*, containing "Some
General Observations on American Custom House Officers and
courts of vice admiralty."   In the same year, Laurens, conservative merchant though he was, became one of the active promoters
of the non-importation association which had for its object the
boycotting of British manufactures and Negro slaves offered for
sale in South Carolina until all of the obnoxious legislation enacted
by the British Parliament since 1763, including the Townshend
Acts, should be repealed.   In 1765, Laurens could not bring himself to vote for delegates to the Stamp Act Congress; in 1769, he

[32] To Ross & Mill, Oct. 31, 1769.
[33] To Richard Grubb, Mch. 4, 1769.
[34] To Rev. Richard Clarke, Aug. 25, 1770.

still had little patience with Christopher Gadsden and the "mouth-ing Liberty Boys"; but when there came a parting of the ways such names as those of Henry Laurens and his brother James, both among the wealthiest merchants, and Miles Brewton, one of the largest slave merchants in Charleston, lent prestige to the radical cause. It was through the efforts of such men as these that the South Carolina Association became one of the most effec-tive on the continent.[35]

[35] The South Carolina Non-Importation Association probably hurt the business of the British merchants more than did any other American association, for it not only effected a sharp decline in the importation of British manufactures, but it put an absolute stop to the slave trade into Charleston.

CHAPTER X
NON-IMPORTATION AT CHARLESTON

I

The initiative in forming a non-importation association at Charleston, in order to bring about a repeal of the parliamentary revenue acts, was taken by small factors or merchants, by mechanics, and by planters, rather than by the great merchants whose economic interests had not seriously conflicted with those of the British merchants and whose grievances against the home government were of recent date. The small factor, even when he ordered merchandise direct from England, usually engaged in a retail trade, which in general was regarded by the gentlemanly representatives of the British merchants as a menial and degrading employment. The mechanic had a real grievance against the British merchants and their Charleston factors, who were allowed by the British government, almost without let or hindrance, to import vast numbers of slaves into the province. This competition of slave with free labor caused great numbers of the mechanics to emigrate to the northern colonies, where wages were lower but where they could count on employment.

The grievances of the planter antedated the enactment of the Townshend Acts. He chafed under the operation of the law prohibiting further issue of legal tender currency by the provincial legislature, a statute passed to favor the British merchants and their factors in the collection of debts. The money stringency caused by the operation of this law directly affected the planter whose whole crop sent in remittances to England was insufficient to pay his debts, and many of the merchants unable to make collections had gone into bankruptcy. The money stringency was further aggravated by the passage of the Townshend Acts which drained from the province much of the foreign gold and silver for the payment of duties on tea, lead, glass, paper, and painter's colors, so that the editor of the *Gazette* prophesied that "a Spanish dollar, of which we have sent millions to Great Britain, will, in a short time, be found nowhere but in the cabinets of the curious."[1] What made the Townshend Acts still more irritating was that the revenue raised from the duties levied under them was applied by the ministry for the support of "new commissioners of the customs, Placemen, parasitical and novel ministerial" officers, as the preamble of the South Carolina Association set forth, some of whom were hampering the coastal trade by their arbitrary interferences and "sweating" money from honest business people under the color of law.

Massachusetts, or rather Boston, was again the initiator of the movement that resulted in non-importation associations being adopted throughout the American colonies. The circular letter sent to the other colonial assemblies by the legislature of Massachusetts in February, 1768, calling in question the constitutionality of the Townshend Acts and asking for coöperation in order to secure their repeal, resulted in the drawing up of petitions against the acts in each province. These petitions were forwarded to the colonial agents in London to be presented to the king. No action having been taken on them, a committee of Boston merchants sent out a circular letter to the merchants of the port towns urging the adoption of non-importation resolutions agreeing not to import goods from Great Britain until the Townshend Acts were repealed.

The letter from the Boston merchants was received in Charleston in September, 1768, and shortly afterwards (October 18) Lieutenant Governor Bull wrote to the Earl of Hillsborough that "it met with no countenance having been handed from man to man with Silent Neglect."[2] In the winter and spring of 1769, the outlook for the adoption of non-importation resolutions at Charleston was not hopeful, although there was restlessness and discontent because Parliament had failed to act on the American petitions, and isolated efforts were being made by small groups to rouse interest in the non-importation movement. In the *South Carolina Gazette* of February 2, a form of agreement had been published

[1] *S. C. Gaz.*, July 27, 1769.
[2] *P. R. S. C.*, XXXII, 56.

for the non-consumption of imports, in which people were advised to refrain from purchasing new. Negroes and British manufactures, with some exceptions; to manufacture their own and their Negroes' clothes or to patronize the manufactures of the other American colonies; and to discontinue totally the use of mourning, which was under the ban because it was imported from Great Britain.

It was claimed that a number of people acceded to the non-consumption agreement by a show of hands, and there is some reason to believe that this may have been true, for there were schemes on foot for economy, industry, and home manufactures.[3] In order to encourage home manufactures the standing order for wearing wigs and stockings in the assembly was altered so as to allow assemblymen to transact committee business in caps and long trousers. The *Gazette* of March 2 informed its readers that many of the inhabitants of the northern and eastern parts of the province had, during the past winter, clothed themselves in their own manufactures, and that many more would have purchased them if they could have been got; that a great reform was "intended" in the enormous expense of attending funerals, for mourning, scarves, etc., and that Christopher Gadsden, Esq., had lately set a patriotic example by wearing blue homespun at the funeral of "the best of wives" rather than imported black cloth; that Carolina knit stockings were being sold at forty-five shillings a pair in preference to those of a better quality imported; that a subscription was on foot to set up a Manufacturing House in town and there was "in contemplation" the establishment of a paper mill; and, finally, that the legislature had in view the continuing of the bounty on hemp and flax in order that home manufactures might be supplied.

These efforts on the part of a few energetic individuals to rouse the people seemed to be meeting with small response in Charleston and the province in general until the appearance of two letters which came out in the newspapers in June. In the

[3] Schlesinger, *Colonial Merchants*, note, p. 142: "It was claimed that a number of people in different parts of the province did come into the association, proposed on February 2, by a show of hands; but the evidence of this is not very satisfactory." See *S. C. Gaz.*, June 8, 1769.

Gazette of June 1, a letter signed "Planter from the Pedee" called the attention of brother planters to the recent public statement of Lord Hillsborough that the merchants of Charleston had acted "like a wise and prudent people in having treated, according to accounts from hence, the circular letter from the Committee of Boston Merchants with the silent contempt it deserved." The writer inquired whether the merchants, who might in general be called "mere Birds of Passage, come here to make a fortune," or the planters, who were "fixed to the country," would be "the greatest sufferers by the late unconstitutional measures" of Parliament. He advised the planters to wear their old clothes until their own manufactures were established and to purchase, when necessary, the manufactures of the other American colonies. He proposed compelling the merchants to come into a non-importation agreement by refusing to deal with those who imported articles on the list of boycotted goods, "either now or hereafter when matters were settled." Perhaps the fruits of this letter were manifested in those "Societies of Gentlemen," which the *Gazette* of June 15 reported were being formed in town, agreeing "to purchase no kind of British goods that could be manufactured in America and to clothe themselves in homespun as soon as it could be got."

In the *Gazette* of June 22 was published a letter signed "Pro Grege et Rege," the pseudonym of Christopher Gadsden. It was addressed significantly enough "To Planters, Mechanicks, and Freeholders of the province of South Carolina, noways concerned in the Importation of British Manufactures." Importers of European goods were stigmatized as strangers in the province, many of a few years residence, whose private interests "were so glaringly against us," that they had not called a single meeting to confer on the letter of the Boston merchants. It was folly to listen to arguments that the revenue acts were to be repealed. Resolve on non-consumption, Gadsden advised, and the merchants will agree not to import. Appended to the letter was a suggested form of agreement. The next week (June 29) the *Gazette* published a non-importation agreement suitable for working men and farmers. This was the first form of a non-importation agreement acceded to by any considerable number of people and it naturally served the class interests of its promoters, planters and mechanics being allowed to import a list of articles deemed necessary on the plantations and in the shops. They agreed that prices should not advance, that they would practice economy, promote American manufactures, and discard the use of mourning. The agreement was to be in force until the Townshend Acts were repealed, and all were urged to sign it within one month on pain of being boycotted.

The mechanics, whose class interests had not been sufficiently served by the agreement of June 29, met on July 3 and 4 under the Liberty Tree in Mr. Mazyck's pasture and proposed two amendments which were inserted in the agreement. One of these provided that no Negroes should be brought into the province after January 1; the other, that no goods usually imported from Great Britain should be purchased from transient traders. We know why the mechanic objected to the Negro; he seems also to have objected to the transient trader from an economic motive. Mechanics to eke out a living often conducted small retail establishments in connection with their trades. Their competitors in the retail business were the masters of vessels, the chief transient traders, who set up shop on the decks of their vessels where they sold goods wholesale and retail as long as they stayed in port.

Meanwhile, the merchants had held a meeting on June 30 and appointed a committee to draw up a report, after which they adjourned until July 7, when they adopted a non-importation agreement of their own. This agreement was to continue only until January 1, 1771, unless the revenue acts were repealed sooner. The list of goods allowed to be imported was larger than in the other agreement. The mechanics' amendment in regard to Negroes, which in the first form of agreement read: "We will not upon any Pretense whatever, directly or indirectly import, or purchase, any New Negroes or slaves brought into this Province for Sale, from and after the 1st of Jan. 1770," was altered so as to prohibit the importation of Negroes from the West Indies beginning October 1, 1769, and from Africa beginning January 1, 1770. The merchants who conducted the Negro business on a large scale received most of their merchandise direct from Africa, while the smaller factors received most of their human chattels from the West Indies. For the rest, all the terms of the rival agreement were taken over except the pledges for promoting local manufactures and for dispensing with the use of mourning. The merchants added wine to the list of forbidden imports, probably because the heavy duties on wine injured the business of the fair trader and contributed to the prosperity of smugglers.[4]

Charleston, which formerly had no non-importation association when all America was entering into agreements not to import, now had two rival and mutually antagonistic organizations. The mechanics objected to the merchants' resolutions because they gave no encouragement to American manufactures and permitted the continued use of mourning. The merchants complained that the first agreement had been framed to enable planters and mechanics to import articles thought indispensable to them while the merchants received no special favors. It was, they urged, an unjust attempt of one part of the community, whose particular wants had already been served, "to throw a burden on the rest more grievous than ever was conceived by the most arbitrary minister of the most despotic king." The agreement in regard to mourning affected the merchants in particular, because their stores were well stocked with mourning goods.[5]

The mechanics and the planters, however, held the whip hand. The mechanics and other inhabitants of Charleston took lists of the "gentlemen in trade" who had signed the first form of agreement "in order that they might lay out their money with them only." The planters gave orders to their factors not to purchase from, or sell to, any merchants who refused to come into the first association. Such pressure was brought to bear that the merchants made overtures for a joint committee to draft a uniform agreement containing the essentials of the two rival agreements. Accordingly, a new form of agreement was evolved containing most of the provisions of the earlier associations. On July 22 Christopher Gadsden read this new form to an assembly of planters,

[4] S. C. Gaz., July 6 and 13, 1769.
[5] See article signed "Merchants of Charles Town" in S. C. Gaz., July 13.

mechanics and others under the Liberty Tree, once for information, and a second time paragraph by paragraph that objections
might be raised. The whole was voted satisfactory and was signed
by two hundred and sixty-eight people headed by the members of
the assembly.[6]

The subscribers engaged to import no European or East Indian goods from Great Britain or elsewhere, with some allowance
for orders too late to countermand, except "negro cloth, not exceeding 1s.6d per yard, striped Duffils blankets, osnabrugs, coarse
white linens, not exceeding 1s.6d. per yard, canvas, bolting cloth,
drugs and family medicines, plantation and workmen's tools, nails,
firearms, bar steel, gunpowder, shot, lead, flints, wool cards and
card wire, mill and grindstones, fish hooks, printed books and
pamphlets, salt, coals, and salt-petre." The usual prices were to
be maintained, American manufactures were to be promoted, and
mourning apparel was to be dispensed with. Trade with transient
vessels was prohibited, after November 1st, except for salt and
coals; no Negroes were to be imported from the West Indies after
October 1st, 1769, nor from Africa after January 1, 1770; and
wine was not to be imported. Lastly, subscribers were required
to cut off all trade relations with those who refused to sign the
agreement within one month, and delinquent subscribers were to
be treated with the utmost contempt.[7]

The establishment of the South Carolina Non-Importation
Association resulted in a dictatorship in which power was exercised
ostensibly by a General Committee of thirty-nine, consisting of
thirteen planters, thirteen mechanics, and thirteen merchants, who
were charged with the execution of the Association. Real power,
however, was exercised by a few energetic leaders. The "first
movers in the Grand Machine," as named by Bull, were: Mr.
John Mackenzie, a planter, who had been educated at Cambridge;
Thomas Lynch, Esq., another planter, who though "a man of
sense, was very obstinate in urging to extremity any opinion" he
had adopted; and Christopher Gadsden, a factor and the owner
of an extensive wharf at Charleston which was in the process of

[6] *S. C. Gaz.*, July 6 and 13, 1769.
[7] *S. C. Gaz.*, July 27, 1769.

construction, "a violent enthusiast in the cause" who viewed "every object of British moderation and measures with a suspicious and jaundiced eye" and maintained "with great vehemence the most extravagant claims of American exemption." Mr. John Neufville, the Chairman of the Association, was one of those merchants who had sued Daniel Moore, the Collector, for extortion in 1767. He was "rather a man of straw stuck up than a man of real consequence," wrote Bull, "pleased with the office and flattered with his own importance." Among the numerous "subalterns of this Corps" was Peter Timothy, the energetic editor of the *South Carolina Gazette.* These leaders acted as "tribunes of the people" and "directed the motions as they (had) previously settled the matter" at public meetings in taverns or under the Liberty Tree.[8]

The chief means relied upon to enforce the Association were intimidation and economic pressure. One clause of the agreement proscribed all persons who failed to sign the Association within one month. On September 7, when the time limit had expired, handbills were distributed over the city with the names of all non-subscribers, to show the smallness of the number and "to hold them up to view" as men who were not friends of America. At that time only thirty-one persons, exclusive of Crown officials, had refused to sign. And only three or four of these, wrote "Epaminondas" were planters of any property, the rest being with very few exceptions, "little Scotch shopkeepers of no consequence."[9] But two of the most strenuous objectors to the resolutions were planters: William Wragg, who subscribed himself a planter but who frequently advertised European and East Indian goods in the newspapers like a great merchant; and William Henry Drayton, a nephew of Lieutenant Governor Bull and a brilliant, hot-headed young planter of great wealth, who later became one of the most active and capable of the patriot leaders. The names of both these men appeared in the handbills and both issued protests.

How effective proscription by the Association was may be illustrated by the case of Drayton, who had attacked the legality

[8] *P. R. S. C.*, XXXII, 415-416.
[9] *S. C. Gaz.*, Apr. 5, 1770.

of the proscription clause in a letter signed "Freeman" in the *Gazette* for August 3. In this article he asserted that "To stigmatize a man with the infamous name of an enemy to his country can be legally done by no authority but by that of the legislature." After a newspaper controversy with Gadsden over this point, Drayton petitioned the legislature for a redress of the grievances suffered by him under the operation of the Association, stating that by the Resolutions certain men had "illegally confederated and conspired" to distress those who would not accede to the Resolutions within one month; as a result people had been compelled to sign the Resolutions or expose themselves to certain ruin. Drayton himself had not been able to sell his commodities, "which remained upon his hands at great risk and heavy expense" because "when possible purchasers learned whose property they were they immediately declined any further treaty for the purchase of them." He complained that there was no redress to be found in the courts of law, because the majority of the judges had acceded to the Resolutions and were therefore disqualified to act in his case; "so general had been the subscription to the Resolutions," that any jury drawn to try the suit would consist of men under the same disqualification. Drayton's petition, however, was rejected by the legislature without a reading, and the only recourse left him was to have it published in the *Gazette*. On January 4, 1770, Drayton sailed for Europe, a beaten man, on Captain Curling's ship *London*, which was carrying back to England goods proscribed by the Association.[10]

The influence of the conservative element was very perceptible, however, even in 1769. No such disorderly proceedings occurred as disgraced the Stamp Act days. The great merchants, though not hearty "Resolutioners" in the beginning, contributed effectively to bring about moderation. Henry Laurens, a conservative merchant, often presided at meetings under the Liberty Tree and at Dillon's Tavern. Miles Brewton, who could not bring himself to the point of taking up arms against his king in 1775, was an active supporter of the Association in 1769, to his great financial loss, for he was one of the most extensive slave

[10] *S. C. Gaz.*, Dec. 14, 1769; *Boston Chronicle*, January 11, 1770.

212 NON-IMPORTATION AT CHARLESTON

merchants in Carolina. "The conduct of our merchants has been exemplary and consistent, throughout the arduous struggle for constitutional Liberty, and will redound to their lasting Honour," wrote Timothy in the *Gazette* of November 1, 1770.

The Committee of Inspection opened and inspected every package of goods imported from Great Britain and examined weekly the proscribed goods which had been seized and placed in storehouses rented by the Association. Upon one occasion the Committee found that two business firms had opened and disposed of uninspected articles. The members of the firm were haled before the General Committee to show cause why they should not be treated with the utmost contempt and could not give a satisfactory answer. Whereupon the General Committee summoned a special meeting of the people, instead of publishing the names of the delinquents, as the Association prescribed, because it was apprehensive that disagreeable consequences might follow the publication of their names. As a matter of fact, there was much talk in the streets of effigies, tar and feathers, but the offending firms complied with the terms of restitution demanded by the General Committee and the incident was closed.[11]

The comparative moderation that characterized proceedings at Charleston may be illustrated by an incident related in the *South Carolina Gazette* of June 21, 1770. An effigy representing a violator of the Association was exhibited in the pillory near Dillon and Gray's tavern on Broad Street. The attached placard contained a threat to treat with carting, tarring and feathering-every person who presumed to deal with such violators. "At ten o'clock, a venerable old gentleman, cloathed with authority—took it down without the least opposition and secured it in the guard house." It reappeared later and was carted throughout all the principal streets of the town attended "by a prodigious concourse of people." Moderate people were concerned at this exhibition, observed the editor of the *Gazette,* but they concluded "there was no safety in breaking the Resolutions."

Nevertheless there was an iron hand in the velvet glove. When non-importation had fallen through in New York and

[11] *S. C. Gaz.,* May 17, 1770.

Philadelphia and only Boston and Charleston were maintaining their resolutions not to import, Philip Tidyman, a jeweler, became a violator of the Association by receiving goods not ordered by him but consigned to him by some person in England. Upon detection Tidyman fled to a ship in the harbor rather than face the General Committee. He sailed for London carrying with him the case of goods which he had concealed from the Committee, but later printed in the *Gazette* a rather abject apology for his "misbehavior" and was restored to favor.[12]

Economic pressure was the principal weapon used in promoting and maintaining the Association. The subscriber was required to cut off all commercial dealings with the non-subscriber. He could not purchase Negroes or merchandise from him, nor make use of his wharf or docks to land goods or produce, nor hire stores belonging to him, nor buy rice, indigo, or other plantation produce from him. The non-subscribing planter was obliged to ship his own produce and found it hard to secure freight against combinations of subscribers; the merchant found his business ruined.[13] Under such conditions the non-subscriber was not aggressive and found it to his advantage to adhere strictly to the Resolutions, even if he were not a member of the Association.

Charleston was the last of the American ports to give up non-importation, and discipline seems to have been maintained to the end. The *South Carolina Gazette* of October 4, 1770, reported that most of the dry goods stores were nearly empty, but no merchant had proposed that a general importation should take place. "Indeed," says the editor, "should any merchant here Attempt to imitate those of New York the Landed Gentlemen and most considerable Planters seem determined entirely to withdraw their custom from those Houses never to be restored."

The fact that the General Committee was vested with somewhat loosely defined inquisitorial and dictatorial powers to interfere in men's private business, was bound to result in some members being accused of using their official positions to further their private interests. The General Committee advertised Ann

---

[12] *S. C. Gaz.*, Nov. 8, 1770.
[13] *P. R. S. C.*, XXXII, 342.

and Benjamin Mathews, in the *Gazette* of May 31, 1770, "as violators of the Resolutions and as persons audaciously counteracting the united sentiments of the whole body of people, not only in this but in all the Northern provinces, and preferring their own little private advantage to the great good of America." People were cautioned against having any commercial dealings with them and they were pronounced obstinate and inveterate enemies to their country and unworthy of the least confidence and esteem. Mrs. Mathews' defense was given to the public, not by the *South Carolina Gazette*, in which she had been advertised as a delinquent, but by the *South Carolina and American General Gazette*, published by Robert Wells, who had been accused of being lukewarm in his support of the Association and who during the Revolution became a Loyalist.

Mrs. Mathews stated that the merchandise in dispute had been ordered before the Resolutions had been entered and that Captain Curling had been detained by contrary winds and did not arrive until January 11. Soon after the goods arrived the Committee of Inspection had called on her son to see the original order, which he submitted to them; but the Committee had refused to allow the goods to be sold, and insisted that he sign a paper agreeing to store the goods, which he agreed to do without consulting his mother, fearing that he would be advertised. She asked the Committee to reconsider the case and offered to reship the goods if the Committee would indemnify her friend in England through whose endorsement the goods had been obtained. When the goods were becoming damaged, she, in the absence of her son, had opened and sold them because she had no other means of supporting herself or paying the friend who had given security for her in London. She charged that Mr. John Edwards, one of the Committee, had received two cargoes a short time before hers, which she defied to the Committee to say were ordered before hers, and he had been allowed to sell them. Mr. Rutledge had received a pair of horses from London as late as April 13, which had not been reshipped, because they came in consequence of an old order which he could not countermand. Her case was similar to his, but a great difference was being made in the cases because he was a man of spirit who could not be trifled with, while she was a poor widow living a few doors from a leading member of the Committee and thus might take a little cash now and then from some of his customers. Ann Mathews' fight, however, was in vain. Benjamin Mathews could not resist the pressure exerted on him. In the *South Carolina Gazette* of October 4, he made humble confession and sued for pardon.

There are echoes of Ann Mathews' charges in a letter which Lieutenant Governor Bull wrote to the Earl of Hillsborough on October 20, 1770. "It is true," declared Bull, that "many of the Subscribers must submit to fate while the rich leaders enjoy their trade in state; but they suffer by their own act, and comfort themselves with the pleasing delusion that their sufferings are to be the means of bringing the Parliament and the people of Great Britain to comply with the claims of American immunities."[14] In a letter of December 5, Bull wrote to the same gentleman that many merchants were for continuing the Resolutions because their stores were full of goods, and he mentioned by name John Edwards, Hawkins, in company with James Laurens, and John Ward, as merchants charged with continuing to supply their stores.[15]

It is not possible at this late date to establish the truth or falsity of such charges. It is true, however, that not only poor widows and middle class people suffered through the operation of the Association, but some of the highest placed persons at Charleston. The first test case brought before the General Committee was that of Captain Alexander Gillon, a merchant originally from Holland, who was to become commodore of South Carolina's navy during the Revolution. He had received one hundred pipes of wine from Teneriffe which he refused to store and reship on the order of the General Committee, claiming, like Ann Mathews, that the wine had been ordered before the Association had been formed. This occasioned the first call of the inhabitants to meet under the Liberty Tree, "where probably," wrote Henry Laurens in anticipation, "we shall hear the Roaring if not of the Lion, at least,

[14] *P. R. S. C.,* XXXII, 342.
[15] *Ibid.,* 415.

the whelp of a Lion, for I verily believe the people here are in Earnest and will stand firm to the utmost of their limited ability." Gillon was heard with close attention and the matter was afterwards discussed; but when those who were of the opinion that Captain Gillon should be allowed to sell his wine were asked to raise their hands, not a hand was raised. Gillon was required to sign an agreement that he would store his wine until a general importation should take place.[16]

Economic pressure was also brought to bear against recalcitrant colonies who failed to live up to their agreements. Rhode Island and Georgia seem to have been the worst offenders. The Rhode Island merchants had been intimidated into non-importation by threats of boycott from the great trading towns of the North, and Governor Hutchinson said of them that they "professed to join but privately imported to their great gain."[17] Georgia was young and not yet self-supporting, with a large British official class and few who at this time felt themselves to be native Americans. A feeble non-importation association was formed, September 19, 1770, patterned after that of South Carolina. In the spring of 1770 when the slave ships began to arrive and were turned back at Charleston, they made their way to Savannah, where the Georgia merchants purchased the Negroes and attempted to introduce them overland into South Carolina, though without great success, according to the *South Carolina Gazette* (May 17), since the border was narrowly watched by the South Carolina brethren. Also it was said that European and East Indian goods were frequently shipped into Charleston from Georgia in rice casks.[18]

The South Carolina Association took action against Rhode Island and Georgia on June 27, 1770, at a meeting under the Liberty Tree. The resolutions then adopted declared that undoubted intelligence had been received that some of the inhabitants of the colony of Rhode Island had been "guilty of a Breach of their agreement, by Importing British goods while the minds of the country were filled with Anxiety for the Suspending Fate of their Liberties." These Rhode Islanders "ought to be treated as

[16] *S. C. Gaz.*, Jan. 24, 1770; Laurens to Habersham, Jan. 27, 1770.
[17] Schlesinger, *The Colonial Merchants*, 195.
[18] *S. C. Gaz.*, June 28, 1770.

Betrayers of American Liberty until they have made Ample Satisfaction and Atonement for [the] heinous Duplicity of [their] Conduct," and accordingly "all commercial Intercourse & Dealing between us & them shall at once and finally cease."

The resolutions further stated that the people of Georgia had acted a "most singular infamous Part from the first" and therefore "ought not only to be considered under the same Predicament as the deluded people of Rhode Island, but also to be amputated from the rest of their Brethren as a Rotten Part that might spread a dangerous Infection." Breaking off economic relations with Georgia, however, was not easy. The resolutions did not apply to goods already ordered and to be transmitted to that province through the port of Charleston, nor to subscribers who owned estates in Georgia, who were allowed to import the produce of such estates as usual. Also it was found necessary not to allow the resolutions of the 27th of June to extend to vessels which were at least one-half owned in South Carolina, so far as to prevent their entering South Carolina ports in ballast and loading with commodities not excepted by the resolutions. It was not until September 27, 1770, that the order prohibiting the transportation of European goods to Georgia in any of the South Carolina coasting vessels became effective.[19]

The statistics given in the following table show that non-importation was as successful at Charleston as in the other great American ports.[20]

Value of goods in pounds sterling imported into America from England and Scotland from 1768-1771:

	1768	1769	1770	1771
New Eng.	£430,807	£223,695	£394,451	£1,420,119
New York	490,674	75,930	475,991	653,621
Penn.	441,830	204,979	134,881	728,744
Va. & Md.	669,522	714,943	717,782	920,326
Carolina	300,925	327,084	146,273	409,169

From this table it appears that in the several colonies, with the exception of Pennsylvania, the non-importation associations were

[19] S. C. Gaz., June 28 and Aug. 23, 1770.
[20] MacPherson, Annals of Com., III, 486, 494, 508, 518-519.

efficiently enforced for about a year; that if the short period of a year is considered, New York must bear the palm for efficiency of enforcement, its imports from Great Britain falling from £491,774 in 1768 to £75,930 in 1769. But if one considers that non-importation was in force for two years in Pennsylvania, in 1769 and 1770, and that during the first year it imported from Great Britain about half as much as usual, and during the following year about one-third as much, then Philadelphia must take the lead for tenacity of purpose. And enforcement was difficult in Pennsylvania because in the neighboring provinces of Virginia and Maryland the non-importation associations were never really in force. The Charleston association counted heavily upon Philadelphia. When the air was full of reports and rumors, in the fall of 1770, that the associations on the whole continent were breaking up, the editor of the *South Carolina Gazette* wrote: "We do not give up the fair Quaker, although some of her merchants have dishonoured her, under the idle pretence, that the Scotch Factors in Maryland are running away with all their back country custom on one side, while Importers at New York will soon do the same on the other."[21]

In the matter of enforcement of its non-importation agreement, Charleston took its rank along with the other colonial ports, a little ahead of Boston and a little behind Philadelphia. New England reduced its imports from £430,807 in 1768 to £223,695 in 1769; while Carolina imports from England were valued at £327,085 in 1769 and £146,273 in 1770. This remarkable falling off in the importations from Great Britain into the Carolinas is a striking indication of the extent to which the trade of North Carolina was controlled by Charleston, for in North Carolina the Non-Importation Association was entered into only by planters; the merchants unhampered by commitments probably carried on their usual trade.[22]

The statement made in Parliament that the plantation provinces actually increased their importations during this period was emphatically not true of South Carolina, and was not even true

[21] Issue of Nov. 1, 1770. Compare Schlesinger, *Colonial Merchants*, Chs. IV. and V.

[22] *S. C. Gaz.*, May 31, 1770.

of the infant colony of Georgia, which received its imported goods mostly through Charleston and could therefore be controlled by that city. It was true, however, of the provinces of Virginia and Maryland where enforcement of the associations must have been well nigh impossible because of the absence of any one large port, and because the British and Scottish factors were in almost complete control of business.

The exclusion of British manufactures was not specially stressed at Charleston as was the exclusion of wine and slaves. For it was necessary to allow the importation of a comparatively extended list of manufactures in order to win the hearty cooperation of the merchants whose grievances were more recent and less heavy than were those of the planters. In a province where the importation of Negroes was so vast, it was clearly perceived that the most effective weapon to employ against Great Britain was the exclusion of slaves. Said a "Planter from the Pedee," "purchasing Negroes is in fact purchasing British manufactures." And in the year 1770 it was estimated by Lieutenant Governor Bull that the British merchants lost in the province of South Carolina through the resolutions not to import British manufactures or slaves the sum of £300,000 sterling.[23]

The South Carolina Association differed in one significant respect from those formed in the northern colonies. It was to remain in force until all of the acts of Parliament since 1763 regulating American commerce were repealed. When reports came in the spring of 1770 that a bill had been ordered to be brought into the House of Commons to repeal the duty on paper, glass, painter's colors, etc., imported into the British colonies of North America, the South Carolina General Committee immediately forwarded a circular letter to the committees of the other colonies, in which it was asserted that "if any province should take advantage of the repeal of these trifling duties to reopen trade with Great Britain, it would have been infinitely better to have submitted quietly to the yoke from the beginning." The First Continental Congress took the same position in 1774 that South Car-

[23] *S. C. Gaz.*, May 24, 1770.

olina was maintaining in 1770, that is, it demanded the restoration of the commercial system as it had existed before 1764.

By the autumn of 1770 all the American ports except Charleston had abandoned non-importation. On December 13, a final meeting of the association was summoned at the Liberty Tree. A motion was made by a person of no importance that non-importation be abandoned. There was an affirmative response from the assembly of planters, merchants, and mechanics. Whereupon, says Bull, "Mr. Lynch who came 50 miles to Town on purpose exerted all his eloquence and even the trope of Rhetorical Tears for the expiring liberties of his dear country, which the merchants would sell like any other merchandise." His efforts were seconded by two of his brethren who proposed importing goods from Holland; but the strugggle was in vain and non-importation was given up except for tea. It was not, however, until May 30, 1771, that the *South Carolina Gazette* reported that a general importation had taken place and stores that had been quite empty were beginning to fill up.[24]

II

From the spring of 1771 until the fall of 1774 was a time of great business activity. Great quantities of East India tea were being imported despite the non-importation agreement, great numbers of slaves were being brought in and sold at fancy prices, and bills of exchange were selling at a premium, a sure sign that the planter was in debt to the merchant. Then came the Boston tea party and the prosperity of the merchant was soon dissipated.

East India tea went through many hands before it reached the American consumer. First the company brought the tea to England and paid an import duty on it there; then the company offered the tea at auction sales to the English exporters, who bought it and shipped it to their American correspondents; next a duty of three pence per pound was collected on it at the custom houses in America; lastly, the American wholesale dealers sold it to the retailers, and when it finally reached the American consumer it was a high-priced commodity in little demand as long as the cheaper smuggled Dutch tea could be had.

[24] *P. R. S. C.*, XXXII, 434.

Parliament attempted to solve the tea problem and prevent the bankruptcy of the great East India Company in which many high-placed people in England were financially interested, by passing legislation in 1767, 1772, and 1773. The Townshend Acts imposed a duty of three pence per pound on tea imported into America and at the same time took off the heavy tea tax collectible in England. The East India company was allowed to name the set up price of tea at auction sales in England, but was made responsible for any deficiency in the revenue resulting from the discontinuance of the English tea duty. This legislation made tea cheaper in America than in Great Britain temporarily; but it did not accomplish its purpose, for the East India Company when hard pressed by creditors advanced the price of tea at the auction sales and this made the tea again more expensive in America than smuggled tea.[25] In 1772 a drawback of only three-fifths of English duties was allowed and the East India company was no longer responsible for any deficiency in the tea revenue. Again the legislation failed of its object; the warehouses of the company were full of unsalable tea and the company on the verge of bankruptcy. Finally, the Tea Act of May 1773 seemed on the point of accomplishing the two-fold purpose of the British government of removing from Americans the temptation to smuggle by making East India tea as cheap, if not cheaper than the smuggled article, and of enforcing the collection of a parliamentary tax in America.

By this act the three pence duty on tea imported into America was retained; a full drawback of British duties on tea reshipped to America was allowed, and the company was not liable for any deficiency in the tea revenue. At the same time a radical innovation was introduced in that the East India Company was allowed to export its own tea to America and establish warehouses where tea could be sold directly to retailers. In this way two sets of middlemen would be eliminated: the British exporter of tea and the American wholesale importer. The result was that East India tea came to America cheap enough to compete with the smuggled teas; but in the North the economic interests of a powerful class

___

[25] Schlesinger, *Colonial Merchants*, 98.

of business men had been assailed and combinations of importers
were organized to resist the landing of the tea.[26]

At Charleston there was no combination of importers to resist
the execution of the Tea Act; and even the planters seemed at
first reluctant to act. Perhaps their memories of non-importation
were not altogether happy. The Charleston factors in the ordinary course of business had received a great deal of dutied tea
from their English correspondents and were therefore unprepared
to resist the East India Company until they got rid of their stock
on hand. Then, from the point of view of the Charleston factor,
putting up a fight against the tea duty was equivalent to giving
encouragement to a disreputable class of smugglers who were
bringing in wine and tea and underselling the fair trader. The
resisters of the Tea Act seem to have been country factors and
mechanics, who were afraid they would be called on to pay
monopoly prices for tea, and perhaps other commodities, and who
were perhaps not unaccustomed to smuggle a little. From the
first they kept up a persistent but ineffective agitation until they
were finally joined by the planters, who were alarmed for the
safety of their constitutional right to tax themselves and on account
of the coercive policy the British government was pursuing toward
Boston. These classes forced the Charleston factors to enter
agreements to obstruct the sale of tea, and resistance to the East
India Company was only partly successful because of the reluctance
of the merchants to act.

The editor of the *South Carolina Gazette* was on the watch-
tower and sounded the alarm when it was announced in the fall
of seventy-three that the East India Company had been licensed
to export more than half a million pounds of tea to America. But
he was forced to go out of the province for the arguments with
which he sought to inform public opinion. He reprinted therefore
certain pieces from the newspapers of the North signed with such
names as Junius Brutus, Cassius, Hampden, in which the old rally-
ing cry of taxation without representation was sounded again
and the fear of monopoly held up to alarm the public. It was
asserted that the three pence tax on tea was laid for the purpose of

[26] Farrand, "The Taxation of Tea," 1767-1773, *A. H. R.*, III, 266-269.

establishing a precedent for future impositions; that the tax was retained, not for revenue, but to assert the power assumed by Parliament in the Declaratory Act to pass laws binding upon the colonies in all cases whatsoever; that the setting up of tea houses in America was intended to pave the way for introducing factories for other goods which the East India Company imported into England, such as silks, calicoes, spices, drugs, and china-ware.

In spite of Timothy's efforts public opinion was in a state of indecision when Captain Curling's ship, the *London*, with two hundred and fifty-seven chests of East India tea on board, anchored before the town on December 1. At a meeting in the Great Hall over the Exchange, on December 3, it was decided to ask the "gentlemen in trade" to enter a written agreement not to import any more dutied tea; to request the tea consignees, who happened to have been members of the late General Committee, not to accept their commissions and to return the tea in the ship that brought it; and to instruct Captain Curling to take the tea back to England. The meeting of December 3 was evidently poorly attended and its decisions on that account not binding. Therefore another meeting was called for December 14, but insufficient notice had been given and it was necessary to call another meeting for December 17.

At the general meeting of all classes of citizens on December 17, it was discovered that the stumbling block to unanimous agreement on boycotting the dutied tea was, that "many gentlemen in trade had not desisted from importing tea subject to the odious duty from the time it had been imposed to the very day of the Importation by the East India Company." Also a minority of the citizens were experiencing difficulty in understanding why so much noise was being made about buying tea directly from the East India Company. They pointed out that since the breaking through of the non-importation agreement three years before, people had been buying dutied tea from private merchants in Great Britain. In both cases the tax was paid even though Americans were not represented in Parliament. To this dissenting group it seemed that the East India Company had all the rights of a private merchant and should be allowed to land its goods and sell them. Their viewpoint was somewhat analogous to that of certain modern consumers who cannot understand why it is so heinous to buy merchandise from the "foreign" chain stores, where they can get it so much cheaper than from the home merchant. Because of the indecision manifested at this meeting, it was decided to defer the formation of a general agreement until another meeting to take place on January 7. Meanwhile it was resolved that the East India Company's tea imported in Captain Curling's ship ought not to be landed, received or vended in the province; and that no teas ought to be imported by any person whatsoever, while the act imposing the unconstitutional duty remained unrepealed.[27]

On December 21, the legal period of twenty days during which the ship might lie unloaded at the wharf expired, and since no consignees had called for the tea it became the collector's duty to seize it for non-payment of duty. Anonymous letters had been received by Captain Curling threatening to fire his ship unless he removed it from the wharf; by the owners of the wharf threatening to fire that if the ship were not moved; and by masters of vessels whose ships were lying near the tea ship warning them of the danger to which their vessels were exposed by being near a ship with such an odious cargo. The collector became alarmed and applied to the lieutenant governor for protection in the execution of his duty, and Bull notified sheriffs and other peace officers to be in readiness to preserve the peace. But early on the morning of December 22 the tea was landed, carried in a dray to the cellars under the Exchange and stored, the few people astir looking on quietly and offering no opposition. At the same time two consignments of tea from private merchants in London were publicly landed by the owners.[28]

At the meeting on January 7 there were few present except determined opposers of the tea tax, and the meeting was adjourned a fortnight in the hope that the approaching session of the General Assembly would bring many to town who would support radical proposals. Again the plan of the radicals was defeated, for Bull prorogued the legislature until March 1. This necessitated post-

[27] S. C. Gaz., Dec. 6 and 20, 1773; Drayton, Memoirs, 98-99.
[28] S. C. Gaz., Dec. 27; Drayton, Memoirs, 99-100.

poning the general meeting until March 16, when "as great and respectable body of inhabitants as ever assembled in the province" met under the Liberty Tree and subscribed to new resolutions: Until the tea act was repealed no tea should be imported into the province; the East India Company's tea in the cellar under the Exchange should not be sold nor removed from the place where it was stored except to be put on shipboard in order to be carried off the province; no dealings should be permitted with any person who should buy or sell tea contrary to the resolutions. A Committee of five was appointed to execute the agreement.[29]

Another consignment of tea that arrived on June 26 found the Committee unprepared. This tea was landed and stored along with Captain Curling's consignment at the Exchange; but when a third consignment arrived on July 18, the Committee summoned Captain Maitland before it and extracted a promise from him that the tea would either be destroyed or taken back to England. Maitland, however, gave great offense to the Committee and the people, for that very day the tea was landed and lodged in the King's storehouse. "Several hundred men went with great threats in quest of him, in the evening, but as they entered his ship on one side, he went off from the other, and took shelter on board His Majesty's ship Glasgow, then in Rebellion Road, and the next morning his ship was removed from the wharf by Capt. Maltby's Assistant." But it seems that another parcel of tea arrived afterwards and found its way to the King's warehouse.[30]

On Tuesday, November 15, the Committee of Observation was informed that Captain Sam. Ball's recently arrived ship *Britannia* had seven casks of tea on board subject to duty. Ball explained to the General Committee that the tea had been placed on board by his mate without his knowledge and that he had no design to resist the Americans. The importers of the tea signified their readiness to do anything the General Committee thought advisable. Consequently on Thursday at noon an "oblation was made to Neptune," each importer emptying his tea chests

[29] *S. C. Gaz.*, Mch. 21, 1774.
[30] *P. R. S. C.*, XXXIV, 181.

into the sea "in the sight of the Committee and a numerous concourse of people which gave 3 hearty cheers, after the emptying of each chest, and immediately afterwards separating as if nothing had happened." The same date on which the above incident was reported in the *South Carolina Gazette* (November 21), six hundred and sixty-nine pounds of tea which had been smuggled into the town were reshipped for the port whence it came with a caution to the shipper "to venture no more this way." This proves, observed the editor, that "we do not reject dutied tea, in order to countenance the Importation of others."

III

, Business was never normal after the Charleston tea party. Immediately after the passage of the Coercive Acts, radicals, such as Timothy and Gadsden, attempted to revive the non-importation movement and to cut off exports to Great Britain until the "Intolerable Acts" should be repealed. But the non-intercourse proposal was rejected in July at one of the largest public assemblies ever held at Charleston, for such action threatened heavy losses to the merchants and the planters had made a good crop which they wished to ship before taking any drastic action to aid the Bostonians. Therefore the matter was postponed until after the meeting of the Continental Congress, to which Gadsden, Thomas Lynch, Edward Rutledge, John Rutledge, and Henry Middleton were sent as delegates.

One of the first acts of the Continental Congress was to request business men not to send any more orders to Great Britain for goods and to give directions to delay or suspend the execution of all orders already sent until the sense of Congress "on the means taken for the preservation of the Liberties of America" should be made public.[31] The plantation provinces were expected to exert a specially great influence in bringing about the repeal of the offending legislation because of their great direct trade with England. Said Samuel Adams, "The shipping, manufactures, and revenues of England depend so much on the Tobacco and Car-

[31] Extracts from the minutes of the Congress printed in the *S. C. Gaz.*, Oct. 10, 1774.

olina colonies that they alone by stopping their exports could force redress."[32]

But the proposal of a non-exportation agreement was the signal for an outburst of sectional feeling which had been suppressed in the presence of a common danger. To ask South Carolina to break off trade relations with England and the West Indies seemed like an invitation to commit economic suicide. That article of the Association therefore which stated that after the tenth of September 1775, America "will not directly or indirectly export any merchandise or commodity to Great Britain, Ireland, or the West Indies, except rice to Europe" was the occasion of a long and violent debate in Congress.

Christopher Gadsden was willing to expunge the offending phrase "except rice to Europe" but John Rutledge contended for its retention. He argued that the real trade of the northern colonies was not affected by the Association because their direct trade to the mother country was trifling and that they could pay their debts to England as usual by means of their flour and fish trade to the rest of Europe; therefore he saw no reason why South Carolina's trade should be almost ruined because two-thirds of Carolina rice and nearly all its indigo went to England. "The affair seemed to him," he said, "like a commercial scheme among the flour colonies to find a better vent for their flour through the British channel, by preventing if possible any rice from being sent to these markets; and that for his part, he would never consent to the South's becoming dupes to the North—and yielding to their unreasonable expectations."[33]

By October 20, Congress had formed a non-intercourse association for the purpose of distressing the business of the British merchants and the West Indian sugar planters in order to secure their coöperation in bringing about a repeal of the "Intolerable Acts." Resolutions were made not to import any British wares or

[32] *American Archives*, 4th Series, I, 237-238.
[33] E. C. Burnett, Letters of Members of the Continental Congress, I, 85, 86. In 1774 Pennsylvania, the wealthiest of the northern colonies and the one with the least direct trade to Great Britain, sent little more than Georgia to the mother country. Pennsylvania's exports were valued at £69,611 and Georgia's at £67,647; while the trade of the Chesapeake region amounted to £612,030 and Carolina's to £432,302. MacPherson, *Annals of Com.*, III, 564.

merchandise after December 1 until the grievances that had arisen since 1763 should be redressed; and if a repeal of the obnoxious measures had not taken place by the following September 10, not to export any commodities to Great Britain, Ireland, or the West Indies, except rice to Europe. Congress further resolved not to purchase any more Negroes after December 1 "but wholly to desist from the slave trade" and cut off trade relations with anyone concerned in it. American business was to be encouraged by increasing the breed of sheep, encouraging manufactures and discouraging gaming and public amusements.[34]

The Continental Association was to be enforced far more effectively in South Carolina than the Non-Importation Association of 1769-1771 had been. The radicals were again in the saddle. They summoned that extra-legal body, the First Provincial Congress, which met on January 11, 1775, and approved without a dissenting vote the proceedings of the Continental Congress. The principal subject of debate was whether the rice planters should be allowed to ship their rice while the growers of wheat, hemp, tobacco, and indigo were deprived of a market for their commodities. Finally a compromise was arrived at by which the rice planters were to make compensation to the members of the other groups. Two committees were appointed to act in the recess of the Congress—the Council of Safety, in the nature of an executive, and the General Committee, as a legislative body. The radicals also had control of the legislative part of the regular government. The South Carolina assembly supported the declaration of the Continental Congress against every species of extravagance and dissipation by passing a law in the winter of 1775 decreeing that whoever should violate the said Association by any manner of horse racing should forfeit the money he bet and the horse he should run. After the Battle of Bunker Hill, the assembly resolved to have no intercourse or dealing with Poole, which had handled so much Carolina rice, nor hire or load vessels belonging to that port, on account of its representations to Parliament on the fishing trade "to the prejudice of our suffering Brethren in New England."[35]

[34] *Journals of the Continental Congress*, I, 75-8.
[35] Laurens to John Laurens, June 23, 1775.

Democracy was a new social force making its presence felt and playing its part in the effective enforcement of the non-importation agreement. On March 28, 1775, Bull wrote to the Earl of Dartmouth that "the Men of Property begin at length to see that the many headed power the People, who have hitherto been obediently made use of by their numbers & occasional riots to support the claims set up in America, have discovered their own strength & importance, and are not now so easily governed by their former Leaders"; that "many gentlemen living and desirous of continuing to live in Affluence, had tried several times to relax the Non-Importation Article by admitting furniture, plate, etc. for their own use" and were constantly opposed by the mechanics; that the mechanics had refused "to let a gentleman's horse from Antigua be landed even after the Committee of Inspection had voted in the affirmative, the matter was reconsidered and voted in the negative."[36]

By the tenth article of the Continental Association, all goods that arrived before December 1, 1774, and until February 1, 1775 (after which no goods from Great Britain were to be received on any account) were at the option of the importers either to be sent back, stored by the committee of town or county at the risk of the importer till the termination of the agreement, or sold under the direction of the General Committee. In the latter case the importer was paid prime costs and charges and the profits went to the relief of the sufferers by the Boston Port Bill. This, however, was a mere form because no person usually bid beyond the cost and charges and the proprietor received his goods as usual. A considerable quantity of goods arrived at Charleston after December 1 and there were no instances in which the owners of goods refused to put them under the direction of the General Committee.[37]

The non-importation agreement was well enforced, Carolina imports falling from £378,116 in 1774 to £6,245 in 1775. Anticipating, however, a cessation of the export trade in September, South Carolina, like most of the other colonies, exported more to

[36] *P. R. S. C.*, XXXV, 80-81.
[37] MacPherson, *Annals of Com.*, III, 559; Laurens to John Laurens, Jan. 4, 1775; *S. C. Gaz.*, Mch. 6, 1775.

Great Britain in 1775 than ever before in her history, her exports for that year being worth £579,549.[38]

Georgia plantations received most of their supplies from Charleston, and Georgia had not sent delegates to the Continental Congress nor acceded to the Continental Association. On February 8, 1775, the General Committee resolved to cut off all dealings and intercourse with the Georgians, except such as were unavoidable by persons who resided in South Carolina and had plantations in Georgia or debts due them in that province.[39] This gave encouragement to the radical party and the largest district in Georgia sent a delegate to the Second Continental Congress in the spring of 1775; a little later revolutionists seized the powder magazine at Savannah. It was not, however, until July 4, 1775, that Georgia acceded formally to the Association. Meantime a channel of trade was left open of which even some patriot traders in Carolina took advantage. Georgia imports, which were valued at £57,518 in 1774, had reached £113,777 in 1775. The Carolina merchants and planters who owned plantations in Georgia were importing through Georgia ports, and were preparing, after trade relations were completely severed between South Carolina and Great Britain, to export through that channel also. As late as August 2, 1775, Laurens requested a correspondent that if Georgia remained "unrestrained as to points southward of Cape Finisterre," he should charter a ship on his own account and secure a license and certificate to carry rice to Spain and Portugal. This was in expectation that "the ports in South Carolina would be locked up by the joint operation of the Restraining Bill and our own Resolutions."[40]

Back-country trade was greatly interfered with, if not entirely broken up, by the effort of the General Committee to force the backwoodsmen into the Continental Association. The back-countrymen were commonly Loyalists both from motives of fear and economic interest. They were like the burnt child who dreads the fire. They had recently attempted to make and enforce law among themselves when the government in the East seemed too

[38] MacPherson, *Annals of Com.*, III, 564, 585.
[39] *S. C. Gaz.*, Mch. 6, 1775.
[40] To William Manning.

indifferent or too feeble to enforce justice among them. When Governor Montagu in 1770 had employed a coarse and tactless brute named Scoville to enforce regular law among them, they had suffered severely. Consequently, they were wary of opposing regular government by supporting the Provincial Congress and its committees, which they conceived to be bodies similar to their own regulating assemblies. Then many believed that if they acceded to American measures they might forfeit the lands which had been granted them by the king's government. Besides, they had no special liking for the haughty planter with his host of slaves or for the merchant who bought their produce for low prices and charged them high prices for supplies. And Lord William Campbell, the Governor, had sent emissaries among them who told them that the whole dispute was about a trifling tax on tea, which they were not much in the habit of using; that the gentlemen on the sea coast were willing to adopt measures that would involve the country in want of salt, osnaburgs, and other imported articles; and that the expense of the recently raised regiments of rangers was infinitely greater than the trifling taxes imposed by the British Parliament. Besides, the rangers might be used to put down opposition in the back country as well as to oppose the king. Despite the eloquence of the Honorable William Henry Drayton and the Reverend William Tennant, who were sent out by the Council of Safety to explain the nature of the dispute to the back-woodsmen, the people living along the Broad and Saluda refused to sign the Continental Association and signed instead agreements in favor of the king.

When diplomacy failed the Provincial Congress resorted to economic pressure. The General Committee, finding that "divers persons in the remote parts of the province" had neglected to sign the General Association subscribed to by the Provincial Congress on June 4, 1775, resolved that no wagoners or other persons should be allowed to sell or dispose of "Indico, Flour, Hemp, Tobacco, Butter, Deer skins, or any other Merchandize or Produce," until they should give satisfactory proof of having signed the General Association, or a similar association in North Carolina or

Georgia.[41]   But the independent back country farmers were not brought to terms by such economic pressure.   They actively and bitterly opposed the men of the low country in armed combat until the British, upon their arrival in 1779, made the very serious error of assuming that because Dissenters in New England had begun the strife with the mother country, Dissenters everywhere were enemies of the king.   When a meeting house of the Dissenters in Charleston was used as a horse stable and when Major Wemys referred to Presbyterian churches as "sedition shops," allowing his plundering soldiery to burn many of them, the up countryman cast in his lot with the low countryman and contributed powerfully to British defeat in the South by surrounding Ferguson on King's Mountain and destroying his army.

Even before the war came on, regular business was being demoralized by the activity of the profiteer.   The Continental Congress had anticipated that the profiteer, or the engrosser as he was then called, would seize the opportunity of making a fortune by creating artificial scarcity and advancing the price of European goods when the Continental Association should go into effect, Congress was therefore resolved to hold up to odium anyone who took advantage of the scarcity of goods to demand extravagant prices.   Before the Continental Association was adopted in South Carolina, however, mercenary capitalists at Charleston were buying up large quantities of goods and storing them with a view to fixing prices at some future time.   Commissions were also being received from persons in the other colonies to purchase commodities at Charleston for them for a like purpose.   For this reason the General Committee appointed, on October 26, 1774, a special committee to consider measures "to prevent engrossing, exporting or advancing the price of European goods to the prejudice of the people of South Carolina."   The General Committee also published an advertisement in the *South Carolina Gazette* of October 31, requesting merchants, shopkeepers and others to detect engrossers and defeat their mercenary schemes; traders were urged not to take advantage of the public distress.   This was the prelude to the orgy of speculation and profiteering that set in with the war,

[41] *S. C. Gaz.*, Sept. 7, 1775.

driving the old conservative merchants out of business and introducing a new set of daring adventurers, who were willing to take
great risks in the hope of making great gain.

About three months after the publication of the Continental
Association, the merchants of London and other commercial cen-
ters of Great Britain, who had been indifferent to the Coercive
Acts, began to find that the American Association was injuring
their business, and they began a systematic propaganda for repeal
of the legislation of 1774. They sent petitions to the House of
Commons setting forth the distress to which the American Association had subjected their business and praying for a repeal of the
"Intolerable Acts." A little later the sugar planters of the West
Indies presented a like petition for this purpose, showing how
much the sugar plantations, owned mostly by men who resided in
England, contributed to the national wealth and to what an
extent their prosperity depended upon a free and reciprocal intercourse with the North American Provinces.[42]

While these petitions were before Parliament hostilities com-
menced in the North with the battles of Lexington and Bunker
Hill. The colonies had by their own act severed trade relations
with the rest of the empire; they were now actually engaged in
making warfare. The time had passed, so the British authorities
felt, for making concessions, and the time had arrived when coercive measures were absolutely necessary. On October 22, 1775,
the bill "prohibiting all trade and intercourse with the American
colonies in an actual state of rebellion" passed both houses of
Parliament by very large majorities; and the king sent out a small
army "rather to undeceive than to punish" the Americans.[43]

* * * * *

We have found that in the colonial era the Chesapeake and
Charleston districts were alike in that climate and soil predestined
both to a great agricultural development. The fact that Virginia
and Maryland tobacco and Carolina rice and indigo were much
in demand in the European markets bound both these districts to
the mother country by close economic ties. At Charleston, how-

[42] Anderson, *Origins of Com.*, IV, 179-180.
[43] 16 Geo. III, C. V.

ever, a great commercial development took place. The city became the metropolis of the lower South, which thus presented a striking contrast to the predominantly agricultural and almost townless Chesapeake region.

Physical geography determined the character and scope of colonial business. The streams of the Chesapeake country gave direct access to the plantations; business was, therefore, concentrated in the hands of English and Scottish factors who could deal with the planters at their wharves. On the other hand, at Charleston was a good harbor with abundant communication with the hinterland by means of rivers; but the shoal channels of the inland streams did not permit overseas vessels to penetrate the country. Consequently, transportation was carried on by means of small vessels and the business of the native merchants developed considerably. In an age of barter the small factors or merchants came into possession of much of the produce of the country and by withholding rice and indigo from the market they could influence somewhat the price of these commodities. They were able to participate in the benefits of rice speculations. To resist the operation of the Townshend Acts they helped organize the Non-Importation Association at Charleston, which was one of the most effective on the continent, while similar associations in Virginia and Maryland were largely inoperative on account of the geographic situation. Finally, as the Revolution came on, the economic grievances of the small business men found expression in revolt.

In spite of this development on the part of native merchants, the masters of business in the Carolina country, as well as in the Chesapeake region, were the factors of the British merchants, who had command of the shipping and wholesale trade. In the early colonial period, with Charleston as a center, they organized a great fur trade extending as much as a thousand miles into the continent. Later, they were employed principally in shipping rice and indigo to Europe and in selling to the planters slaves from Africa. In the prosperous period before the Revolution the trade territory of Charleston included, besides South Carolina, a large part of North Carolina, Georgia and East and West Florida.

British factors directed the most lucrative branch of foreign commerce, the trade in Negroes from Africa, and they furnished the country with immigrants and indentured white servants. The prevailing social attitude in regard to this traffic in white and black people was determined by a profit consideration. Large fortunes could be made in these lines of business by men of high social rank. The slavery of black men, especially, was regarded as natural, inevitable, and, in some respects, desirable. Even in the eighteenth century, however, there were indications that intelligent men were coming to look upon chattel slavery with abhorrence. The great Charleston factors as a class were zealously loyal to the British Empire whose trade regulations did much to foster their prosperity. Some of them, however, came into sharp conflict with corrupt British officials charged with the execution of the laws relative to smuggling, and they suffered such losses in property and dignity that when the quarrel with the mother country resulted in an appeal to arms, they cast in their lot with the rebellious Americans.

BIBLIOGRAPHY

I. PRIMARY SOURCES. UNPRINTED

A. In the South Carolina Historical Commission, Columbia.
Journals of the Commons House of Assembly, 1759-1775. Originals and copies.
Journals of the Minutes of the Council, 1760-1774. Originals and copies.
Journals of the Indian Commissioners, 1750-1765. Originals. Cited as Indian Books.
Public Records of South Carolina (British Transcripts), vols. 28-36 covering years 1758-1782. Cited as P. R. S. C.

B. In the Charleston Library, Charleston.
Elfe, (Wm.). Cabinet-maker, MSS. Account Book, 1768-1776.

C. The Archives of the South Carolina Historical Society, Charleston.
A Beaufort Merchant's Account Book, 1785-1790.
Merchant's Day Book, Charles Town, S. C., March, 1764-December 31, 1766.
Miscellaneous Business Papers of Manning, Miller and Chesnut, unsorted.
Kershaw Papers, containing notes, accounts, receipts, etc., given by Joseph Kershaw. In the possession of Mrs. Harriet Kershaw Leiding, Charleston.
Laurens MSS. Letter books, account books, notes, and miscellaneous manuscripts of Henry Laurens, known as the Laurens Papers, 1747-1792. References to Laurens are to this collection unless stated otherwise in the notes.

D. At the Court House, Charleston.
Inventory and Will Books, Probate Judge's Office, 1776-1778, 1783-1786.

II. PRIMARY SOURCES. PRINTED

A. MAGAZINES AND NEWSPAPERS

The European Magazine and London Review, published by the Philosophical Society of London. London, 1782-1798, 25 vols.

BIBLIOGRAPHY 237

The Gentleman's Magazine. London, 1731-1817, 120 vols.
The Political Magazine for October, 1780. London, 1780-1791.
The American Museum, or Universal Magazine. 12 vols. Philadelphia, 1787-1792.
The South Carolina Historical and Genealogical Magazine, published by the South Carolina Historical Society. Vols. IX, XIII, XIV, XV, XVI contain some source material.
The South Carolina Gazette, 1760-1788 (1732-1788). The name was changed after the war to the Gazette of the State of South Carolina.
The South Carolina Gazette and Country Journal, 1765-1775.
The South Carolina and American General Gazette, 1766-1775, 1776-1780, 1781.
The Georgia Gazette (Savannah): Reproductions for 1763-1770. Library of Congress.

B. DOCUMENTS, COLLECTIONS, AND SURVEYS

America

American Archives, Peter Force, ed. Tracts and other Papers relating Principally to the Origin, Settlement and Progress of the Colonies in North America from the Discovery of the Country to the year 1776, 4 vols. Washington, 1830-1846.
American Tracts, 4 vols. Printed for J. Almon. London, 1766.
A Century of Population Growth, 1790-1900. Statistics compiled by Wm. S. Rossiter. Washington, Government Printing Office, 1909.
American Population Before the Federal Census of 1790. E. B. Greene and V. D. Harrington. New York, 1932.

Georgia

Collections of the Georgia Historical Society. Savannah, 1840-1878.
The Colonial Records of the State of Georgia, 21 vols., Asa D. Candler, ed. Atlanta, 1904-1910.

North Carolina

The Colonial Records of North Carolina, 10 vols., William Saunders, ed. Raleigh, 1886-1890.

238   BIBLIOGRAPHY

South Carolina

Brevard, Joseph. Digest of the Public Statute Law of South-Carolina, 1692-1813, 3 vols. Charleston, 1814.

Carroll, B. R., Historical Collections of South Carolina, 2 vols. New York, 1836.

Cooper, Thomas and McCord, Daniel, Statutes at Large of South Carolina, 10 vols., 1836-1840.

Donnan, Elizabeth, Documents Illustrative of the History of the Slave Trade to America, Carnegie Series, No. 409. Washington, 1930.

South Carolina Historical Collections; Collections of the South Carolina Historical Society. Charleston, Richmond, 1857-1897.

Gibbes, R. W., ed., Documentary History of the American Revolution, 1764-1776, 3 vols. New York, 1853-1857.

First Census of the United States, Heads of Families, South Carolina. Washington, Government Printing Office, 1907-1908.

Grimke, John F., ed., Public Laws of the State of South Carolina from its first establishment as a British Province Down to the Year 1790. Philadelphia, 1790.

Moore, Frank, ed., Materials for History. New York, 1861. Contains some of the correspondence of Henry Laurens during the Revolutionary War.

Ordinances of the City Council of Charleston, Digests for 1783-1818, Archibald E. Miller, Printer. Charleston, 1818.

Ordinances of the City Council of Charleston, Digests, 1783-1844. Charleston, 1844.

Phillips, U. B., ed., Plantation and Frontier, 2 vols. (In Documentary History of American Industrial Society). Cleveland, 1910.

Weston, P. C., ed., Documents Connected with the History of South Carolina. London, 1856.

C. CONTEMPORANEOUS HISTORY, DESCRIPTION AND
OTHER WRITINGS

Anderson, Adam, Origins of Commerce, 4 vols. London, 1787-1789.

Chalmers, George, An Introduction to the History of the Revolt of the American Colonies, etc. Boston, 1845.

Charleston Yearbooks, 1883, 1884, 1885.

De Brahm, John Gerar William, History of the Province of Georgia. Wormsloe, Georgia, 1849.

Drayton, John, A View of South-Carolina, as Respects Her Natural and Civil Concerns. Charleston, 1802; Memoirs of the American Revolution from its commencement to the year 1176, etc., 2 vols. Charleston, 1821.

Edwards, Bryan, History, Civil and Commercial, of the British Colonies in the West Indies, 4 vols. Philadelphia, 1806. First edition, London, 1793.

Hewatt, Alexander, An Historical Account of the Rise and Progress of .the Colonies of South Carolina and Georgia, 2 vols. London, 1779.

Laurens, Henry, Extracts from the Proceedings of the High Court of Vice-Admiralty, in Charles-Town, . . . 1767 and 1768: Some General Observations on American Custom-House Officers. Printed by David Bruce. (Pamphlets) Charlestown, 1769.

Leigh, Egerton, The Man Unmasked. Charles-Town, 1769. (Pamphlet)

McCall, Capt. Hugh, The History of Georgia, Containing Brief Sketches of the Most Remarkable Events of the Present Day (1784). Atlanta, 1909.

MacPherson, David, Annals of Commerce, 4 vols. London, 1805.

Pitkin, Timothy, A Statistical View of the Commerce of the United States. Hartford, 1816.

Pownal, Thomas, The Administration of the Colonies, 2 vols. London, 1768.

Ramsay, David, M.D., The History of the Revolution of South-Carolina, from a British Province to an Independent State, 2 vols. Trenton, 1785.

——The History of the American Revolution, 2 vols., Philadelphia, 1789.

Raynal, Abbé, A Philosophical and Political History of the Settlements and Trade of the Europeans in the East and West Indies. Translated from the French by J. O. Justamond, F. R. S., 8 vols. London, 1783.

Romans, Bernard, A Concise Natural History of East and West Florida, vol. I, New York, 1775. Vol. II apparently never published.

Sheffield, John, Observations on the Commerce of the American States. London, 1783. (Pamphlet)

Young, Arthur (?), American Husbandry, 2 vols. London, 1775.

D. CORRESPONDENCE, DIARIES, MEMOIRS, REMINISCENCES, BOOKS OF TRAVEL

Bartram, William, Travels Through North and South Carolina, Georgia, East and West Florida. Philadelphia, 1791.

Burnett, E. C., Letters of Members of the Continental Congress, 4 vols. Washington, 1921.

Chastellux, Marquis de, Travels in North America in the Years 1780, 1781, and 1782, 2 vols. London, 1787.

Elliott, Jonathan, The Debates in the Several State Conventions, etc., 5 vols. Washington, 1836-1845.

Fraser, Charles, Reminiscences of Charleston. Charleston, 1854.

Jefferson's Writings, Ford, P. L., ed. 10 vols. New York, 1892-1899.

Johnson, Joseph, Traditions and Reminiscences, Chiefly of the American Revolution in the South. Charleston, 1851.

La Rochefoucauld-Liancourt, Travels Through the United States of North America, the Country of the Iroquois, and Upper Canada, in the Years 1795, 1796, and 1797; with an Authentic Account of Lower Canada. London, 1799.

Mereness, Newton D., ed., Travels in the American Colonies. New York, 1916. Of especial interest is the Journal of Lord Adam Gordon, a British officer who traveled in America in 1762-66.

Michaux, F. Andre, Travels to the Westward of the Alleghany Mountains. London, 1805.

Pinckney, Mrs. Eliza (Lucas), Journal and Letters of Eliza Lucas. Wormsloe, Ga., 1850.

Quincy, J., Journal of Josiah Quincy, Junior, 1773. Mass. Hist. Society Proceedings, XLIX, 424-481.

Schaw, Janet, Journal of a Lady of Quality; Being the Narrative of a Journey from Scotland to the West Indies, North Carolina and Portugal in the Years 1774 to 1776, cited by Evangeline Walker Andrews and Charles M. Andrews. New Haven, 1921.

Schoepf, Johann David, Travels in the Confederation, 1783-1784, translated and edited by Alfred J. Morrison. 2 vols. Philadelphia, 1911.

Smyth, John Ferdinand D., A Tour in the United States of America: Containing an Account of the Present Situation of That Country; the Population, Agriculture, Commerce, and Manners of the Inhabitants, etc., 2 vols. London, 1784.

Sparks, Jared, ed., The Diplomatic Correspondence of the American Revolution, 12 vols. Boston, 1829-1830.

Stork, William, ed., A Description of East-Florida, with a Journal, Kept by John Bartram, of Philadelphia, Botanist to His Majesty for the Floridas. London, 1769.

Thomas, E. S., Reminiscences of the Last Sixty-five Years, Commencing with the Battle of Lexington. Hartford, 1840.

Washington, President Washington's Diaries, 1791 to 1799, translated and compiled by Jos. Hoskins. Summerfield, N. C.,

Watson, Elkanah, Men and Times of the Revolution, or Memoirs of Elkanah Watson, . . . from 1777 to 1842. New York, 1857.

Webster, Journal of a Voyage to Charlestown, in So. Carolina by Pelatiah Webster, Southern History Association Publications, II (1898), 131-148.

Wharton, Francis, ed., Revolutionary Diplomatic Correspondence of the United States. Washington, Government Printing Office, 1889.

Winterbotham, William, An Historical, Geographical, Commercial, and Philosophical View of the United States of America and of the European Settlements in America and the West-Indies, 4 vols. New York, 1796.

III. SECONDARY AUTHORITIES

Adams, James T., Provincial Society, 1690-1763. New York, 1927. In a History of American Life edited by A. M. Schlesinger and Dixon Ryan Fox.

Andrews, C. M., The Colonial Background of the American Revolution. New Haven, 1924.

——Colonial Commerce, American Historical Review, XX (October, 1914), 43-63.

242   BIBLIOGRAPHY

Ashe, Samuel A., History of North Carolina, 2 vols. Greensboro, 1908-1925.
Baldwin, S. E., American Business Corporations before 1789, American Historical Association Annual Report (1902), I, 253-274.
Ballagh, J. C., An Introduction to Southern Economic History—The Land System, American Historical Association Annual Report (1897), 103-129.
Bancroft, George, A History of the United States, 10 vols. Boston, 1859-1875.
Bassett, J. S., The Regulators of North Carolina (1765-1771), American Historical Association Annual Report (1894), 141-212.
——The Relation between the Virginia Planter and the London Merchant. American Historical Association Annual Report (1901), I, 551-575.
Beer, George L., British Colonial Policy, 1754-1765. New York, 1907; The Commercial Policy of England toward the American Colonies, Columbia University Studies, III, No. 2. New York, 1893.
Bell, H. C., The West India Trade before the American Revolution, American Historical Review, XXII (January, 1917), 272-287.
Brevard, Caroline Mays, A History of Florida from the Treaty of 1763 to Our Own Times, 2 vols. Deland, Fla., 1924, Florida State Historical Society.
Brooke, Richard, Esq., F.S.A., Liverpool as it was During the Last Quarter of the Eighteenth Century. Liverpool, 1853.
Campbell, Richard L., Historical Sketches of Colonial Florida. Cleveland, Ohio, 1892.
Chancellor, Wm. E. and Hewes, Fletcher W., The United States, 2 vols. New York, 1904-1905.
Channing, E., A History of the United States, 6 vols. New York, 1905-1925.
Clark, Washington A., A History of the Banking Institutions Organized in South Carolina, Prior to 1860. Columbia, 1922.
Crane, Verner, The Southern Frontie , 1670-1732, Duke University Press. Durham, N. C., 1928.
Darby, William, Memoir of Florida. Philadelphia, 1821.
Davis, Joseph Stancliffe, Essays in the Earlier History of American Corporations. Cambridge, 1917.

Doggett, Carita, Dr. Andrew Turnbull and the New Smyrna Colony of Florida. The Drew Press, Florida, 1919.

Donnan, Elizabeth, The Slave Trade into South Carolina before the Revolution, American Historical Review, XXXIII (July, 1928), 804-828.

Dubois, W. E. B., The Suppression of the African Slave Trade to the United States, Harvard Historical Studies, I. New York, 1896.

Elzas, Barnett A., The Jews of South Carolina. Philadelphia, 1905.

Faulkner, Harold U., Economic History of the United States. New York, 1928.

Farrand, Max, The Taxation of Tea, 1767-1773, American Historical Review, III (January, 1898), 266-269.

Fisher, Willard C., American Trade Regulations before 1789, Papers American Historical Association, III, No. 2, 223-249.

Forbes, James Grant, Sketches, Historical and Topographical, of the Floridas; More Particularly of East Florida. New York, 1821.

Giesecke, A. A., American Commercial Legislation before 1789, University of Pennsylvania Studies, Philadelphia, 1910.

Greene, Evarts B., Provincial America. New York, 1905.

Gregg, Alexander, History of the Old Cheraws. New York, 1867.

Hirsch, Arthur H., The Huguenots of Colonial South Carolina, Duke University Press. Durham, N. C., 1928.

Kirkland, T. J., and Kennedy, R. M., Historic Camden, 2 vols., Part I, Colonial and Revolutionary. Columbia, 1905.

Logan, John H., History of the Upper Country of South Carolina. Charleston, 1859. First volume published; remaining MS. is in the Draper Collection of the Wisconsin State Historical Society.

Lord, Eleanor L., Industrial Experiments in the British Colonies, Johns Hopkins Studies, Extra vol. (1898), 69-70.

McCrady, Edward, The History of South Carolina Under the Royal Government, 1719-1776. New York, 1899.

——Slavery in the Province of South Carolina, 1670-1770, American Historical Association Annual Report (1895), 631-673.

Mills, Robert, Statistics of South Carolina. Charleston, 1826.
Osgood, Herbert L., The American Colonies in the Eighteenth Century. New York, 1924.
Phillips, U. B., American Negro Slavery. New York, 1918.
——The Slave Labor Problem in the Charleston District, Political Science Quarterly, XII, No. 3.
——The South Carolina Federalists, American Historical Review, XIV (April, 1909), 429-543; XIV (July, 1909), 731-743.
Porcher, Frederick A., The History of the Santee Canal, published by the South Carolina Historical Society, 1903. (Pamphlet)
Ravenel, Harriott Harry (Mrs. St. Julien), The Life and Times of William Lowndes. Boston, New York, 1901.
——Charleston, the Place and the People. New York, 1906. lina. New York, 1906.
Salley, A. S., Jr., A History of Orangeburg County, South Carolina. Orangeburg, 1898.
——The Introduction of Rice Culture into South Carolina, South Carolina Historical Commission Bulletin. Columbia, 1919.
Schaper, William A., Sectionalism and Representation in South Carolina. Washington, Government Printing Office, 1901.
Schlesinger, Arthur M., The Colonial Merchants and the American Revolution, 1763-1776. New York, 1918.
——"The Uprising Against the East India Company," Political Science Quarterly, XXXII (1917), 60-79.
Smith, William R., South Carolina as a Royal Province, 1719-1776. New York, 1903.
Sprunt, James, Chronicles of the Cape Fear. Raleigh, 1914.
Thomas, Isaiah, The History of Printing in America. Worcester, 1810.
Wallace, David Duncan, The Life of Henry Laurens, with a Sketch of the Life of Lieutenant-Colonel John Laurens. New York, 1915.
Williams, Gomer, History of the Liverpool Privateers and Letters of Marque with an Account of the Liverpool Slave Trade. Liverpool, 1897.

INDEX

ABBEVILLE County, S. C., 29, 31
Adams, James Truslow, on prices in North Carolina, 38
Adams, John, on cheap foreign molasses as an ingredient of American independence, 179
Adams, Samuel, and the formation of a non-importation association at Boston, 70; quoted, 191, 226
Admiralty Courts, established under the Townshend Acts, 190-191; cases before, 192-199; Henry Laurens' pamphlets on, 200
Agriculture. See also Rice and Indigo. In the Carolina low country, 26-28; in the Carolina up-country, 30-31; trade in British America subordinated to, 55; colonial and modern in South Carolina compared, 57; estimates of profits from, 60-61
Alabama, 44, 169
"A Lady of Quality," quoted, 7, 39, 40, 106, 142
Albemarle Sound, 37
Altamaha River, 42, 66, 111
America, emigration from, to Georgia, after the Revolution, 7; appearance of, at Wilmington, 7; commerce of colonial, to Great Britain, 10; general character of business in colonial, 79-82
Amherst, General, 182
Amsterdam, 17, 51
Ancrum, Lance and Loocock, 89, 90
Ancrum, William, 90
Andrews, C. M., on one cause of immigration to America, 113
Ann, ship, trial of, 198-199
Antigua, 50, 106, 161
Apalachicola River, 44
Archdale, Governor of South Carolina, 169
Ashley River, first settlement of Charleston on, 4; colonial Charleston on,

5; residences on, 58; Col. Washington's plantation across, 151
Asia Minor, 46
Asiento, 70
Assize of Bread, 23
Augusta, Fort. See Fort Augusta.

BACK country trade. See also Kershaw, Joseph. Development of, 34; and the prospective Charleston factor; barter in, 91
Bacon Ridge, S. C., 88
Bakers on strike, 23-24
Baltimore, mentioned, 3; population, 5; and Irish immigration, 114
Barbadoes, 5, 50
Barter, in the coastal trade, 65-66; in colonial business, 67-68; in the back country trade, 91
Bartram, William, naturalist, entertained on a cattle ranch, 31
Beaufort, port of South Carolina, reason for removal of settlement on Port Royal, 4; size of, in 1784, 7; Fort Littleton at, 13; flour inspection at, 31; shipyard at, 62; Charleston stores at, 88; Merchant's Account Book, 91; slave trade, 133; rice shipments from, 156; smuggling at, 181
Bell, William, merchant of Philadelphia, 95
Bill of Exchange, mentioned, 49, 68; the merchant as banker, establishing a balance, drawing and selling tne, 74-75; example of a, 75; negotiability of the, on the West Indies and the northern colonies, 76; exchange on, 76-78; protesting the, 78; interest on, 78
Birmingham, population, in 1761, 16; slave trade, 125, 135
Black Mingo River, 6
Black River, 6

Bloody Point, 63
Boone, Governor of South Carolina,
111, 165, 176, 182
Bordeaux, 50, 114
Boston, mentioned, 4, 83, 154; popula-
tion, 16; as hemp market, 31; Bull,
on principles imbibed from Rhode
Island and, 187; Admiralty Court set
up at, 190; as initiator of non-importation, 191, 204; Christopher on
the letter from the merchants of,
206; and Charleston last to give up
non-importation, 213; enforcement of
non-importation at, 218
Boundary, between South Carolina and
Georgia, 42; between South and
North Carolina, 36
Bounty, bounties, South Carolina and
British on various commodities, 31;
South Carolina, on flour and hemp,
31; South Carolina on hemp and
naval stores, 36; British and South
Carolina, on indigo, 50, 52, 54, 162,
167; South Carolina, on the importation of immigrants and indentured
servants, 111, 120; British, on silk
and wine produced in the southern
colonies, 117
Brahm, William Gerard de, on stock
raising in Georgia, 32; plantation
estimates of, 59-60
Brands, for cattle, horses, hogs, 33;
for Negro slaves, 136; for Indian
slaves and skins, 174
Brazil, 137
Bremen, 153
Brewton, Miles, Charleston merchant,
mentioned, 131, 144; supports non-
importation in 1769, 202, 211
Bristol, population, in 1761, 16; slave
trade, 125, 135; freight rates to,
153; slave and rice trade, 157
Broad River, 6, 35, 36, 111, 117
Brother's Endeavor, schooner, 66
Broughton Island Packet, trial of, 196;
plantation, 66
Brunswick, N. C., 38, 40
Bull, Stephen, planter, petitions for
Georgia lands, 42

Bull, William, Lieutenant Governor of
South Carolina, quoted, 11, 12, 13;
population estimates of, 15; petitions
for Georgia lands, 42; quoted, 48;
refuses extra-legal money, 1774-
1775, 73-74; tries in 1760 to raise
one thousand men to go against the
Cherokees, 110; on the settlement
of upper Carolina, 112; recommends
to the assembly to appropriate money
to pay for provisions for French
Protestants, 115; on annual slave
importation into South Carolina, after
1763, 127; statistics for slave trade,
133; on grasshoppers as enemies of
indigo, 163; on Charleston's trade
with the Cherokees, after 1763, 170;
on smuggling in South Carolina,
181; on attitude of the people of
South Carolina toward the Stamp
Act, 186-187; and the Stamp Act
riots, 187-188; and Dougal Campbell, 188; on the reception at
Charleston of the Massachusett's circular letter, Feb., 1768, 204; on the
real leaders of non-importation, 209-
210; uncle of William Henry Drayton, 210; makes charges against
leaders of the Non-Importation Association, 215; on losses incurred by
British merchants through the South
Carolina Non-Importation Association, 219; on the break up of the
Non-Importation Association, 220;
and the landing and storing of tea,
Dec. 22, 1773, 224; on democracy
in enforcing non-importation in
1774, 229
Bull's Island, 7
Bunker Hill, battle of, 228, 233

CALHOUN, Captain Patrick, 116
Camden, on the Wateree, 6; flour in-
spection at, 31; Charleston stores at,
88; and Joseph Kershaw, 88-91
Campbell, Dougal, Clerk of Common
Pleas, 188-189
Campbell, Lord William, Governor of
South Carolina, 46, 231

248 INDEX

Council of Safety, 228
Country Factor. See Factor, country.
Cowes, mentioned, 50; port handling Carolina rice, 157
Cowles and Company, Bristol, 198
Cowpens and Blackstock, battles of, 32
Credit System. See also Plantation Business. Described, 55-56; situation in Virginia and South Carolina compared, 56
Creek Indians, 169, 170, 176, 177
Cross Creek, now Fayetteville, 39

DARIEN, Ga., 41, 42, 65
Dartmouth, Earl of, 73, 229
Deerskins. See Skin Trade.
Dentistry, 79
Dinwiddie, Governor of Virginia, 12
Dismal Swamp canal, 37
Domestic Slave Trade. See Negro Slaves
Donnan, Elizabeth, controverted, 131
Dorchester, S. C., 88
Drayton, John, 61, 76, 151
Drayton, William, Chief Justice of Florida, 46
Drayton, William Henry, proscribed by the South Carolina Non-Importation Association, result of boycott, 210-211; sent by the Council of Safety to explain the nature of the dispute to the backwoodsmen, 231
Duncan, Sir William, 76

EAST Florida, as trade territory of Charleston, 3, 25; land grants, 45, 46; types of settlements in, 46; collapse of the "boom" in, 47; and the Charleston merchants, 47; Laurens and trade in, 65, 98; Indian trade, 169
East India Company, efforts of, to escape bankruptcy, acts of Parliament concerning tea, 1767, 1772, 1773, 220-221; becomes exporter of tea, union of northern merchant against shipments of, 221-222; organization of resistance to at Charleston, 222;

arguments used to arouse colonial opposition to, 222-223
Edenton, N. C., 37, 75
Edward Wilkinson and Company, Indian trading firm, 176
Edwards, Fisher and company, 121, 131
Edwards, John, Charleston merchant, 214, 215
Elfe, Thomas, cabinet-maker, 103-104
Eli Kershaw and Company, 89
Elizabeth River, 37
England, competes for Carolina with France and Spain, 7-8; industrial supremacy of, and indigo, 8; trade of American colonies to, 8 et seq.; commercial war with Spain, 1713-1739, 70-71; slave trade of, 124 et seq.; policy of, in regard to the slave trade into South Carolina, 127
Exchange. See Bill of Exchange.

FACTOR, Charleston, mentioned, 8; and East and West Florida trade, 47; his business defined, 49-51; career of John Hopton, typical, 51-53; plantation business of, 53-61; shipping business of, 61-67; and means of exchange, 67-78; and the wholesale trade, 82-83; and the retailers, 83-84; and the foreign slave trade, 94-95
Factors, Country. See also Retailers. And internal trade, 49; and the shipping business, 62; as initiators of the non-importation movement, 203; and the Charleston tea party, 222-226
Factors, English and Scottish, 3-4, 219; classes of, in Charleston District, 49
Fayetteville, N. C. See Cross Creek.
Fire Prevention. See Charleston, city.
First Continental Congress. See Continental Congress, First.
Fisher, William, Philadelphia merchant, 118, 198
Flanders, 50, 154
Florida. See also East Florida and West Florida. Location of Carolina

1769, 207; contest with merchants over non-importation, 207-209

Mellichamp, Thomas, discovers new method of producing flora indigo, 165

Merchants, British prosperity in relation to rice, 8; and boat ownership, 64; as bankers, 74; and Charleston factors, 83; and the import trade, 83; favored provincial duty on the importation of slaves, 127; and methods of selling slaves, 141-142; and rice speculation, 159-160; propaganda of, for repeal of "Intolerable Acts," 233

Merchants, country. See also Retailers. And the shipping business, 62, 84, 85

Mexico, 44

Middleton, Henry, delegate to the First Continental Congress, 226

Minorca, Island of, 47

Mississippi (state), 44

Mobile, mentioned, 44; Indian trade of, 48, 169; smuggling at, 181

Moncks Corner, S. C., 87

Montagu, Governor of South Carolina, 188, n. 14; 231

Moore, Daniel, Collector of the Port of Charleston, career of, 193-198

Mosquito Inlet (Ponce de Leon Inlet), 46

Moultrie, John, Lieutenant Governor of Florida, 46

NAVAL stores, production of, in North Carolina, 39; Gov. Tryon's report on, 40-41; inspection of, in North Carolina, 41

Negro clothing. See Clothing, Negro.

Negro, free, problem of, 101-102

Negro, slaves, number employed on typical plantation, 26; diet of, 28, 95; as article of merchandise—the domestic slave trade, 97-99; as tradesmen, system of hiring out, 99-102; social and economic effects of employing Negroes as tradesmen, 102-105; as market people, 106-108

Neufvilel, John, 210

Neuse River, 37

New Berne, N. C., 37

New Bordeau, S. C., 116

New England, and Sabbath observance, 19; traders and North Carolina trade, 37-38; trade of, towns, 83; effect of enforcement of revenue laws of 1764 on trade of, 180; ships and Stamp Act riots at Charleston, 187; forms non-importation association, 191; enforcement of non-importation in, 217-218; mentioned, 232

Newfoundland, 9

New Orleans, 44

Newport, R. I., 126

New Smyrna, Fla., 46

New York (city), mentioned, 4; shipping compared to Charleston's, in 1732, 10; population, in 1786, 16; as cattle and hog market for upper Carolina, 34; mentioned, 50; Carolina tourists and, 68; mentioned, 83; trade with Charleston retailers, 83; Stamp Act Congress at, 185; abandonment of non-importation in, 212; enforcement of non-importation at, 217-218

Ninety-Six, S. C., 29, 59, 175

Non-Importation Association, South Carolina, delay in organizing plantation provinces accounted for, 171-192; Laurens and the organization of, 202; effectiveness of, 202, n. 35; formation of, 203-210; enforcement of, 210-217; comparative statistics for enforcement of, and the other American associations, 217-219; and the slave trade into South Carolina, 219; distinguishing marks of, 219-220; break up of, 220

Non-Importation, in 1765, 185, n. 9

Non-Importation, 1774-1775. See Tea.

Norfolk, 3, 37

North Carolina, trade territory of Chesapeake District, 3; trade territory of Charleston District, 3, 25; only good harbor at Wilmington, 7; export trade, 10; Charleston's control of trade in, 11; cattle and hog raising in, 31-35; and Santee canal,

254

INDEX

34; back country trade of, 35, 36; land grants in, 36; physical geography and trade in, 36-38; Albemarle section, 37; Neuse River section, 37; Cape Fear section, 38-39; lumbering and production of naval stores, 39-41; overseas trade, statistics for, 41; circulation of South Carolina paper money in, 71; non-importation in, 218

Northern colonies, Wilmington's trade to, 7, 39; character of trade of, to Great Britain, 8-9; corn of, 28; upper Carolina settled by emigrants from, 29, 112; flour from, 31, 92; decline of Charleston's import trade to, 34; West Florida exports to, 44; traders of, raise objection to parliamentary rice legislation of 1764, 54, n. 4; trade of country factors to, 83-84; manufactures of, after Revolution, 92; southern mechanics migrate to, on account of Negro competition, 106; character of frontier of, 110; freight rates on rice to, 153-154; smuggling by traders of, 179

Ogechee River, 32

Oswald, Richard, English slave merchant, plantation in East Florida, 46; letter to, quoted, 47; declined to invest in South Carolina back country, 58-59; sends out Ratsel and Gervais to South Carolina, 86; social rank as slave merchant, 145

Paine, Thomas, quoted, 112
Pamlico Sound, 37
Patrols and night watches, 14
Patroon, explanation of term, 86, n. 7
Pedee River. See Great Pedee River.
Penn, William, merchant of St. Augustine, 121
Pennsylvania, western, trade territory of Chesapeake District, 3; shipping, 10; emigration from, to upper Carolina, 29; as rice market, 156; en-

forcement of non-importation in, 217-218

Pensacola, capital of West Florida, settlements in, advantages of location, 44; road established between St. Augustine and, 48; fur trade. 48, 169; smuggling in Indian trade at, 181

Pensacola Packet, 47

Petersburg, Va., 37

Philadelphia, mentioned, 4, 81, 95, 151; shipping to England compared to North Carolina's, 10; population, in 1786, 15; as market for Carolina hemp, 31; as cattle and hog market for South, 34; and Carolina tourists, 68; colonial dentist visits, 79; country factors' trade with, 83; flour, 92; price of mechanic work at, 103; Charleston communicates with Europe by way of, in summer, 154; vice admiralty court set up at, 191; abandonment of non-importation at, 212-213; enforcement of non-importation at, 217-218

Pine Tree Hill. See Camden.

Pine Tree Store, 89

Pitt, William, 179

Plantation, plantations, Bowland, at Rocky Point, off the Cape Fear, 13; Hunt Hill, N. C., 40; as investments, 58-61; Mepkin, on Cooper River, 61; Henry Laurens', 61; Broughton Island, Ga., 66; as field for retail and wholesale trade, 92-94; Wright's Savannah, Ga., 94; the Lucas, at Wappo, 117; Silk Hope, on Cooper River, 117

Plantation Business, and the Charleston factor, 53; inter-relation of climate, soil, rice and indigo, and Negro slaves, in development of, 53; legislation to promote, 53-55; credit system in, 55-56; liquor in, 93-94; under operation of the Townshend Acts, 195-197

Planter, Carolina, prosperity of, dependent on rice, 8; martial spirit of, 13; and the credit system, 55-56; and the shipping business, 61-62;

Royal African Company, 135

Rutherford, John, 39

Rutledge, Edward, delegate to First Continental Congress, 226

Rutledge, John, delegate to Stamp Act Congress, 186; delegate to First Continental Congress, 226; argues for rice exemption, 227

ST. Augustine, bar before, capital of East Florida, population, in 1763, 44; naval value of, 44-45; road established between Pensacola and, 48; mentioned, 50, 65; Laurens forwards "parcel" of Negroes to, 98; mentioned, 121; "expresses" from Charleston advertise slaves in, 133-134; mentioned, 148

St. Johns River, 46, 47

St. Michael's church, 16, 17, 18, 22, 187

St. Philip's church, 18, 21, 58

St. Simon's Island, Ga., 42

Saltilla River, 42

Saluda River, 6, 34

Sampit River, 6

Santee canal, 7, 34

Santee River, branches of, 6; and Santee canal, 7, 34; townships laid out along, 111

Savannah, port of Georgia, 4; location, trade subsidiary to Charleston, 7; population, in 1784, 7; and trade of western Georgia, 36; mentioned, 58, 75, 133, 194, 216

Savannah River, meanders of, 6; Savannah on, 7; forts on, 12; cattle ranch on, 31-32; Bloody Point on, 63; townships laid out along, 111

Schaw, Janet. See "A Lady of Quality."

Schoepf, J. D., German traveller, quoted, 19, 21, 101

Scotch-Irish, 29, 112

Scotland, Chesapeake District's trade to, 11; emigration from, to South Carolina, 30; mentioned, 50

Sheffield, Lord, on character of business in southern colonies, 83

Shipbuilding, in the Chesapeake District, 11; in northern colonies, 31; in South Carolina, 62-63

Shipping Business, and the Charleston factor, 49; capital required for, 51; rivalry in, 61-62; number and size of vessels employed in trade of Charleston, 63-64; boat ownership, 64; duties and drawbacks on intercolonial, 65; captain of merchant vessel as merchant, 66

Ships, vessels, tonnage of, entering Charleston harbor, 4; number and size of, employed in Charleston's export trade, 11, 64; number employed in Georgia trade, 1762-1772, 43; number employed in West Florida trade to Great Britain, in 1767, 48; classes employed in trade of South Carolina, 63-64; the Maria Wilhelmina, 64; ownership of, 64-65

Shubrick, Thomas, 42

Silk and wine culture, 36-37, 46

Skin Trade, forts for protection of, 12; decline of Charleston's 29, 34, 169; Georgia exports of deerskins, 1760-1770, 43; of West Florida, 44; extent of Charleston's, 169; value of exports, 1747, 1748, 1769, 170; three periods in management of, 170-171; conduct of business in middle period, 1729-1763, 171-175; British policy in regard to, after 1763, 175; re-organization of Indian business, 176; stores, regulations of traders, 176-177; smuggling in, 181-182

Slave trade, domestic. See Negro Slaves.

Slave trade, foreign, and the Charleston factor, 49, 94; European participation in, statistics, 124-125; public sentiment in regard to, in England and the United States, 125; English cities engaged in, 125, 135; Liverpool's pre-eminence in, 125-126; American participation, 126; effect of wars of Great Britain on, 1702-1763, 126; character of period

ing, 223-226; an "oblation to Neptune," 225-226

Tea party, Charleston. See Charleston tea party.

Tennessee, trade territory of Chesapeake District, 3; tobacco in, 10; emigration from South Carolina into, 108; mentioned, 169

Thomas and Roger Smith (slave merchants), 147

Tidyman, Philip, 213

Timothy, Ann, 82

Timothy, Peter, mentioned, 82, 130, 133; on smuggling at Charleston, 181; leader in the non-importation movement, 210; on the conduct of merchants in 1769, 212; and resistance to the East India Company, 222-223; and Gadsden attempt to revive non-importation in 1773, 226

Torrans, Gregg, and Poaug, immigrant business of, 114-117; slave business of, 138-139

Townshend Acts, and the installation of lamps at Charleston, 20; and business depression, 63; drains hard money from colonies, 68; courts set up under, 190-191; directed at commercial provinces, parts of acts that affected plantation provinces, 191; resistance to, in New England and South Carolina compared, 191-192

Trade, back country. See back country trade.

Tryon, Governor of North Carolina, 40-41

Turnbull, Doctor Andrew, 46

Turtle River, 42

Tuscarora Indians, 71

U P-COUNTRY, Carolina, settlement of, productions and society in, legislation for development of, 29-30; cattle and hog raising in, 31-33; transportation, 33-36

V ENDUE sales, 86

Vera Cruz, 44

Vice Admiralty. See Admiralty Courts.

Vienna, S. C., 31

Village and crossroads' stores, 88

Virginia, part of Chesapeake District, 3; export trade to Great Britain, 9 et seq.; and North Carolina trade, 10; trade to Scotland and West Indies, 10-11; emigration from, to upper Carolina, 29; as hog market for North Carolina, 33; debtor situation in, 56; barter in, after Revolution, 67; wholesale trade in, 83; enforcement of non-importation in, 217-219

W ACCAMAW River, 6, 11

Wagoning, 35-36

Wall of Charleston, 4, 12

Wallace, D. D., author of Life of Henry Laurens, controverted, 153-154

Wambaw, schooner, 65, 195-196

War of Jenkins' Ear, 71

Wasana, S. C., 46

Washington, Col. William, rice planter, 151

Wateree River, 6, 34, 89, 111

Webster, Peletiah, 58, 138

Wells, Robert, 214

West Florida, part of Charleston District, 25; territory included in, economic reasons for acquisition of, 44; acquisition, and the Charleston skin trade, 169

West Indies, Wilmington's trade to, 7, 39; trade of northern colonies to, 9, 34; trade routes leading to, 9; Virginia trade to, 10; as market for southern lumber, cattle, hogs, 32, 33; Charleston's provision trade to, 34; Georgia trade to, 39; West Florida exports to, 43; John Hopton's voyage to, 51; coastal trade to, 66; negotiability of bills of exchange on, 76; business of country factors with, 83; clothing of slaves in, 94; installment payment for Negroes introduced from, 140; prejudice against "seasoned" Negroes from, 142;